A GUIDE TO HEALTHY EATING

Heart Smart®
COOKBOOK
THIRD EDITION

In partnership:
Henry Ford Health System
and the Detroit Free Press

A portion of the proceeds associated with the sale of each Heart Smart® Cookbook III will be used to help provide heart-related care to patients in need at Henry Ford Health System.

ISBN: 978-0-937247-79-2

$23.95

A key to reading this book:

Throughout the recipes of Heart Smart® Cookbook III, you'll find helpful tips. Here's what the accompanying icons represent:

Number of servings you should expect a given recipe to generate

Time it will take to prepare and cook the recipe

Any additional tips from the Free Press Test Kitchen that might help

Icons by David Pierce / Detroit Free Press

Table of Contents

Acknowledgments

This book would not have been possible without the combined efforts of Steve Dorsey, vice president of research and development for the Detroit Media Partnership, and Steven Keteyian, PhD, program director of Preventive Cardiology for the Henry Ford Health System. Their vision and expertise helped make this book a reality.

The Detroit Free Press and Henry Ford Health System would like to thank those who supported and assisted us in producing this book.

A special thank you to chef Frank Turner, director of Culinary Wellness at Henry Ford West Bloomfield Hospital, for contributing eight great recipes found throughout this cookbook.

EDITORS:

Susan M. Selasky, Detroit Free Press

Darlene Zimmerman, registered dietitian, Heart Smart® Program

WRITERS:

Detroit Free Press: Susan M. Selasky, test kitchen director and food writer

Henry Ford Health System: Darlene Zimmerman, registered dietitian, Heart Smart® Program; Jonathan Ehrman, PhD, associate program director Preventive Cardiology; Clinton Brawner, clinical exercise physiologist, and Amy Lehto, exercise physiologist

SPECIAL SUPPORT:

Detroit Free Press: Laurie Delves, books coordinator; Rose Ann McKean, photo research; photo department; Kathy O'Gorman, food editor; Steve Dorsey, Amy Huschka and Morgan Phillips, designers; Erin Hill Perry, copy editor; David Pierce and Martha Thierry, illustrations and graphics; Charnae Sanders, Tania Lee and Aaron Snyder, 2011 summer apprentices; Chuck Whitman, Erin Fuhs and Ken Elenich, photo technicians,

Henry Ford Health System: Yvonne Moses, registered dietitian, Heart Smart® Program; Jody Bott, marketing manager; Anu Reddy, social media and web services specialist; Dave Olejarz, manager, Media Relations; Sally Ann Brown, senior public relations specialist; Melissa Van Zant, supervisor, Preventive Cardiology; Lishawn Kidd, secretary; Henry Ford Heart Smart® registered dietitians and dietetic interns; Bethany Thayer, registered dietitan, director of Wellness Programs and Strategies, and Jeremy Abbey, CEC.

Foreword

Today, more and more people are learning about the important role that proper nutrition and physical activity play in their health. There are many things each of us can do to improve our health and prevent disease.

It is with great pleasure that Henry Ford Health System offers Heart Smart® Cookbook III to assist you with making the proper nutrition changes needed to improve your health and well-being. Heart Smart® Cookbook III is Henry Ford Health System's third installment in what spans almost 25 years of providing nutrition information and recipes to help people make healthier food and lifestyle choices.

Henry Ford Health System's ultimate commitment is to be your partner in wellness. At Henry Ford Health System, we offer many community-based programs that provide meaningful opportunities to help individuals attain and maintain good health now and in the future.

We trust that the information and recipes in Heart Smart® Cookbook III will help you on your journey to wellness and reduce your overall risk for heart disease, cancer, diabetes and other chronic diseases. From cover to cover, we encourage you to enjoy the many wonderful heart healthy recipes that await you.

To your good health,

Nancy M. Schlichting
Chief Executive Officer
Henry Ford Health System

Robert G. Riney
President & Chief Operating Officer
Henry Ford Health System

Kimberlydawn Wisdom, MD, MS
Senior Vice President, Community Health & Equity
and Chief Wellness Officer
Henry Ford Health System
Michigan's First Surgeon General

Heart Smart® Healthy Eating Habits for Life

Every day, you make choices to protect yourself and your family. You lock your doors, wear a helmet riding your bike and tell your kids not to talk to strangers. But what are you doing to protect you and your family from developing major chronic diseases?

Diet-related chronic diseases — cardiovascular disease, high blood pressure, diabetes, cancer and osteoporosis — cost billions of dollars in health care every year. According to the latest Dietary Guidelines for Americans from the U.S. Department of Agriculture and U.S. Department of Health and Human Services, 37% of adults have cardiovascular disease and 34% have high blood pressure, the latter being a major risk factor for heart disease, stroke, congestive heart failure and kidney disease. Nearly 11% of adults have diabetes, with the vast majority of those cases being type 2 diabetes, a disease that is heavily influenced by an unhealthy diet and lack of physical activity. Approximately 41% of men and women will be diagnosed with cancer during their lifetime. And one of two women and one in four men 50 years and older will have an osteoporosis-related fracture in their lifetime.

Concerning heart disease, four out of 10 adults in the U.S. older than 40 will experience a heart attack or be diagnosed with a blockage in the vessels that supply blood to the heart. Lifestyle-related factors that increase your risk for a heart attack or stroke include cigarette smoking, high blood pressure, diabetes, unhealthy blood cholesterol levels, obesity and physical inactivity. The majority of people who experience a heart attack have at least one of these risk factors. As shown in the figure at right, these factors are common in the U.S., with 37% having two or more of them. In addition, nearly three out of four adults have high blood pressure, unhealthy blood cholesterol, or smoke cigarettes. As you might expect, these risk factors are becoming increasingly common in younger adults and children.

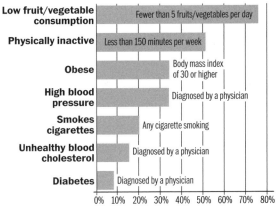

Percent of Adults in the U.S. with Important Risk Factors or not Achieving Important Lifestyle Goals

- Low fruit/vegetable consumption — Fewer than 5 fruits/vegetables per day
- Physically inactive — Less than 150 minutes per week
- Obese — Body mass index of 30 or higher
- High blood pressure — Diagnosed by a physician
- Smokes cigarettes — Any cigarette smoking
- Unhealthy blood cholesterol — Diagnosed by a physician
- Diabetes — Diagnosed by a physician

0% 10% 20% 30% 40% 50% 60% 70% 80%

Sources: Centers for Disease Control and Prevention. Surveillance for Certain Health Behaviors Among States and Selected Local Areas — United States, 2008. MMWR 2010;59(No. SS-10).

Lloyd-Jones D, et al.; on behalf of the American Heart Association Statistics Committee and Stroke Statistics Subcommittee. Heart disease and stroke statistics—2010 update: A report from the American Heart Association. Circulation. 2010;121:e46–e215.

While the numbers are staggering, the fight against most of these devastating diseases often starts at your kitchen table. What you choose to eat every day can in part, determine your risk of developing these life changing illness. A healthy way of eating shouldn't begin after a heart attack or a hip fracture; it should be a lifelong commitment that starts at a young age.

At Henry Ford Hospital's Edith and Benson Ford Heart & Vascular Institute, we believe that all Americans older than two years of age can benefit from eating a Heart Smart® diet. Our healthy eating recommendations and weight management program are based on those of major health organizations including the American Heart Association, the National Cancer Institute, the American Diabetes Association, the U.S. Department of Agriculture and U.S. Department of Health and Human Services and American Dietetic Association.

Seven Steps to Eating Heart Smart®

Eat More Fruits and Vegetables

Whether your goal is to reduce the risk of heart disease, high blood pressure or cancer, the evidence is overwhelming that the most powerful preventive foods can be found in the produce aisle. Fruits and vegetables provide a number of nutrients that are lacking in the diet of most Americans, including folate, magnesium, potassium, dietary fiber and vitamins A, C and K. Additionally, most fruits and vegetables are naturally low in calories, fat and sodium and are cholesterol-free.

Fill half your plate with fruits and vegetables at every meal, striving to eat at least 2 ½ cups of vegetables every day along with 2 cups of fruit. Choosing fruits and vegetables vibrant in color helps obtain important nutrients.

Choose More Whole Grains

The health benefits of eating whole grains continue to make headlines. Turns out, people who consume more whole grains tend to have a lower risk for heart disease, diabetes, digestive disorders such as diverticulosis (a condition where tiny sacs form on the intestinal wall as it weakens), constipation and some forms of cancer. Fiber-containing foods such as whole grains help provide a feeling of fullness that can help with managing body weight. Whole grains also provide magnesium, a mineral needed for the building of healthy bones.

Researchers suspect the health benefits attributed to whole grains comes from the combination of phytochemicals, vitamins, minerals and dietary fiber they provide. One key recommendation promoted by the latest U.S. Dietary Guidelines for Americans is to make sure that half your grain choices throughout the day are whole grains. That means choosing whole-wheat bread rather than wheat or white bread, brown rice instead of white rice, and oatmeal over a sugar soaked cereal.

Opt for Low-Fat and Fat-Free Dairy Foods

Dairy foods are well known for improving bone health, especially in children and adolescents, but they also are associated with a reduced risk of cardiovascular disease, type 2 diabetes and lower blood pressure in adults.

Milk and other dairy foods provide calcium, potassium and vitamin D, all nutrients that are vital for good health. Calcium is needed for building and maintaining strong bones and teeth. Potassium-rich diets may help maintain a healthy blood pressure, and vitamin D is required for optimum absorption of calcium.

It is especially important for parents to establish the habit of feeding milk to their young children, as those who consume milk at an early age are more likely to continue that habit into adulthood. Family members older than two should opt for fat-free, ½% and/or 1% milk. These options provide little or no artery-clogging saturated fat and less cholesterol when compared to 2% and whole milk.

Because they are nutritionally similar to milk, soy beverages fortified with calcium and vitamins A and D are considered part of the Dairy Group.

Select Lean Cuts of Meat

You can still enjoy beef, pork, lamb and veal on a heart healthy diet. In fact, the American Heart Association says that meat has a place on your plate, as long as it is lean and the daily portion does not exceed two, three-ounce servings (a total of 6 ounces of cooked meat) for the day. A deck of cards or a woman's palm represents a three-ounce portion.

In addition to protein, meat provides essential nutrients such as iron, zinc, magnesium and vitamin B12. However, depending on the cut and portion size, meat can also provide a significant amount of saturated fat as well as dietary cholesterol.

Enjoy a Variety of Seafood

Research on the health benefits of adding fish to your weekly menu continues to mount. The studies are so promising that the latest U.S. Dietary Guidelines encourage Americans to consume at least eight ounces of fish, particularly fatty fish, every week to promote heart health.

Naturally fatty fish, such as salmon, trout, sardines and Atlantic or Pacific mackerel, provides the most omega-3 fatty acids. While the health benefits of consuming more omega-3 fatty acids are still being studied, the research is pretty clear that increased intake of omega-3 fatty acids helps reduce the risk for heart attack and death from heart disease.

Keep Tabs on Your Sodium Intake

If you're one of the 74.5 million adults in this country with high blood pressure, the amount of sodium you eat is an important consideration. The American Heart Association recommends a maximum daily sodium intake of 2,300 milligrams — the amount of sodium in just one teaspoon of salt. A further reduction to no more than 1,500 milligrams of sodium a day applies to those who are 51 and older, African Americans or anyone with high blood pressure, diabetes or chronic kidney disease.

One eating pattern, called the DASH (Dietary Approaches to Stop Hypertension) diet, significantly reduced blood pressure in people with and without hypertension. The DASH plan emphasizes fruits, vegetables, fat-free and low-fat dairy products, whole grains, seafood, poultry, beans, nuts and seeds, along with lower intakes of sodium, red and processed meats and sweets.

The best place to start with lowering your sodium intake is to rely less on processed foods and spend more time in the kitchen with this cookbook preparing your own meals.

Choose Healthy Unsaturated Fats over Saturated and Trans Fats

While the American Heart Association recommends keeping total fat intake to between 25 and 35% of your daily calories (about 55 to 78 grams of total fat each day if you consume 2,000 calories), they emphasize that the type of fat consumed has a greater impact on your heart health.

A higher intake of most saturated fatty acids is associated with higher levels of total blood cholesterol and harmful low-density lipoprotein (LDL) cholesterol, a scenario that sets the stage for a greater risk of heart disease. Saturated fats are found in fatty animal products such as well-marbled meat, poultry skin, butter and whole-milk products. Health organizations recommend reducing saturated fat intake to no more than 7 to 10% of daily calories or no more than 15 to 22 grams saturated fat each day. A double scoop of your favorite premium ice cream will cost you about 22 grams of saturated fat.

Trans fatty acids (trans fats), found primarily in commercial products made with or fried in partially hydrogenated vegetable oils, also increase blood cholesterol. The American Heart Association recommends limiting trans fats to no more than 1% of total calories. That's about two grams of trans fat a day for someone consuming 2,000 calories. A small order of french fries likely has 3 or 4 grams of trans fat.

When substituted for saturated and trans fats in the diet, monounsaturated and polyunsaturated fats may actually lower harmful LDL cholesterol. Olive oil, peanut oil, canola oil and most nuts are high in monounsaturated fat. Foods rich in polyunsaturated fat include vegetable oils (e.g. corn, soybean and sunflower) and many nuts and seeds.

While a nutritious eating plan is key to achieving a healthier lifestyle, maintaining a healthy body weight, being physically active and not smoking are important, too. The good news is that it is never too early or too late to make changes that improve your health and well-being.

The ultimate goal of our Heart Smart® Cookbook III is to help you do just that — improve your health and the health of your family by enjoying great tasting food. In addition to our new and delicious recipes, this book offers meal planning strategies, supermarket shopping tips, recipe makeover secrets and common sense do's and don'ts when eating out.

Achieve and Maintain a Healthy Body Weight

Living Heart Smart® includes trying to achieve an optimum body weight. Being overweight is common in the United States – 68% of Americans are overweight, and one in every three children is overweight or obese.

The most common method used to determine weight status is called the Body Mass Index, or BMI. BMI uses your height and weight to determine whether you are at a healthy weight, overweight or obese. To determine your BMI, use this equation:

$$BMI = \frac{Weight\ in\ lbs.\ x\ 703}{(Height\ in\ inches)\ x\ (Height\ in\ inches)}$$

You also can go to www.henryford.com/weightprogram to access an easy-to-use BMI calculator.

The following table of BMI values also lists the corresponding weight categories:

BMI Value	Weight Category
< 18.5	Underweight
18.5 – 24.9	Healthy weight
25.0 – 29.9	Overweight
30.0 or higher	Obese weight

If your BMI is 25.0 or greater you should consider yourself at an increased risk for diseases and conditions related to being overweight. The higher your BMI is above 25.0, the higher your risk. In most people, an elevated BMI is due to too much body fat.

However, some people believe that even though their BMI is over 25, it is because they are just very muscular or "big boned" — not overly fat. An easy way to figure out whether this is the case is to take a tape measure, and place it around your waist, about an inch below your belly button. If the measurement is 35 inches or more for a woman or 40 inches or more for a man, and your BMI is over 25, you very likely have too much fat.

The health risks associated with being overweight or obese are:

- Death
- Heart disease and heart failure
- Stroke
- High blood pressure

- Diabetes
- Cancer (several forms)
- Osteoarthritis
- Metabolic syndrome

Learn More

Learn more about the Henry Ford Weight Management Program by scanning this QR code with your smartphone. To download a free QR code scanner, visit your smartphone's application store.

Heart Smart® Weight Loss

When selecting a plan to lose weight, it is important to keep in mind several points:

- Any strategy must include changes in diet, exercise habits and overall lifestyle.

- The strategy you choose should be healthy — for your heart and for preventing and treating other overweight related conditions. Any plan that allows or suggests you eat a lot of fat, particularly saturated and/or trans fat, should be avoided. Any plan that focuses on a single food or very few types of foods — for example, an all juice diet or the grapefruit diet — also should be avoided.

- Losing weight often is considered easier than keeping it off. A well-rounded weight-loss plan must include, from the very beginning, strategies aimed at maintaining weight loss.

- Consider getting help for your efforts. While some people are successful losing weight on their own, most studies suggest that the majority of people who have lost at least 30 pounds and kept it off for at least five years involved professional help. Help also should include people in your personal life, including family and friends.

- Finally, you must be fully committed to be successful.

So let's explore the different types of weight management options.

Self-help options These do-it-yourself options range from books, CDs, videos and online resources with self-designed plans. The quality of these options varies greatly. Some are based on sound scientific and behavioral principles and methods that have proven effective; others are gimmicks, fad diet plans or overly aggressive exercise plans that are usually ineffective in the long term. When attempting to sort through these self-help options, remember the old adage that "if it sounds to good to be true, it probably is."

Commercial-type programs Representing both for-profit and non-profit companies, these programs typically have store fronts and offer services over the phone or Internet. For-profit programs can be expensive and may be staffed by medical professionals (physicians, nurses, dietitians) or inexperienced people who joined the program and were successful. Depending on the company, services range from basic diet planning and counseling to restrictive diets designed for rapid and significant weight loss.

Clinical programs These programs typically assist individuals regardless of whether they plan to lose a little (25 pounds) or a lot (more than 100 pounds) of weight. Henry Ford Hospital offers effective clinical programs staffed by health care professionals who not only specialize in working with overweight individuals, but also those with health-related conditions such as diabetes, high blood pressure and high cholesterol. For more information, visit www.henryford.com/weightprogram.

Watch This!

Scan this QR code with your smartphone to watch the Heart Smart® video.

Surgical programs Surgery is restricted only to people who meet certain criteria. These include a BMI higher than 40 or a BMI higher than 35 with a medical condition such as diabetes or high blood pressure. While surgery has the best long-term results for weight loss and maintenance, prospective patients must realize that weight gain after surgery is still possible. Therefore, those who have had surgery must adhere to a healthy diet and exercise program to maintain their weight loss. There are several types of surgery available with varying rates of success. Go to www.henryford.com/dearobesity.

The Value of Exercise for Weight Loss and Maintenance

Exercise alone is an inefficient method for weight loss. Regular exercise, combined with low calorie eating is key to long-term weight management and is the biggest predictor of success for long-term weight maintenance. It also improves your overall health and accelerates weight loss. Go to www.henryford.com/prevent for information about the Henry Ford exercise program.

The type of exercise best suited for you depends on what you're trying to achieve. Cardiovascular exercise is best for burning calories. Strength training, or resistance training helps to maintain lean muscle mass during periods of significant weight loss. Both are important and provide health benefits. The table below provides some specific information about exercise.

Type	Type	Days per week	Time/Amount
Cardiovascular exercise	• Walking, biking, jogging, swimming, etc. • Focus on one exercise per day but each can be performed during a week	Min. = 5 Max. = 7	• Goal of 60 minutes • May need to start with 15 or 30 minutes total if you have not exercised in a while • Can be completed throughout the day in smaller segments
Resistance exercise	• Machine weights, calisthenics, resistance bands • Focuses on major muscles of arm and legs	Max. = 3	• 2 to 3 sets of each exercise for 10 to 15 repetitions • Perform for each major muscle group of arms and legs, resting each muscle group a day before repeating

Losing weight the Heart Smart® way can lead to a lifetime of health. The most important steps are to select a program best for you and to learn to live the rest of your life at a healthy weight. You can do it and Heart Smart® is here to help you succeed.

Planning to Eat Heart Smart®

Move over food guide pyramid, there's a new healthy eating icon. A colorful four-part plate with a side of dairy has pushed the old food guide pyramid off the table. The new image, called My Plate, is split into four sections — fruits, vegetables, grains, protein and a separate circle for dairy.

The graphic makes it clear that fruits and vegetables should make up half your meal, with vegetables playing a dominant role. Grains and proteins (fish and meat, for example) should occupy the other half, with grains having a slight advantage.

This easy-to-understand layout depicts what constitutes a healthy meal. Whether you are at the grocery store, at a restaurant or in your kitchen preparing dinner, the new food plate graphic serves as a constant reminder of what proportions of foods are recommended for good health.

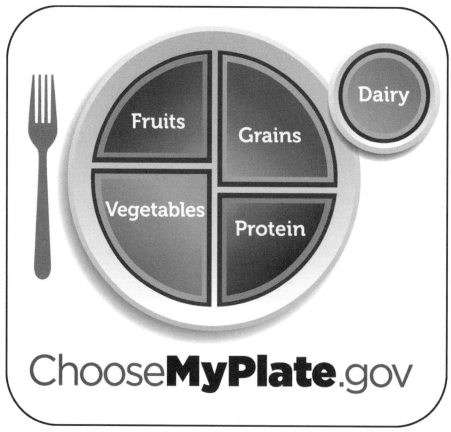

Source: United States Department of Agriculture.
Available at www.choosemyplate.gov

The Choose My Plate graphic and the Nutrition Facts label serve as useful tools when planning healthy meals.

Understanding the Nutrition Facts label and the ingredients list on food packages can help you evaluate and compare the nutrient content of the foods you eat.

Serving Size and Servings per Container
At the top of the label the serving size is listed along with the number of servings in the container. The nutrition information that follows is based on one serving. Eat two servings and get twice the calories, fat and other nutrients.

Calories and Calories from Fat
The label lists the number of calories and the number of calories from fat in one serving.

Total Fat, Saturated Fat, Trans Fat, Cholesterol and Sodium
To help reduce your risk of heart disease and other chronic diseases, use this section to select foods that are lowest in total fat, saturated fat and trans fat, cholesterol and sodium. For healthy adults, use the % Daily Value (listed at the right) as a general guide to determine if a food is high or low in a nutrient — 5% or less is low, 20% or more is high.

Total Carbohydrate, Dietary Fiber and Sugars
Healthy, fiber-rich carbohydrates include fruits, vegetables, legumes (dried beans and peas) and whole grains. The grams of sugar listed on the label isn't necessarily an indication of added sugar. A better way to select foods with limited added sugar is to check the ingredient list. Brown sugar, corn syrup, dextrin, fructose, high-fructose corn syrup, honey, invert sugar, malt syrup, maltose, maple syrup, molasses, raw sugar, sucrose and sugar all are considered added sugars. Finding these ingredients at the top or front of the ingredient list means lots of extra sugar and calories.

Protein
Because protein requirements vary between adults and children, and men and women, a % Daily Value is not provided. When choosing protein-rich foods, such as fish, meat, poultry, legumes and dairy products; make choices that are lean, low-fat or fat-free.

Vitamins and Minerals
Vitamins A and C, calcium and iron are often listed on food labels. Choose foods with a higher % Daily Value for these nutrients.

Nutrition Facts
Serving Size 1 cup (228g)
Servings Per Container 2

Amount Per Serving

Calories 260	Calories from Fat 120

	% Daily Value*
Total Fat 13g	20%
Saturated Fat 5g	25%
Trans Fat 2g	
Cholesterol 30mg	10%
Sodium 660mg	28%
Total Carbohydrate 31g	10%
Dietary Fiber 0g	0%
Sugars 5g	
Protein 5g	

Vitamin A 4%	•	Vitamin C 2%
Calcium 15%	•	Iron 4%

* Percent Daily Values are based on a 2,000 calorie diet. Your Daily Values may be higher or lower depending on your calorie needs.

	Calories:	2,000	2,500
Total Fat	Less than	65g	80g
Sat Fat	Less than	20g	25g
Cholesterol	Less than	300mg	300mg
Sodium	Less than	2,400mg	2,400mg
Total Carbohydrate		300g	375g
Dietary Fiber		25g	30g

Calories per gram:
Fat 9   •   Carbohydrate 4   •   Protein 4

Claims made on food packages such as low-fat or reduced-sodium can only be used if the food meets government definitions. Here are some common claims and their meaning.

Fat

Fat-free	Less than 0.5 grams fat per serving
Low-fat	3 grams or less fat per serving
Reduced-fat	Product must contain 25% less than the regular version
Light, lite	At least one-third fewer calories per serving than a comparison food, OR 50% less fat than a comparison food, OR 50% less sodium than a comparison food, OR Can refer to the color or texture of a food if clearly stated such as light brown sugar

Saturated fat

Saturated fat-free	Less than 0.5 grams saturated fat per serving
Low saturated fat	1 gram or less saturated fat per serving and 15% or less calories from fat

Cholesterol

Cholesterol-free	Less than 2 milligrams cholesterol and 2 grams or less saturated fat per serving
Low-cholesterol	20 milligrams or less cholesterol and 2 grams or less saturated fat per serving

Sodium

Sodium-Free	Less than 5 milligrams sodium per serving
Very-Low Sodium	Less than 35 milligrams sodium per serving
Low-Sodium	140 milligrams or less sodium per serving

Fiber

High fiber	5 grams or more fiber per serving
Good source of fiber	2.5 to 4.9 grams fiber per serving

Calories

Calorie-free	Less than 5 calories per serving
Low-calorie	40 calories or less per serving
Sugar-free	Less than 0.5 grams sugar per serving

So, you have the My Plate icon firmly embedded in your mind and a basic understanding of the food label, but still struggle as you move through the grocery store. Take the guesswork out of grocery shopping and use our guide.

Heart Smart® Grocery Shopping Guide

Fruits and Vegetables

Current guidelines encourage adults to consume at least 2 ½ cups of vegetables every day and 2 cups of fruit. According to the Centers for Disease Control and Prevention, 75% of Americans fall short of this goal. To maximize the nutritional value of any meal, enjoy a variety of brightly colored fruits and vegetables. As you make your way through the produce aisle, consider the five color groups.

Red: Beets, cherries, cranberries, pink grapefruit, pomegranate, raspberries, red apples, red grapes, red onions, red peppers, rhubarb, strawberries, tomatoes, watermelon

Orange and Yellow: Apricots, cantaloupe, carrots, corn, grapefruit, mangoes, oranges, papayas, peaches, pineapple, winter squash, sweet potatoes, yellow peppers

Green: Asparagus, avocados, broccoli, Brussels sprouts, green beans, green grapes, green peppers, honeydew melon, kiwi, leafy greens, peas

Blue and Purple: Blackberries, blueberries, eggplant, plums, prunes, purple cabbage, raisins, purple grapes

White, Tan and Brown: Bananas, brown pears, cauliflower, dates, onions, mushrooms, turnips, parsnips, bananas, pears, white peaches

Remember that canned products count, too. In most cases, canned (and frozen) fruits and vegetables are nutritionally comparable to fresh. Once cans are sealed and heat processed, the food maintains its nutrient quality for about two years.

Choose canned fruit packed in 100% fruit juice or water instead of syrup. When buying canned vegetables, choose ones with no added salt.

Breads, Cereals and Grains

The 2010 U.S. Dietary Guidelines from the U.S. Department of Agriculture and U.S. Department of Health and Human Services encourage Americans to make at least half their daily grain choices whole grains. A whole grain is made up of three parts: the bran, the endosperm and the germ. The bran or outer layer provides fiber; the endosperm or middle layer contains mostly carbohydrates and protein, with small amounts of B vitamins; and the germ or inner part contributes trace minerals, healthy fats, B vitamins and antioxidants. When grains are milled or refined the bran and germ are removed along with their nutrients and much of the fiber.

Choose grain products that name a whole-grain ingredient first on the list. Being first on the list tells you that it is the predominant ingredient in the food by weight.

One slice of bread, about 1 cup of breakfast cereal, or a ½ cup of cooked cereal, rice, or pasta counts as one serving.

Bread: Make sure the first ingredient on the ingredient list is a whole grain such as whole-wheat flour or crushed whole-wheat. Choose breads that contain no more than 3 grams of total fat per slice (1 ounce) and at least 3 grams dietary fiber. Don't assume breads labeled multi-grain, stone ground or wheat contain whole grains; read the label to make sure.

Cereal: Choose cereals that have a whole grain listed as a first ingredient such as whole oats, contain no more than 3 grams of total fat and at least 3 grams of dietary fiber per serving. Many nutrition experts recommend no more than 8 grams of sugar per serving or 12 grams if the cereal contains dried fruit such as raisins. Go as low as you can with added sugar and add your own sweetness by tossing sliced or dried fruit into your cereal bowl.

Other Grains: Other whole grains to consider include whole-wheat flour, brown or wild rice, bulgur (cracked wheat), buckwheat, millet, whole oats, oatmeal or rolled oats, quinoa, whole-grain barley, whole-grain cornmeal, whole-wheat pasta and popcorn.

Watch This!

Scan this QR code with your smartphone to watch the Heart Smart® video.

Milk, Yogurt and Cheese

Milk, yogurt and cheese provide many essential nutrients including calcium, potassium, vitamin D and protein. The recommended number of servings from this food group depends on your age. Children 2 to 3 years old should have 2 cups per day, 4- to 8-year-olds should have 2 ½ cups every day and everyone else should opt for 3 cups daily. One cup of yogurt and 1 ½ ounces of cheese is the equivalent to one serving of milk.

Milk: Choose fat-free (skim) or low-fat (½ or 1%) milk. If you are lactose intolerant, drink smaller amounts of milk at a time, try lactose-free skim milk or fortified soymilk.

Yogurt: Opt for low-fat or fat-free varieties. Check the label to see that you are getting a healthy dose of calcium. An 8-ounce container of yogurt should provide at least 30% of the Daily Value for calcium and a 6-ounce container should provide at least 25%. To keep the sugar content down, buy plain low-fat or fat-free yogurt and add your own fruit.

You also might try fat-free or low-fat Greek-style yogurt. Thicker and creamier than traditional yogurt, Greek yogurt has a texture similar to custard or sour cream. This rich texture is achieved through a straining process, which removes more whey and water from the yogurt.

Greek yogurt contains almost twice the amount of protein as traditional yogurt and about half the amount of sodium. One nutritional disadvantage is its calcium content. Due to the straining process, 8 ounces of plain Greek yogurt has about 150 milligrams of calcium compared to 450 milligrams of calcium in the same amount of traditional yogurt.

Cheese: Choose low-fat and reduced-fat varieties. A low-fat cheese has 3 grams of fat or less per ounce and a reduced-fat cheese will range from 4 to 7 grams of fat per ounce.

Meat, Poultry, Seafood, Eggs and Legumes

Beef, pork, lamb and veal provide essential nutrients including iron, zinc and key B vitamins.

And if you select lean cuts, trim external fat, and cook without adding fat, there is no reason not to include meat in your diet.

Meat: Lean cuts of beef will have the words round or loin in the name, such as eye of round, top round, round tip or tenderloin. For pork and lamb, look for loin or leg cuts such as pork tenderloin, loin chops or leg of lamb. When purchasing veal, look for loin chop, cutlet or rib roast.

Poultry: Skinless chicken breasts, turkey breasts and turkey cutlets remain the leanest poultry choices. If you would prefer to cook poultry with the skin on, that's fine. Just be sure to remove the skin before eating it because poultry skin provides saturated fat. If you are using ground turkey or chicken as an alternative to ground beef, make sure you purchase ground poultry that does not contain poultry skin.

Seafood: The 2010 Dietary Guidelines encourage Americans to consume at least 8 ounces of seafood each week. Fish is low in saturated fat, and it provides beneficial omega-3 fatty acids. Consuming about 8 ounces of fish each week is associated with a reduced risk of cardiac deaths among people with and without pre-existing heart disease.

Eggs: Thanks to its high cholesterol content, eggs (specifically egg yolks) have had a rather unhealthy reputation in the past. The American Heart Association still recommends limiting cholesterol consumption to less than 300 milligrams per day for healthy people and no more than 200 milligrams a day for those with heart disease or an elevated bad LDL cholesterol. However, they no longer have a recommended limit on egg yolk consumption.

One egg contains 75 calories along with vitamin B12, iron, vitamin D, zinc, folate and choline, an essential nutrient that may play a role in memory function, fetal brain development and in the prevention of heart disease. Eggs also provide lutein and zeaxanthin, two carotenoids that may reduce the risk of age-related macular degeneration, the leading cause of blindness in older adults.

There is no need to eliminate eggs from your diet. Just keep in mind that one large egg yolk contains about 200 milligrams of dietary cholesterol. Moderating your cholesterol consumption elsewhere in your food plan likely will be necessary.

Legumes

Legumes (dried beans, peas and lentils) have emerged as an extremely versatile food with an excellent nutritional reputation. Legumes provide a healthy dose of soluble fiber, which may help reduce the risk of heart disease by lowering the bad LDL cholesterol. Beans also are low in fat, cholesterol-free and rich in protein, folate, iron and zinc.

Legumes are the family of edible seeds that come from plants with pods. Black beans, kidney beans, navy beans, soybeans, split green or yellow peas, chickpeas (garbanzo beans) and lentils are examples. Legumes are, by far, the best plant source of protein. Most legumes are available dried or canned.

Watch This!

Scan this QR code with your smartphone to watch the Heart Smart® video.

Fats and Oils

Most major health organizations recommend limiting total fat intake to no more than 25 to 35% of your daily calories. That percentage translates to 56 to 78 grams of total fat each day if you consume about 2,000 calories. A 12-ounce broiled T-bone steak alone has about 58 grams of total fat.

While the total amount of fat you eat is an important, the types of fat you consume have a greater impact on your health.

Saturated Fat: Saturated fats typically are solid at room temperature and occur naturally in animal foods. Well-marbled meats, full-fat dairy products such as whole milk, cream, ice cream, cheese and butter supply saturated fats, as do tropical oils like coconut, palm kernel and palm. Consuming a diet rich in saturated fat can raise bad LDL cholesterol levels, increasing heart disease risk.

Trans Fat: Trans fats (or trans fatty acids) are created when an oil is partially hydrogenated. Most of the trans fats we eat come from commercially fried and baked foods, stick margarines and foods containing partially hydrogenated oils. Trans fats act like saturated fats and raise bad LDL cholesterol levels, increasing the risk for heart disease. They also lower the good HDL cholesterol.

When selecting margarine (or any food), check the food label for options that list 0 grams of trans fat per serving. Liquid squeeze, spray bottle, and most tub margarine will meet that criteria. Stick margarine typically has 1 or 2 grams trans fat per serving. Also, make sure the margarine you choose has no more than 2 grams of saturated fat per serving and lists a liquid oil rather than a partially hydrogenated oil as the first ingredient.

Monounsaturated and Polyunsaturated Fat: When substituted for saturated and trans fats in the diet, these fats may actually lower harmful LDL cholesterol. Olive oil, peanut oil, safflower oil, canola oil and nuts are high in monounsaturated fat. Foods rich in polyunsaturated fat include corn, soybean, sunflower oils and many types of nuts and seeds.

Use all types of fats in moderation and choose monounsaturated and polyunsaturated fats over saturated and trans fats.

A Note about Water

While the question of how much water should a person drink may seem rather simple, the answer is not as straightforward. The truth is, your water needs depend on many factors, including your health, activity level, and even where you live. A reasonable guideline for the average healthy adult is about 8 cups per day.

Summing It Up

A healthy eating pattern emphasizes nutrient-dense foods such as vegetables, fruits, whole grains, fat-free and low-fat dairy products, seafood, lean meats and poultry, eggs and legumes (dried beans and peas). It also includes reducing your intake of sodium, unhealthy fats, added sugars and refined grains. Eating healthy is not about deprivation, it's about choosing wisely from a wide variety of the foods you enjoy.

Watch This!

Scan this QR code with your smartphone to watch the Heart Smart® video.

Eating Out Heart Smart®

According to the National Restaurant Association's (NRA) most recent Restaurant Industry Forecast, consumers spend 49% of their food budget in restaurants. On a typical day, restaurant industry sales total $1.7 billion. On a positive note, the NRA also found that seven out of 10 consumers say they are trying to eat healthier when dining out today than they did two years ago. And restaurant operators say their customers are ordering healthier items and paying more attention to the nutritional content of food.

With a little knowledge, you can put together a healthier meal no matter where you're dining.

Before you arrive

- Choose a restaurant that sets you up for success — one that offers healthier fare or can meet your special requests.

- Try not to arrive famished. Resisting high-calorie, high-fat foods becomes a challenge when you're hungry.

- Know before you go. Most chain and fast food restaurants have nutrition information available on the Internet. Finding out how much fat is in the double cheeseburger might help you consider a healthier choice. At the restaurant, ask whether nutrition information is available.

- If you know you will be dining out, try to make healthier choices for the rest of the day.

Make your meals lower in fat and sodium

- Foods that are baked, broiled, grilled, poached, roasted, steamed or stir-fried in a small amount of oil tend to be lower in fat than items that are deep-fried, pan-fried or sautéed.

- Ask that butter or margarine, gravies, sauces, salad dressing or sour cream be served on the side.

- When ordering pizza, choose vegetable toppings instead of meat toppings. If you must have meat, consider the leaner choices of ham and Canadian bacon. Request that your pizza be made with less cheese or reduced-fat cheese. Ask for whole-wheat crust.

- Remove visible fat from meat, as well as the skin from poultry, before eating.

- Fish is a good choice as long as it's grilled, baked or broiled. Butter and tartar sauce add extra fat and calories, and cocktail sauce adds extra sodium.

- Order sandwiches and hamburgers without high-fat accompaniments such as mayonnaise, cheese or bacon.

- Beware of entree salads made with high-fat cheese, lunchmeat, eggs and regular salad dressing. They can contain more fat and calories than a deluxe hamburger.

- Watch out for high sodium buzzwords such as smoked, pickled, broth, tomato sauce or juice, and barbecue, cocktail, soy and teriyaki sauce.

- Avoid grabbing the salt shaker once your food arrives.

Choose your calories carefully

- Make water, fat-free or low-fat milk, unsweetened tea or other drinks without added sugars your beverage choice.

- Alcoholic drinks can carry a heavy calorie tag. A large margarita or daiquiri can have as many calories as your main course.

- A bread basket may contain 400 to 1,000 calories; a basket of tortilla chips can have 700 to 900 calories. Take a handful of chips or one roll and ask your server to remove the basket.

- For dessert, opt for fresh fruit, sorbet, sherbet, or frozen low-fat or fat-free yogurt.

Boost the nutritional value

- Opt for steamed or grilled vegetables, or a baked potato instead of french fries or coleslaw.

- Request whole-wheat bread for sandwiches or toast.

- Choose brown rice and whole-grain pasta — instead of white rice and pasta — for a fiber boost.

- Try vegetarian menu options that focus on vegetables, legumes and whole grains.

Pay attention to portion sizes

- Ask for a half- or lunch-size portion, as they tend to be smaller.

- Avoid the value meal upgrade. As tempting as is may be to super-size the fries, burger or soft drink for a mere 50 cents, there is no savings when it comes to your health.

- Resign from the clean plate club. It's OK to leave food behind.

- If you enjoy leftovers, ask your server to bring a to-go container with your meal so you can immediately put half of it aside.

- It's important to understand what healthy food portions really look like, the following visuals can provide some guidance.

Food	Healthy Portion Looks Like
1 serving cooked vegetables	½ baseball
1 serving raw leafy salad greens	1 baseball
1 piece fresh fruit	1 baseball
1 serving cooked pasta, rice, hot cereal	½ baseball
1 serving mayonnaise or margarine	3 dice
1 portion cooked meat, poultry, seafood	Deck of cards, size of a woman's palm
1 ounce cheese	4 dice or two thumbs
1 serving ice cream or frozen yogurt	½ baseball

About Our Recipes

At Heart Smart® we know that eating well and living well go hand in hand. As we celebrate the publication of this latest cookbook, know that our commitment to providing great-tasting and great-for-you recipes has never been stronger.

As you cook your way through this book, remember that the recipes are not just for those with heart disease, but for anyone trying to eat healthier. We hope you will be intrigued by and excited about serving these recipes to anyone wanting to benefit from good, healthy, great tasting food.

With each recipe, you will find a nutritional analysis and cooking tips from the Detroit Free Press Test Kitchen. While every effort has been made to provide accurate nutrition information, many variables account for a wide range of nutrient values in food. Therefore, nutritional analyses should be considered approximate. Also, keep in mind the following as you review the recipe and nutrition information:

- Each analysis is based on a single serving, unless otherwise indicated.

- Ingredients listed as optional are not included in the analysis, unless otherwise noted.

- When a recipe lists two or more ingredient options, the first option listed is used in the nutritional analysis.

- Can sizes often change over time. This is especially true with canned beans, soups and vegetables. If you cannot find the exact can size as stated in the recipe, look for the closest one.

- Meats are analyzed as cooked and lean, with all visible fat removed.

- To keep the sodium content of our recipes as low as possible, yet still full of flavor, we use low-sodium and reduced-sodium products and add salt sparingly to recipes.

- Margarine used in our recipes should be labeled 0 grams trans fat. This is not to be confused with fat-free or light margarine. Most tub margarines are acceptable, whereas stick margarines likely contain trans fat.

- Because we want your time in the kitchen preparing nutritious and delicious recipes to be a success, the recipes in this cookbook have been tested.

How To's from the Authors

Follow the author's on the Heart Smart® Blog by scanning this QR code with your smartphone. To download a free QR code scanner, visit your smartphone's application store.

Appetizers and Snacks

Appetizers and Snacks

In the car, at the office or in front of the television — snacking is part of the American lifestyle. Unfortunately, most traditional snack foods carry a high fat and calorie price tag and offer little of health-promoting nutrients.

But, with a little planning, snacks can be healthy. They can provide nutrients, such as vitamins A and C, calcium and fiber, without lots of fat or too many calories. These six Heart Smart® snack tips can make between-meal eating a valuable part of your family's diet.

Focus on the food groups. Boost the nutritional quality of your diet by choosing snacks from several food groups. It's a great way to add fruits, vegetables, low-fat milk and whole grains to your diet.

Take a handful, not a bowl full. Eat snack-size portions. Remember, snacks aren't meal replacers. They're smaller portions of food to quench hunger pangs.

Store the snacks. Placing snacks within reach of the recliner encourages mindless eating. Make snacking a conscious activity by keeping the bag of chips or canister of cashews in the kitchen cupboard and not at your fingertips.

Veg out. Appetizers and snacks are great opportunities to sneak some vegetables into your diet. Many of the recipes you'll find in this section feature vegetables — Artichoke and Red Pepper Pizza Bites, Corn and Tomato Salsa and Easy Cheesy Zucchini Squares are just a few. Also, fresh vegetables, such as carrot sticks and broccoli florets, serve as wonderful dip and salsa holders. Our Hummus Bi Tahini and White Bean Spread are great with celery sticks, and the Crab Dip is fabulous on top of cucumber slices.

De-fat dips. When preparing creamy dips and spreads that contain sour cream, mayonnaise or cheese, opt for fat-free or reduced-fat versions of those ingredients. We were able to create a wonderful Spinach Artichoke Dip with reduced-fat sour cream and fat-free mayonnaise.

Buy baked. When purchasing potato chips, crackers or tortilla chips, grab the baked or reduced-fat version. Baked tortilla chips are perfect for our Mexican Layered Dip.

Artichoke and Red Pepper Pizza Bites

This recipe follows the Nutrient Rich Foods approach. It's a positive way of eating that focuses on a food's complete nutrient package. It is designed to help people choose nutrient-dense foods from all five food groups, without labeling them good or bad. We made this pizza snack more nutrient-rich by opting for vegetable toppings instead of fatty meats and cut down on the amount of cheese to lower the fat content.

 16 (2 bites per serving)   **60 mins total**

Ingredients

1 tablespoon cornmeal

1 pound pizza dough, thawed

4 cloves garlic, peeled, minced

2 tablespoons olive oil

1 teaspoon dried basil or 1 tablespoon fresh basil, minced

½ teaspoon fennel seed

¼ teaspoon salt

¼ teaspoon freshly ground black pepper

1 cup sliced mushrooms

½ red bell pepper, chopped

1 jar (6 ounces) marinated quartered artichoke hearts, drained and chopped

½ cup thinly sliced red onion

½ cup coarsely chopped black olives

1 ¾ cups (about 6 ounces) shredded part-skim mozzarella cheese

Directions

Preheat oven to 425 degrees.

Dust a jelly roll pan (15 ½-by-10 ½-by-1-inch) with cornmeal to prevent dough from sticking. Begin stretching dough to cover as much of the pan as possible, being careful not to tear the dough. Allow the dough to rest while preparing other ingredients.

In a small bowl, combine garlic, oil, basil, fennel seed, salt and black pepper; set aside. Just before the ingredients are ready to be layered on the dough, give the dough one final stretch.

Spread the oil and garlic mixture over the dough. Layer the mushrooms, red bell pepper, artichoke hearts, red onion and black olives on the dough and sprinkle with the cheese. Bake until golden brown, about 14 to 18 minutes, and cut into 32 small squares.

Cook's note: To avoid soggy pizza bites, drain artichoke hearts well and pat dry with paper towel.

Nutritional info (per serving)

Calories.......................125	Sodium ....222 mg
From fat.................36%	Cholesterol ....102 mg
Fat ....5 g	Calcium ....102 mg
Saturated................2 g	Fiber ....1 g
Trans ....0 g	Food exchanges
Carbohydrates ....15 g	½ starch, 1 vegetable,
Protein ....6 g	1 fat

Corn and Tomato Salsa

Snack when you're hungry rather than when you're bored, frustrated or stressed. Choose snacks that add fruits, vegetables, low-fat milk and whole grains to your diet. A serving of this Corn and Tomato Salsa is a delicious way to sneak a vegetable serving into your eating plan.

 8 (¼-cup servings)   30 mins total

Ingredients

½ cup cooked corn kernels

½ cup diced ripe tomato

¼ cup diced red bell pepper

¼ cup diced cucumber, seeded

¼ cup finely chopped red onion

2 tablespoons red wine vinegar

2 tablespoons tomato juice

2 tablespoons minced jalapeño pepper

1 tablespoon lemon juice

1 tablespoon olive oil

1 clove garlic, peeled, minced

1 teaspoon dried basil

½ teaspoon ground cumin

½ teaspoon chili powder

¼ teaspoon salt

¼ teaspoon dried thyme

¼ teaspoon ground black pepper

Pinch of cayenne pepper

Directions

In a glass bowl, combine all ingredients. Stir well. Refrigerate for at least 30 minutes to allow flavors to blend. Stir well before serving.

Watch This!

Scan this QR code with your smartphone to watch the Heart Smart® video.

Nutritional info (per serving)

Calories	32	Sodium	73 mg
From fat	56%	Cholesterol	0 mg
Fat	2 g	Calcium	6 mg
Saturated	0 g	Fiber	1 g
Trans	0 g	Food exchanges	
Carbohydrates	4 g	1 vegetable	
Protein	1 g		

Crab Dip

Horseradish is a fat-free, low-sodium root that adds distinctive, pungent flavor to sauces, spreads, salad dressings and dips, such as this Crab Dip. Horseradish can be purchased as a fresh, whole root or grated and bottled. Bottled horseradish is white if preserved in vinegar or red if preserved in beet juice.

High-quality horseradish should have a sharp, penetrating aroma and a hot, biting taste. As bottled horseradish ages, it darkens in color and loses its pungency.

 12 (¼-cup servings) **15 mins total**

Ingredients

2 cups low-fat cottage cheese

4 tablespoons reduced-fat cream cheese

1 tablespoon Worcestershire sauce

2 teaspoons lemon juice

1 teaspoon horseradish

1 teaspoon dry mustard

¼ teaspoon hot pepper sauce

¼ teaspoon salt

Dash ground black pepper

1 can (6 ounces) crabmeat, drained

2 green onions, washed, ends removed, finely diced

Directions

In a food processor or blender, combine cottage cheese, cream cheese, Worcestershire sauce, lemon juice, horseradish, dry mustard, hot pepper sauce, salt and pepper. Blend until smooth. Transfer to a medium bowl and stir in crabmeat and green onions. Cover and refrigerate 5 hours or overnight. Serve with fresh vegetables or whole grain crackers.

Nutritional info (per serving)

Calories	55
From fat	33%
Fat	2 g
Saturated	1 g
Trans	0 g
Carbohydrates	2 g
Protein	8 g
Sodium	281 mg
Cholesterol	17 mg
Calcium	43 mg
Fiber	0 g

Food exchanges
  1 lean meat

Cranberry Salsa with Cinnamon Chips

Mangoes supply an ample amount of soluble fiber, which helps to reduce the amount of cholesterol in blood. An average-sized mango supplies more than 60% of the RDA for vitamin C and is one of the few low-fat foods with a respectable amount of vitamin E.

When selecting a mango, look for fruit with unblemished, yellow skin blushed with red. A ripe mango will have a full, fruity aroma and is ready to eat when it is slightly soft to the touch and yields to gentle pressure, like a ripe peach.

 10 (¼-cup servings) 45 mins total

Ingredients

1 can (16 ounces) whole cranberry sauce

½ cup finely diced English cucumber, peeled if desired

½ cup peeled and chopped mango

1 tablespoon finely diced red onion

1 jalapeño pepper, seeded and finely diced

1 tablespoon fresh lime juice

Vegetable oil cooking spray

6 (8-inch) low-fat flour tortillas

1 tablespoon granulated sugar

½ teaspoon ground cinnamon

Test Kitchen Tip

Mangos have a long, flat seed that runs the length of the fruit making it hard to cut in half. Peel the fruit using a paring knife and locate the seed by cutting a piece off the bottom of the mango so you can see where the seed is. Cut the mango lengthwise from top to bottom on one side as close to the seed as possible. Do the same on the other side.

Directions

In a large bowl, mix cranberry sauce, cucumber, mango, red onion, jalapeño and lime juice. Refrigerate at least 1 hour before serving.

To make the chips, preheat oven to 350 degrees. Spray both sides of each tortilla with cooking spray and cut them into 8 wedges.

In a large plastic, sealable bag, combine sugar and cinnamon; add tortilla wedges, seal the bag and shake to coat.

Place wedges on a baking pan in a single layer. Bake them for 8 to 10 minutes or until wedges are crisp and dry.

Cool and store tortillas in an airtight container until ready to serve with cranberry salsa.

Nutritional info (per serving)

Calories.........................149
    From fat 6%
Fat ....1 g
    Saturated...............0 g
    Trans ....0 g
Carbohydrates ....34 g
Protein ....2 g
Sodium ....191 mg
Cholesterol ....0 mg
Calcium ....39 mg
Fiber ....1 g
Food exchanges
    1 starch, 1 fruit

Creamy Black Bean Dip

Eating beans, peas and lentils provide generous amounts of fiber. Three tablespoons, one serving of this dip, contains 2 grams of fiber. Bump up the fiber by serving carrots or red pepper strips with the dip. This dip tastes even better the second day.

 9   **20 mins total**

Ingredients

1 can (15 ounces) black beans, rinsed and drained

Juice of one lime (about 1 tablespoon)

2 ounces reduced-fat cream cheese, softened

¼ cup medium or hot salsa

3 tablespoons diced red onion

1 tablespoon jalapeño pepper, diced

½ teaspoon ground cumin

½ teaspoon chili powder

1 clove garlic, peeled, minced

¼ teaspoon salt

¼ teaspoon ground black pepper

Directions

Place beans and lime juice in a food processor and pulse until smooth. Add cream cheese and continue to process until smooth. Transfer dip to a bowl and add the salsa, red onion, jalapeño, cumin, chili powder, garlic, salt and pepper. Stir until well-blended. Refrigerate at least 2 hours or overnight before serving. Serve with fresh vegetables, whole-wheat pita bread or baked tortilla chips.

 Test Kitchen Tip

Canned beans can be high in sodium. Rinsing them rids them of some of the sodium.

Nutritional info (per serving)

Calories.........................59
    From fat.................15%

Fat ....1 g
    Saturated.................1 g
    Trans ....0 g

Carbohydrates ....9 g

Protein ....3 g

Sodium ....151 mg

Cholesterol ....4 mg

Calcium ....26 mg

Fiber ....2 g

Food exchanges
    2 vegetable

Easy Cheesy Zucchini Squares

Zucchini's principal nutrition attribute is its low calorie content. Because this summer squash is more than 95% water, it has just 19 calories per cup. Zucchini provides a good source of vitamin C, fiber, potassium and magnesium.

 8 60 mins total

Ingredients

Vegetable oil cooking spray

¾ cup fat-free egg substitute

⅓ cup plain bread crumbs

¼ teaspoon salt

⅛ teaspoon black pepper

Dash of hot red pepper sauce (such as Tabasco sauce)

2 ½ cups grated zucchini

1 cup (4 ounces) shredded reduced-fat sharp cheddar cheese

¼ cup grated onion

Directions

Preheat oven to 350 degrees. Coat a square 8-by-8-inch pan with cooking spray. In a large bowl, beat egg substitute with an electric mixer until it is slightly foamy.

Add bread crumbs, salt, pepper and red pepper sauce, and beat 1 additional minute.

Stir in zucchini, cheese and onion. Mix all ingredients until well blended. Pour mixture into the pan.

Bake for 35 to 40 minutes or until the top is golden brown. Remove the pan from oven, and let it stand 10 minutes. Cut into 16 squares (2 squares per serving).

Test Kitchen Tip

Choose zucchini no more than 6 or 7 inches long and 1 to 2 inches in diameter. Large zucchini have more seeds, tough rinds, stringy, coarse flesh and a slightly bitter taste. The skin should be shiny and free of cuts, bruises and decay.

Nutritional info (per serving)

Calories	85
From fat	32%
Fat	3 g
Saturated	2 g
Trans	0 g
Carbohydrates	6 g
Protein	7 g
Sodium	274 mg
Cholesterol	10 mg
Calcium	125 mg
Fiber	1 g

Food exchanges
1 lean meat, 1 vegetable

Easy Spinach Cottage Cheese Bake

A growing body of research suggests that calcium, from three or four daily servings of low-fat dairy foods, may help regulate your body's fat-burning machinery. Studies have found that in a reduced-calorie diet, weight and body fat go down as calcium intake goes up. Current recommendations encourage adults to consume 1,000 to 1,200 milligrams of calcium each day. As a point of reference, one cup of nonfat yogurt has about 450 milligrams of calcium, one cup of skim milk has about 300 milligrams. One serving of this Easy Spinach Cottage Cheese Bake has 264 milligrams of calcium.

 10   1 hour 10 mins total

Ingredients

Vegetable oil cooking spray

1 container (16 ounces) low-fat cottage cheese

1 package (10 ounces) frozen chopped spinach, defrosted and squeezed dry

¾ cup (3 ounces) shredded reduced-fat sharp cheddar cheese

¾ cup diced red bell pepper

1 egg

¾ cup fat-free egg substitute

¼ cup plain bread crumbs

3 tablespoons grated Parmesan cheese

Directions

Preheat oven to 350 degrees.

Coat a 9-inch pie plate with nonstick cooking spray.

In a large bowl, combine the cottage cheese, spinach, cheddar cheese, red pepper, egg, egg substitute, bread crumbs and Parmesan cheese. Mix all ingredients until well blended. Pour into the prepared pie plate. Bake for 45 minutes or until center is set. Let stand 10 minutes before serving.

Nutritional info (per serving)

Calories	101	Sodium	352 mg
From fat	27%	Cholesterol	30 mg
Fat	3 g	Calcium	141 mg
Saturated	2 g	Fiber	1 g
Trans	0 g		
Carbohydrates	5 g	Food exchanges	
Protein	12 g	1 lean meat, 1 vegetable	

Heart Smart® Guacamole

Avocados offer many nutritional benefits. Folate, vitamin B6, niacin, potassium and fiber are a few nutrients in ample supply. Although avocado is high in fat, its fat is mostly monounsaturated. Research suggests that using monounsaturated fats in place of saturated fats can help lower LDL (bad) cholesterol levels. However, because avocados also are high in calories, it makes sense to enjoy this fruit in moderation. This guacamole is great served with fresh vegetables.

 12   15 mins total

Ingredients

2 ¼ cups diced avocado (2 avocados)

⅓ cup reduced-fat sour cream

1 tablespoon lime juice

⅓ cup salsa

3 tablespoons finely diced red onion

1 tablespoon finely diced jalapeño pepper

1 clove garlic, peeled, minced

¼ teaspoon salt

6 ounces baked tortilla chips

Directions

In a medium-size bowl, mash avocados and sour cream until fairly smooth. Stir in lime juice, salsa, onion, jalapeño pepper, garlic and salt. Cover and refrigerate 1 to 2 hours before serving. Serve with baked tortilla chips. One serving consists of 2 ½ tablespoons guacamole and ½ ounce of baked tortilla chips.

Nutritional info (per serving)

Calories	113
From fat	40%
Fat	5 g
Saturated	1 g
Trans	0 g
Carbohydrates	16 g
Protein	2 g
Sodium	179 mg
Cholesterol	3 mg
Calcium	40 mg
Fiber	3 g
Food exchanges	
1 starch, 1 fat	

Test Kitchen Tip

Choose avocados that are unblemished and feel heavy for its size. The skin should be dark purplish. A ripe avocado should yield slightly to gentle pressure. If pressing leaves a small dent in the fruit, it's probably too ripe for slicing but great for mashing and making guacamole. If pressing leaves a large dent, the fruit is overripe and will likely have black, unusable flesh.

Hummus Bi Tahini

This thick Middle Eastern dip is made from mashed chickpeas (also called garbanzo or ceci beans) seasoned with lemon juice, garlic, salt and olive oil. When tahini — a thick paste made of ground sesame seed — is added, it becomes hummus bi tahini. By omitting olive oil, reducing the tahini slightly and cutting the salt in half we created a Heart Smart® version.

 12 (¼-cup servings)   10 mins total

Ingredients

2 cans (15.5 ounces each) chickpeas (garbanzo beans), drained and rinsed

½ cup fresh lemon juice

2 cloves garlic, peeled, minced

½ teaspoon salt

5 tablespoons tahini

Directions

In a blender or food processor, purée the chickpeas and lemon juice. In a small bowl combine the garlic and salt; blend in tahini. Add tahini mixture to the chickpea mixture and blend until it's smooth.

Test Kitchen Tip

Let the kids use hummus as a vegetable dip or pita bread companion or you can use it as a sandwich spread. If you want to add a flavor twist to this traditional hummus recipe, add finely chopped roasted red bell pepper.

Nutritional info (per serving)

Calories......................100
    From fat.................45%

Fat ....5 g
    Saturated...............0 g
    Trans ....0 g

Carbohydrates ....12 g

Protein ....4 g

Sodium ....177 mg

Cholesterol ....0 mg

Calcium ....31 mg

Fiber ....3 g

Food exchanges
    1 starch, 1 fat

Layered Mexican Dip

Nutrient-dense foods, such as the beans in this recipe, provide generous amounts of vitamins, minerals, dietary fiber and relatively few calories. To get the most nutrition out of your calories, go to www.NutrientRichFoods.org. It offers many tools and tips, as well as a guide to reading food labels.

Nutritional info (per serving)

Calories	176	Sodium	381 mg
From fat	20%	Cholesterol	9 mg
Fat	4 g	Calcium	98 mg
Saturated	1 g	Fiber	4 g
Trans	0 g		
Carbohydrates	31 g		
Protein	6 g		

Food exchanges
1 starch, 2 vegetable, 1 fat

 16   30 mins total

Ingredients

1 can (16 ounces) fat-free refried beans

1 minced chipotle pepper in adobo sauce

2 tablespoons lime juice, divided

1 teaspoon ground cumin

½ teaspoon chili powder

2 to 3 dashes Tabasco sauce, optional

½ cup medium or hot salsa, divided

1 cup diced avocado

½ cup reduced-fat sour cream

½ cup (2 ounces) reduced-fat sharp cheddar cheese

½ cup diced tomato

¼ cup sliced green onions

3 tablespoons diced black olives

1 jalapeño pepper, diced

16 ounces baked tortilla chips

Directions

In a medium bowl, stir together refried beans, chipotle pepper, 1 tablespoon lime juice, cumin, chili powder, Tabasco sauce and 2 tablespoons salsa.

In a small bowl, toss avocado with the remaining 1 tablespoon of lime juice; cover and set aside. Spread bean mixture in a 10-inch quiche dish. Spread sour cream on top of bean layer. Continue layering with cheddar cheese, tomatoes, avocado, green onions, black olives, jalapeño pepper and remaining salsa. Refrigerate 2 hours before serving. Serve with baked tortilla chips or fresh vegetables. The nutrition analysis includes 1 ounce of baked chips per serving.

Test Kitchen Tip

Look for canned chipotle peppers in adobo sauce in most grocery stores. Chipotle peppers are smoked jalapeños and can be very hot. One pepper provides a lot of heat. Freeze any leftover, with some of the sauce in ice cube trays. Once the individual cubes are frozen, pop them out and store in freezer quality sealable bags.

Michigan Apple Salsa

Salsas are a great low-calorie dip to serve with baked tortilla chips or over fish, chicken or turkey. This salsa, developed by chef Frank Turner, director of Culinary Wellness at Henry Ford West Bloomfield Hospital, uses Michigan apples, which are one of the state's largest fruit crops. They're unique because there are many varieties, all with their own flavor profiles.

 16 (¼-cup servings) **15 mins total**

Ingredients

2 medium red Michigan apples (Empire, Gala, Ida Red, Jonathan or Rome work well)

2 tablespoons lime juice

½ cup chopped orange segments

½ cup finely chopped onions

½ cup finely chopped green pepper

1 jalapeño pepper, chopped

1 clove garlic, peeled, minced

2 tablespoons chopped cilantro

1 tablespoon apple cider vinegar

½ teaspoon ground cumin

1 teaspoon vegetable oil

Directions

Core and dice apples into ¼-inch pieces. Place in a large bowl and toss immediately with lime juice. Stir in orange segments, onion, green pepper, jalapeño pepper, garlic, cilantro, apple cider vinegar, cumin and vegetable oil. Chill for 2 hours before serving.

Test Kitchen Tip

To get more juice of lemons or limes, roll them on the counter, pressing down on them with the palm of your hand. This breaks down the cells. You also can microwave them first for 15 to 20 seconds.

Nutritional info (per serving)

Calories.........................27	Sodium ....1 mg
From fat...................0%	Cholesterol ....0 mg
Fat.................................0 g	Calcium ....7 mg
Saturated ....0 g	Fiber ....1 g
Trans ....0 g	Food exchanges
Carbohydrates ....6 g	½ fruit
Protein ....0 g	

Watch This!

Scan this QR code with your smartphone to watch the Heart Smart® video.

Pizza Pinwheels

This appetizer is quick and easy to prepare. It's best served warm.

 8 (2 pinwheels per serving) **30 mins total**

Ingredients

Vegetable oil cooking spray

1 can (about 13 ounces) refrigerated pizza dough

¼ cup pizza sauce

¼ cup chopped fresh basil

⅓ cup thinly sliced red onion

½ teaspoon dried oregano

1 cup shredded mozzarella cheese

1 tablespoon Parmesan cheese

Directions

Preheat oven to 400 degrees.

Coat a baking sheet with vegetable oil cooking spray, and set it aside.

Unroll pizza dough and spread it with pizza sauce. Sprinkle chopped basil, red onion, oregano and mozzarella cheese on top. Start rolling dough, from the long end, jellyroll style.

Slice into 1-inch pieces and place them on the prepared baking sheet. Sprinkle with Parmesan cheese. Bake for 12 minutes.

Remove pinwheels from the oven and serve warm.

Nutritional info (per serving)

Calories	133	
From fat	27%	
Fat	4 g	
Saturated	2 g	
Trans	0 g	
Carbohydrates	18 g	
Protein	7 g	

Sodium	275 mg
Cholesterol	9 mg
Calcium	105 mg
Fiber	1 g
Food exchanges	
1 starch, 1 fat	

Roasted Tomato Salsa

The American Institute for Cancer Research recommends that at least two-thirds of your plate be filled with vegetables, fruit, whole grains and legumes. This recipe is a delicious way to sneak in a couple vegetable servings. It's great with baked tortilla chips or as a vegetable dip and is a delicious accompaniment to chicken or fish.

 12 (⅓-cup servings)  **60 mins total**

Ingredients

Parchment paper or vegetable oil cooking spray

10 plum tomatoes, quartered

1 green pepper, quartered, seeded

½ red onion, peeled, quartered, plus ¼ cup finely diced red onion

1 tablespoon olive oil

⅓ cup chopped cilantro

2 tablespoons jalapeño pepper, minced

3 cloves garlic, peeled, minced

2 tablespoons lime juice

1 tablespoon white vinegar

1 tablespoon sugar

½ teaspoon ground cumin

½ teaspoon salt

Pinch of cayenne pepper

Nutritional info (per serving)

Calories	43
From fat	21%
Fat	1 g
Saturated	0 g
Trans	0 g
Carbohydrates	8 g
Protein	1 g
Sodium	88 mg
Cholesterol	0 mg
Calcium	18 mg
Fiber	2 g

Food exchanges
2 vegetable

Directions

Preheat oven to 425 degrees. Line a jelly roll pan (15-by-10-by-1-inch) with parchment paper or coat with vegetable oil cooking spray.

In a large bowl, toss the tomatoes, green pepper and red onion that is quartered with olive oil. Pour onto the prepared jelly roll pan.

Bake uncovered for 20 to 30 minutes or until vegetables soften. Remove from oven and cool completely. Place roasted vegetables in a blender or food processor. Cover and process the vegetables until blended but still chunky. Place it in a large glass bowl and add cilantro, remaining ¼ cup finely diced red onion, jalapeño pepper, garlic, lime juice, vinegar, sugar, cumin, salt and cayenne pepper. Refrigerate at least 1 hour to allow flavors to blend. Stir well before serving.

Spinach Artichoke Dip

Fat-trimming tricks for turning a typically fat-filled spinach artichoke dip included using reduced-fat cream cheese, reduced-fat sour cream and fat-free mayonnaise. We also reduced the amount of Parmesan cheese. Those simple changes slashed more than 50 calories from each serving and reduced the fat content by more than half without compromising flavor.

 10 (¼-cup per serving)  45 mins total

Ingredients

4 tablespoons (2 ounces) reduced-fat cream cheese, softened

½ cup reduced-fat sour cream

¼ cup fat-free mayonnaise

1 tablespoon fresh squeezed lemon juice

1 can (13.75 ounces) quartered artichoke hearts, drained and well-rinsed

½ package (10 ounces) chopped frozen spinach, thawed

½ cup grated Parmesan cheese

¼ cup chopped onion

1 clove garlic, peeled, minced

¼ teaspoon black pepper

Directions

Preheat oven 375 degrees.

In a large bowl, using an electric mixer, cream together cream cheese, sour cream, mayonnaise and lemon juice. Cut artichoke hearts into quarters and squeeze excess liquid from spinach. Using a large spoon, gently incorporate artichoke hearts, spinach, Parmesan cheese, onion, garlic and pepper into cream cheese mixture. Transfer dip into an oven-safe dish and bake uncovered until heated through and bubbly, about 25 minutes.

Nutritional info (per serving)

Calories..........................70
    From fat 51%

Fat ....4 g
    Saturated................ 2 g
    Trans .... 0 g

Carbohydrates .... 5 g

Protein .... 4 g

Sodium .... 175 mg

Cholesterol .... 14 mg

Calcium .... 92 mg

Fiber .... 1 g

Food exchanges
    1 vegetable, 1 fat

Spinach Pie Roll-Ups

This recipe is a great appetizer for a potluck. For easier slicing, cool each roll for 15 minutes and use a serrated knife.

 15 (2 pieces per serving)   1 hour 10 mins total

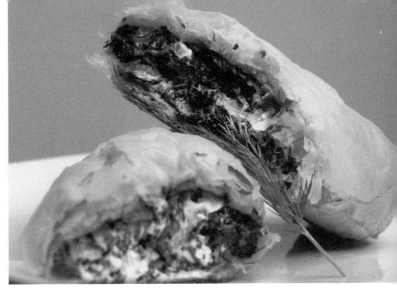

Ingredients

Parchment paper or vegetable oil cooking spray

3 cups diced onion

2 cloves garlic, peeled, minced

1 tablespoon olive oil

2 packages (10 ounces each) frozen chopped spinach, defrosted and squeezed dry

½ cup finely chopped fresh parsley

3 tablespoons finely chopped fresh dill weed

2 tablespoons lemon juice

1 egg

1 egg white

¾ cup low-fat ricotta cheese

1 cup crumbled feta cheese

½ teaspoon salt

½ teaspoon ground black pepper

12 sheets phyllo dough

3 tablespoons trans fat-free margarine, melted

Nutritional info (per serving)

Calories....................... 116	Sodium .... 265 mg
From fat 39%	Cholesterol .... 22 mg
Fat .... 5 g	Calcium .... 113 mg
Saturated................ 2 g	Fiber .... 2 g
Trans .... 0 g	Food exchanges
Carbohydrates .... 12 g	2 vegetable, 1 fat
Protein .... 6 g	

Directions

Preheat oven to 350 degrees. Line a sided baking sheet with parchment paper or spray with vegetable oil cooking spray.

In a nonstick skillet over medium heat, sauté onion and garlic in olive oil about 5 minutes or until onion is tender. Add spinach, parsley, dill weed and lemon juice and continue cooking an additional 2 to 4 minutes or until the mixture looks dry. Remove from heat and set aside.

In a large bowl, slightly beat egg and egg white. Add ricotta cheese, feta cheese, salt and black pepper; stir to combine. Add spinach mixture to the cheese mixture and stir until well blended.

Note that this recipe makes three spinach pie rolls. Using 4 sheets of phyllo for each spinach pie roll, lightly spray each sheet of phyllo with the cooking spray, stacking one layer on top of the next. Place one third of the spinach filling mixture on the long end of the prepared phyllo sheets and roll up, folding the sides. Place spinach pie roll seam-side down on large baking sheet lined with parchment paper. Repeat the procedure, making two additional rolls. Brush the top and sides of each roll with the melted margarine.

Bake for 30 to 40 minutes or until phyllo is crisp and golden brown. Remove from oven and allow to rest 10 to 15 minutes before slicing. Cut each spinach pie roll into 10 pieces. One serving consists of 2 pieces.

White Bean Spread

When using fresh rosemary, be sure to chop and crush the leaves thoroughly. The needle-like leaves are quite tough and do not soften during cooking. Even dried rosemary needs to be crushed or crumbled. Rosemary's pungent, piney flavor pairs well with poultry, fish, lamb, beef and game, especially when roasting. It also enhances soups, stuffings, dressings, egg dishes, vegetables such as tomatoes, spinach, peas and mushrooms, and dips and spreads like this White Bean Spread.

 12   10 mins total

Ingredients

2 cans (15.5 ounces each) cannellini beans, drained and rinsed

2 tablespoons red wine vinegar

2 tablespoons water

2 tablespoons olive oil, divided

2 cloves garlic, peeled, finely minced

¼ teaspoon salt

1 teaspoon minced fresh rosemary

⅛ teaspoon paprika

Directions

In a blender or food processor, puree beans, vinegar, water and 1 tablespoon olive oil.

In a small bowl combine the garlic, salt and rosemary. Add garlic mixture to cannellini bean mixture and pulse until blended. When ready to serve, drizzle the spread with the remaining tablespoon of olive oil and sprinkle with paprika. Serve spread with whole-wheat pita bread or fresh vegetables.

Nutritional info (per serving)

Calories.........................68
  From fat 40%

Fat ....3 g
  Saturated................0 g
  Trans ....0 g

Carbohydrates ....11 g

Protein ....4 g

Sodium .... 212 mg

Cholesterol ....0 mg

Calcium .... 36 mg

Fiber ....4 g

Food exchanges
  ½ starch, ½ fat

Test Kitchen Tip
Because the sprigs of rosemary are sturdy you can use them like a skewer. Thread rosemary sprigs through small cut potatoes or other vegetables and grill them.

Breads and Breakfast

Breads and Breakfast

For years, Mom told us breakfast was the most important meal of the day. Well, she was right. A healthy breakfast gives you the energy to get your day started and provides important vitamins and minerals your body needs.

Breakfast literally means "to break the fast." After eight or more hours without food, the body is essentially a cold furnace that needs to be lit. Breakfast kicks the brain into gear and keeps us alert throughout the morning.

For children and teens, a morning meal is especially important. According to the American Dietetic Association, those who regularly eat breakfast tend to perform better in school, often scoring higher on tests. Children who eat breakfast are more likely to meet the recommended levels of calories, protein, vitamins and minerals compared to those who skip breakfast.

Another benefit to eating breakfast just might show up on the bathroom scale. Many studies have found that breakfast eaters are less likely to be overweight. One theory suggests that eating a healthy breakfast can reduce hunger throughout the day.

Breakfast eaters may have an easier time reducing their risk of heart disease because they tend to consume less fat during the day. And, compared to breakfast skippers, breakfast eaters tend to have lower blood cholesterol levels.

A healthy breakfast does not have to be time consuming to make or eat. Quick energy-boosting breakfasts can be as simple as cold cereal with skim milk and fruit, a whole-grain toaster waffle topped with warmed applesauce, raisins and cinnamon, or a toasted bagel topped with a thin smear of peanut butter and banana slices and a glass of skim milk.

And when you have the time to make breakfast, consider Ricotta Cheese Pancakes with Strawberry Rhubarb Compote which are packed with vitamin C and provide a good source of calcium. The Vegetable Frittata offers a great way to sneak some vegetables into your diet. And the Sunshine Muffins are sure to become a family favorite. Many of the quick breads in this chapter are ideal because you can make and freeze them.

Almond Strawberry Smoothie

This quick-to-make smoothie uses almond milk, which has a mild, slightly nutty aroma. Flavor options include plain, vanilla and chocolate. Almond milk is a nondairy beverage made by crushing almonds, steeping them in water, then straining and pressing them to extract their liquid.

Eight ounces of almond milk contains 25% of the daily needs for vitamin D and 30% of calcium needs, which is what you'll find in cow's milk.

Look for almond milk alongside traditional milk in the refrigerator case or in an aisle, packaged in a shelf-stable, aseptic carton.

 3    **10 mins total**

Ingredients

1 cup unsweetened almond milk (such as Blue Diamond Almond Breeze Original Almond Milk)

1 cup low-fat vanilla yogurt

7 or 8 large frozen strawberries

1 frozen banana

1 tablespoon sugar

1 teaspoon vanilla extract

Directions

In a blender, combine almond milk, yogurt, strawberries, banana, sugar and vanilla extract. Cover and process until smooth. Pour into glasses and serve immediately. Each serving is about 1 cup.

Nutritional info (per serving)

Calories	154
From fat	12%
Fat	2 g
Saturated	1 g
Trans	0 g
Carbohydrates	29 g
Protein	5 g
Sodium	105 mg
Cholesterol	4 mg
Calcium	296 mg
Fiber	2 g

Food exchanges
1 fruit, 1 milk

Apple-Stuffed French Toast

As researchers and health professionals continue to seek answers for safe and effective weight-loss options, one thing remains clear: Enjoying a healthy diet, especially one that includes fruit and fiber-rich foods such as whole grains, vegetables and legumes, is key to a healthy life.

To increase your fruit and fiber intake, give this Apple-Stuffed French Toast a try. One serving provide 1 ½ servings of fruit and five grams of fiber.

 4   **2 hours total**

Ingredients

Vegetable oil cooking spray

8 slices cinnamon raisin bread without icing (such as Sun Maid)

3 tablespoons sugar

½ teaspoon ground cinnamon

1 ¼ cups shredded apple (about 2-3 medium apples)

3 ounces reduced-fat cream cheese, softened

1 egg

¾ cup skim milk

1 tablespoon vanilla extract

Nutritional info (per serving)

Calories....................... 328	Sodium .... 331 mg
From fat.................22%	Cholesterol .... 69 mg
Fat .... 8 g	Calcium .... 120 mg
Saturated................ 4 g	Fiber .... 5 g
Trans .... 0 g	Food exchanges
Carbohydrates ....54 g	2 starch, 1 ½ fruit,
Protein .... 10 g	1 meat, 1 fat

Directions

Spray an 8- or 9-inch square baking dish with cooking spray. Place four slices of raisin bread in a single layer in the bottom of the dish.

In a small dish or measuring cup, combine sugar and cinnamon. Set aside 1 tablespoon of the cinnamon sugar mixture in a separate container. Peel apples and shred them. Squeeze excess liquid from the shredded apples.

Add cinnamon sugar mixture (minus the 1 tablespoon) to the grated apples and stir to combine. Evenly divide apple mixture over the four slices of raisin bread and spread to cover each slice. Top apples with the remaining four slices of raisin bread.

In a large bowl, beat cream cheese at medium speed of mixer until smooth. Add egg, milk and vanilla; mix well. Pour egg mixture over raisin bread. Refrigerate at least 45 minutes or overnight.

To bake, preheat oven to 350 degrees. Sprinkle top of the French toast with the reserved tablespoon of cinnamon sugar mixture.

Bake uncovered for 35 to 40 minutes or until set. Remove from oven and serve.

Blueberry Streusel Muffins

To lower the fat content of your favorite recipe, it's easy to change a few ingredients. The fat in each one of these muffins was slashed by 6 grams simply by replacing one whole egg with two egg whites, using applesauce instead of canola oil and skim milk instead of whole milk. Reduced-fat cream cheese also was an easy replacement for full-fat cream cheese.

 12 45 mins total

Ingredients

Vegetable oil cooking spray or foil muffin tin liners

2 tablespoons trans fat-free margarine

2 tablespoons reduced-fat cream cheese

¼ cup applesauce

¾ cup sugar

2 egg whites

1 egg

2 teaspoons vanilla extract

2 cups all-purpose flour

2 teaspoons baking powder

¼ teaspoon salt

½ cup skim milk

1 cup fresh blueberries

2 tablespoons brown sugar

¼ teaspoon ground cinnamon

Directions

Preheat oven to 375 degrees.

Spray a 12-count muffin pan with vegetable oil cooking spray or line with foil muffin liners. (When baking low-fat muffins, foil liners work better than paper liners.)

In a large bowl, cream together margarine and cream cheese. Add applesauce and sugar and continue beating until light and creamy. Add egg whites, egg and vanilla, beating well. In a separate bowl, combine flour, baking powder and salt; mix well. Stir flour mixture into egg mixture alternately with milk. Fold in blueberries. Spoon batter into prepared muffin cups.

In a small bowl or measuring cup, combine brown sugar and cinnamon and sprinkle topping evenly over unbaked muffins. Bake 20 to 25 minutes or until a wooden pick comes out clean.

Nutritional info (per serving)

Calories	178
From fat	15%
Fat	3 g
Saturated	1 g
Trans	0 g
Carbohydrates	33 g
Protein	4 g
Sodium	145 mg
Cholesterol	20 mg
Calcium	37 mg
Fiber	1 g

Food exchanges
1 starch, 1 fruit, 1 fat

 Test Kitchen Tip
You can toss blueberries with a small amount of flour before gently folding them into batter. This prevents blueberries from sinking to the bottom of muffins.

 Watch This!
Scan this QR code with your smartphone to watch the Heart Smart® video.

Carrot Pineapple Bread

While carrots provide a host of beneficial nutrients such as potassium, vitamin C, vitamin K and fiber, the beta carotene content is off the charts. A hefty 1 ½ cups of grated carrots goes into this bread. Another bonus is these loaves freeze well.

 2 loaves (12 slices each)   1 hour 35 mins total

Ingredients

Floured baking spray

¼ cup canola oil

6 ounces low-fat vanilla yogurt

1 ¾ cup sugar

1 large egg

3 egg whites

1 tablespoon vanilla extract

2 cups all-purpose flour

1 cup white whole-wheat flour (such as King Arthur white whole-wheat flour)

Glaze

½ cup confectioners' sugar

3 tablespoons water

2 teaspoons baking powder

½ teaspoon baking soda

⅛ teaspoon salt

1 tablespoon ground cinnamon

1 teaspoon ground nutmeg

1 ½ cups finely grated carrots

1 can (8 ounces) crushed pineapple packed in juice, drained

⅔ cup walnuts, chopped

Directions

Preheat oven to 350 degrees.

Spray two 8-by-4-inch loaf pans with floured baking spray and set aside.

In a large mixing bowl, beat canola oil and yogurt with an electric mixer on medium speed; add sugar and beat well. Add egg, egg whites and vanilla extract and beat well. In a separate bowl, combine the all-purpose flour, white whole-wheat flour, baking powder, baking soda, salt, cinnamon and nutmeg. Stir flour mixture into sugar mixture until just moistened, being careful not to over mix. Gently fold in grated carrots, pineapple and walnuts.

Pour batter into the prepared loaf pans and bake for 40 to 50 minutes or until a wooden pick inserted in center comes out clean.

To prepare the glaze, combine confectioners' sugar and water and stir until smooth. Spread glaze over the top of each loaf while it is still warm. Cool bread in the pans on a wire rack for 20 minutes. Remove bread from the pans and cool completely on a wire rack.

Test Kitchen Tip

Store carrots in a plastic bag in the refrigerator's vegetable bin. Unwrapped carrots left at room temperature lose sweetness and crispness. If carrots do become limp, re-crisp them in a bowl of ice water. Don't store carrots near apples. Apples release ethylene gas that can give carrots a bitter taste.

Nutritional info (per 1-slice serving)

Calories	180	Sodium	78 mg
From fat	25%	Cholesterol	9 mg
Fat	5 g	Calcium	30 mg
Saturated	1 g	Fiber	1 g
Trans	0 g	Food exchanges	
Carbohydrates	32 g	2 starch, 1 fat	
Protein	3 g		

Cherry Walnut Scones

The original triangular scone was made with oats and baked on a griddle. Today's versions are mostly flour-based and baked in the oven. For scones with crusty tops and bottoms but soft sides, place the scones close together on your baking sheet. Place scones a few inches apart if you want the tops, bottoms and sides to be crusty. Scones are best eaten the day they're baked. They can be frozen.

 16 55 mins total

Ingredients

Vegetable oil cooking spray

2 cups all-purpose flour

1/2 cup plus 1 tablespoon sugar, divided

1 tablespoon baking powder

1/2 teaspoon salt

1/4 cup canola oil

3/4 cup low-fat buttermilk

1 teaspoon orange zest

3/4 cup dried cherries

1/4 cup walnuts, chopped

Directions

Preheat oven to 350 degrees. Coat a baking sheet with vegetable oil cooking spray. In a large bowl, mix the flour, 1/2 cup sugar, baking powder and salt.

Pour canola oil into the dry ingredients and mix well to a crumb consistency.

Add buttermilk and orange zest and knead dough to combine, about 12 times. The dough will be quite sticky. Continue kneading to work in the cherries and walnuts.

Divide dough in half. Place each half on a floured surface and lightly sprinkle it with enough flour to form dough into a circle about 7 inches in diameter.

Sprinkle remaining 1 tablespoon of sugar on top of the scone circles.

Cut each circle into 8 wedges, as you would a pizza.

Place scone wedges on cookie sheet and bake for 15 minutes or until they are lightly golden brown. Remove from oven and serve.

Nutritional info (per serving)

Calories......................150	Sodium ....131 mg
From fat................30%	Cholesterol ....0 mg
Fat ....5 g	Calcium .... 36 mg
Saturated ....0 g	Fiber ....1 g
Trans ....0 g	
Carbohydrates ....25 g	Food exchanges
Protein ....3 g	1 1/2 starch, 1 fat

Test Kitchen Tip

Overworking the dough creates a heavy, dense scone, so handle it as little as possible. When the dough forms a moist clump, transfer it to a lightly floured surface. Also, use as little flour as possible, as too much flour produces a tough scone.

Chocolate Chip Banana Muffins

The banana's best-known nutrient is potassium, a mineral that helps regulate body fluid balance and transmits nerve impulses and muscle contractions. Potassium also plays a role in blood pressure.

Choose bananas that are firm, plump, brightly colored and free of bruises and blemishes. Avoid bananas with a dull, grayish hue; these have been stored at very cold temperatures and will not ripen properly. Two large bananas should yield about 1 cup of mashed bananas.

Test Kitchen Tip

Tossing the chocolate chips with a small amount of flour before adding them to the batter helps prevent them from sinking to the bottom.

 16   1 hour total

Ingredients

Floured baking spray

¼ cup trans fat-free margarine

2 ounces reduced-fat cream cheese

¾ cup sugar

1 egg

½ cup skim milk

1 tablespoon vanilla extract

1 ¾ cups all-purpose flour

1 teaspoon baking powder

½ teaspoon baking soda

¼ teaspoon salt

1 cup mashed ripe bananas

½ cup mini chocolate chips

Directions

Preheat oven to 350 degrees. Coat a muffin pan with floured baking spray.

In a large bowl, cream together margarine, cream cheese and sugar with an electric mixer. Add egg, milk and vanilla extract. Continue to beat until combined.

In a separate bowl, combine flour, baking powder, baking soda and salt. Add the wet ingredients to the dry ingredients and stir until just moistened. Fold in bananas and chocolate chips. Divide batter, filling muffin cups two-thirds full. The batter will yield 16 muffins.

Bake 20 to 25 minutes or until a wooden pick inserted in the muffin comes out clean. Loosen and place muffins onto cooling rack.

Nutritional info (per serving)

Calories......................159
    From fat.................23%

Fat ....4 g
    Saturated ....2 g
    Trans ....0 g

Carbohydrates ....27 g

Protein ....3 g

Sodium .... 133 mg

Cholesterol ....16 mg

Calcium .... 23 mg

Fiber ....1 g

Food exchanges
    1 starch, ½ fruit, 1 fat

Fall Fruit Compote

With just 125 calories per ⅓ cup serving and no fat, this compote is terrific warm or cold. Serve the compote on top of oatmeal, yogurt or whole-grain waffles. Peeling the apple and pear is optional.

 6   35 mins total

Ingredients

1 cup water

¼ cup packed brown sugar

½ teaspoon ground ginger

½ teaspoon ground cinnamon

1 ½ cups seedless red grapes, halved

1 ½ cups diced apple

1 cup diced pear

5 dried apricots, diced

¼ cup apricot preserves

Directions

In a medium saucepan, combine water, brown sugar, ginger and cinnamon; bring to a boil. Cook 1 minute, stirring constantly. Add grapes, apple, pear and dried apricots. Reduce heat to medium and cook 25 minutes or until thickened, stirring occasionally. Remove from heat and stir in apricot preserves.

Serve this compote warm or cold.

 Test Kitchen Tip
If your brown sugar is hard, don't fret. Place the brown sugar in a microwave-safe bowl and microwave on high in 30 second increments until it softens.

Nutritional info (per serving)

Calories	125
From fat	0%
Fat	0 g
Saturated	0 g
Trans	0 g
Carbohydrates	32 g
Protein	1 g
Sodium	8 mg
Cholesterol	0 mg
Calcium	19 mg
Fiber	3 g
Food exchanges	
2 fruit	

Watch This!

Scan this QR code with your smartphone to watch the Heart Smart® video.

French Toast Casserole

This recipe goes together in a snap. And, it's terrific when you need to feed a crowd. You can substitute a multi-grain baguette for the bread if desired.

 12   1 hour 25 mins total

Ingredients

Vegetable oil cooking spray

10 cups 1-inch cubed sturdy white bread (about 16 one-ounce slices)

⅓ cup raisins

1 block (8 ounces) reduced-fat cream cheese, softened

4 eggs

1 cup fat-free egg substitute

1 ½ cups skim milk

⅔ cup fat-free half-and-half

1 ¼ cups maple syrup, divided

1 teaspoon vanilla extract

1 teaspoon cinnamon

Directions

Preheat oven to 375 degrees.

Coat a 13-by-9-inch baking dish with cooking spray. Place bread cubes and raisins in the dish and gently toss.

In a large bowl, beat cream cheese at medium speed until smooth.

Add eggs, one at a time, mixing well after each addition. Add egg substitute and mix well.

Add milk, half-and-half, ½ cup maple syrup, vanilla and cinnamon; mix well. Pour mixture over bread in the baking dish.

Bake uncovered for 35 to 45 minutes or until set. Remove from oven and serve with remaining maple syrup.

Test Kitchen Tip
Freeze the bread slices for about 15 minutes so it's easier to cube them. Stack the slices and then cut into cubes.

Nutritional info (per serving)

Calories...................... 289
   From fat................. 22%
Fat .... 7 g
   Saturated .... 3 g
   Trans .... 0 g
Carbohydrates .... 47 g
Protein .... 10 g
Sodium .... 398 mg
Cholesterol .... 84 mg
Calcium .... 143 mg
Fiber .... 1 g
Food exchanges
   2 starch, 1 fruit,
   1 lean meat, 1 fat

Lemon Poppy Seed Pancakes with Blueberries

One serving of these lemony pancakes is a hearty four pancakes topped with fruit. Blueberries pack a good antioxidant punch, but you can substitute any favorite berries or fruit. Topping the pancakes with fruit is a good way to add in a fruit serving.

4   **45 mins total**

Ingredients

¾ cup skim milk

2 tablespoons lemon juice

1 egg

2 tablespoons trans fat-free margarine, melted

1 teaspoon vanilla extract

1 cup all-purpose flour

2 tablespoons brown sugar

½ teaspoon baking powder

½ teaspoon baking soda

¼ teaspoon salt

1 teaspoon poppy seeds

1 teaspoon lemon zest

Vegetable oil cooking spray

1 ⅓ cups fresh blueberries

1 tablespoon powdered sugar

Nutritional info (per serving)

Calories....................... 233	Sodium .... 385 mg
From fat................. 19%	Cholesterol .... 53 mg
Fat .... 5 g	Calcium .... 97 mg
Saturated................. 1 g	Fiber .... 2 g
Trans .... 0 g	Food exchanges
Carbohydrates .... 39 g	2 starch, ½ fruit, 1 fat
Protein .... 7 g	

Directions

In a small bowl, stir milk and lemon juice and let stand for 10 minutes to curdle. Whisk in egg, melted margarine and vanilla extract. In a separate bowl, combine flour, brown sugar, baking powder, baking soda, salt, poppy seeds and lemon zest until well combined. Pour milk mixture into flour mixture and whisk until batter is just combined being careful not to over mix.

Spray a nonstick skillet with vegetable oil cooking spray and warm over medium heat. Once hot, ladle ⅛ cup of batter per pancake into the skillet. Turn pancake when top forms bubbles and edges appear cooked, about 2 minutes. Briefly cook second side, just long enough to brown. Repeat with remaining batter to yield 16 pancakes. Serve 4 pancakes per serving topped with blueberries and sprinkled with powdered sugar.

Oatmeal Pancakes with Blueberry Sauce

Oats are outstanding. As a whole grain, they offer impressive levels of protein, thiamine, iron, selenium and soluble fiber, which are credited with helping lower blood cholesterol levels. In pancakes, oats are mixed in with all-purpose and white whole-wheat flour.

 8   1 hour total

Ingredients

1 package (12 ounces) frozen blueberries

⅓ cup granulated sugar

1 tablespoon lemon juice

1 tablespoon cornstarch

3 tablespoons water

¾ cup quick-cooking oats

½ cup white whole-wheat flour

½ cup all-purpose flour

¼ cup packed brown sugar

1 teaspoon baking powder

½ teaspoon baking soda

¼ teaspoon salt

1 cup low-fat buttermilk

1 egg

1 tablespoon canola oil

1 tablespoon vanilla extract

Vegetable oil cooking spray

Nutritional info (per 3 pancake serving)

Calories	207	Sodium	214 mg
From fat	17%	Cholesterol	28 mg
Fat	4 g	Calcium	62 mg
Saturated	1 g	Fiber	3 g
Trans	0 g	Food exchanges	
Carbohydrates	39 g	1 ½ starch, 1 fruit, ½ fat	
Protein	5 g		

Directions

To prepare blueberry sauce, combine blueberries, sugar and lemon juice in a saucepan and heat over medium heat. Allow mixture to gently simmer for 20 to 25 minutes. In a small bowl combine cornstarch and water and stir until dissolved. Reduce heat to medium-low and add cornstarch mixture to blueberry mixture, stirring constantly. Cook 1 minute on medium-low heat.

Remove sauce from heat and allow to cool while preparing the pancakes.

In a large bowl, combine dry oats, whole wheat flour, all-purpose flour, brown sugar, baking powder, baking soda and salt; mix well.

In a medium bowl, whisk together buttermilk, egg, oil and vanilla. Pour buttermilk mixture over dry ingredients and stir until batter is just combined.

Spray a nonstick skillet with cooking spray and set over medium-high heat. When hot, spoon 2 tablespoons of batter onto pan. Turn pancake when top forms bubbles and edges appear cooked. Briefly cook second side, just long enough to brown. Repeat with remaining batter.

Test Kitchen Tip

Fresh or frozen blueberries are antioxidant superstars. Freeze fresh blueberries by rinsing them and patting them dry. Place on a tray and freeze to almost solid. Store in freezer bags up to one year.

Oatmeal Raisin Mini Muffins

When substituted for artery-clogging saturated fat such as butter, monounsaturated and polyunsaturated fats may lower harmful LDL cholesterol. Canola oil used in these Oatmeal Raisin Mini Muffins, is high in monounsaturated fat. Olive oil, peanut oil and most nuts are also high in monounsaturated fat. Foods rich in polyunsaturated fat include vegetable oils, such as corn, soybean and sunflower, and many nuts and seeds. These make a great grab-and-go snack.

 8 30 mins total

Ingredients

Floured baking spray

½ cup raisins

½ cup all-purpose flour

½ cup quick-cooking oats

½ cup granulated sugar

1 teaspoon ground cinnamon

1 teaspoon baking powder

¼ teaspoon baking soda

¼ teaspoon salt

1 egg

¾ cup low-fat vanilla yogurt

2 tablespoons canola oil

1 teaspoon vanilla extract

Directions

Preheat oven to 400 degrees.

Spray a 24-count mini muffin tin with the floured baking spray.

In a large bowl, combine raisins, flour, oats, sugar, cinnamon, baking powder, baking soda and salt; set aside. In a separate bowl, whisk together egg, yogurt, canola oil and vanilla. Add wet ingredients to dry ingredients and stir until just moistened. Using a tablespoon, divide batter among the prepared muffin cups.

Bake 12 to 14 minutes or until a wooden pick inserted in the muffin comes out clean. Loosen and place muffins onto cooling rack.

Nutritional info (per 3 muffin serving)

Calories	183
From fat	25%
Fat	5 g
Saturated	0 g
Trans	0 g
Carbohydrates	32 g
Protein	4 g
Sodium	155 mg
Cholesterol	27 mg
Calcium	59 mg
Fiber	1 g

Food exchanges
1 starch, 1 fruit, 1 fat

Pear Bread

This bread was a Best of the Free Press Test Kitchen recipe for 2008. It's great lightly toasted and served with tea. You can freeze it for up to 3 months.

 2 loaves (12 slices each)　 **1 hour 35 mins total**

Ingredients

Floured baking spray

¼ cup canola oil

½ cup low-fat vanilla yogurt

1 ¾ cups sugar

1 large egg

3 egg whites

1 tablespoon vanilla extract

2 cups all-purpose flour

1 cup white whole-wheat flour (such as King Arthur white whole-wheat flour)

2 teaspoons baking powder

½ teaspoon baking soda

⅛ teaspoon salt

2 teaspoons cinnamon

2 cups peeled and chopped pears

⅔ cup chopped pecans

Directions

Preheat oven to 350 degrees.

Spray two 8-by-4-inch loaf pans with the baking spray and set aside.

In a large mixing bowl, beat canola oil and yogurt with an electric mixer on medium speed; add sugar and beat well. Add egg, egg whites and vanilla extract and beat well.

In a separate bowl, combine all-purpose flour, whole-wheat flour, baking powder, baking soda, salt and cinnamon. Stir flour mixture into sugar mixture until just moistened, being careful not to over mix. Gently fold in the pears and pecans.

Pour batter into prepared loaf pans and bake for 50 to 60 minutes or until a wooden pick inserted in center comes out clean. Cool bread in the pans on wire rack for 20 minutes. Remove bread from pans and cool completely on wire rack.

Nutritional info (per 1-slice serving)

Calories....................... 173	Sodium .... 74 mg
From fat................. 26%	Cholesterol ....9 mg
Fat .... 5 g	Calcium .... 27 mg
Saturated ....1 g	Fiber .... 2 g
Trans .... 0 g	Food exchanges
Carbohydrates ....30 g	1 starch, 1 fruit, 1 fat
Protein .... 3 g	

 Test Kitchen Tip

You can toast most nuts to intensify flavor. Because the nutty flavor will be stronger, you can use fewer nuts in most recipes.

Poppy Seed Bread

Let your family try this bread before you tell them it's a healthier version. The original Poppy Seed Bread recipe from Darlene Zimmerman's aunt, Sister Carol Kowalski, called for whole milk, ½ cup oil and eggs. It also contained 12 grams of fat per slice. A recipe makeover, six attempts in all, reduced the fat per slice to just 4 grams without comprising flavor.

 14   **2 hours 20 mins total**

Ingredients

Vegetable oil cooking spray

2 tablespoons trans fat-free margarine

2 tablespoons (1 ounce reduced-fat cream cheese

1 cup granulated sugar

1 large egg

2 teaspoons vanilla extract

2 teaspoons almond extract

Glaze

½ cup powdered sugar

3 tablespoons fresh squeezed orange juice

1 cup all-purpose flour

1 cup white whole-wheat flour (such as King Arthur white whole-wheat flour)

1 tablespoon poppy seeds

2 teaspoons baking powder

½ teaspoon baking soda

⅛ teaspoon salt

1 cup skim milk

1 tablespoon trans fat-free margarine, melted

½ teaspoon almond extract

Directions

Preheat oven to 350 degrees. Spray a 9-by-5-inch loaf pan with cooking spray and set aside.

In a large mixing bowl, beat margarine and cream cheese with a mixer on medium speed; add sugar, beating well. Add egg, vanilla extract and almond extract and beat well.

In a separate bowl, combine all-purpose and whole-wheat flour, poppy seeds, baking powder, baking soda and salt. Add flour mixture to cream cheese mixture alternately with milk, mixing well after each addition.

Pour batter into prepared loaf pan and bake for 50 to 60 minutes or until a wooden pick inserted in center comes out clean.

To prepare glaze, in a small bowl, combine powdered sugar, orange juice, melted margarine and almond extract.

While bread is still warm, spread glaze over the top of the loaf. Cool in pan on a wire rack for 20 minutes. Remove bread from pan and cool completely on wire rack.

Nutritional info (per 1-slice serving)

Calories.........................177
    From fat.................20%

Fat ....4 g
    Saturated.................1 g
    Trans ....0 g

Carbohydrates ....33 g

Protein ....3 g

Sodium ....155 mg

Cholesterol ....17 mg

Calcium ....43 mg

Fiber ....0 g

Food exchanges
    2 starch, ½ fat

Ricotta Cheese Pancakes with Strawberry Rhubarb Compote

Rhubarb is intensely tart and usually combined with sugar in many recipes. In this Strawberry Rhubarb Compote, the tart rhubarb is paired with sweet strawberries and sugar.

 6 (3 pancakes)   35 mins total

Ingredients

¾ cup all-purpose flour

2 tablespoons sugar

1 teaspoon baking powder

½ teaspoon baking soda

¼ teaspoon salt

1 cup skim milk

½ cup low-fat ricotta cheese

1 egg

1 teaspoon vanilla extract

1 teaspoon lemon zest

Vegetable oil cooking spray

Compote

1 cup strawberries, hulled, sliced

1 cup diced rhubarb

⅓ cup sugar

2 tablespoons water

2 teaspoons fresh lemon juice

Directions

In a large bowl, combine flour, sugar, baking powder, baking soda and salt; mix well.

In a medium bowl, beat together milk, ricotta cheese, egg, vanilla and lemon zest. Pour milk mixture over dry ingredients and stir until batter is just smooth.

Spray a nonstick skillet with cooking spray and set over medium heat. When hot, spoon ⅛ cup batter onto pan. Turn pancake when top is covered with bubbles and edges appear cooked. Briefly cook second side, just long enough to brown.

Repeat with remaining batter.

To prepare the compote, place strawberries, rhubarb, sugar and water in a medium saucepan and bring to a boil over medium heat, stirring continuously. Cook until thickened, about 10 to 15 minutes. Remove from heat and stir in lemon juice. Serve on pancakes.

Nutritional info (per serving)

Calories..........................174
    From fat.................10%

Fat ....2 g
    Saturated.................1 g
    Trans ....0 g

Carbohydrates ....33 g

Protein ....6 g

Sodium ....291 mg

Cholesterol ....41 mg

Calcium ....127 mg

Fiber ....1 g

Food exchanges
    1 starch, 1 fruit,
    ½ lean meat

Test Kitchen Tip

Fresh rhubarb is perishable and should be refrigerated, tightly wrapped in a plastic bag, for up to three days. If the leaves are attached, cut them off before storing in the refrigerator. Never eat the leaves, raw or cooked, because they are highly toxic.

Watch This!

Scan this QR code with your smartphone to watch the Heart Smart® video.

Strawberry and Yogurt-Filled Crêpe

Dessert crêpes are often filled with jam or fruit, rolled or folded and sometimes flamed with brandy. Savory crêpes can be filled with various meats, smoked fish, cheese or vegetables and are sometimes topped with a sauce. These crêpes make a simple, somewhat elegant breakfast.

 4 (2 crepes)   1 hour 15 mins total

Ingredients

1 cup skim milk

1 egg

2 egg whites

4 teaspoons canola oil, divided

2 teaspoons vanilla

²/₃ cup all-purpose flour

2 tablespoons sugar

⅛ teaspoon salt

1 ½ cups low-fat vanilla yogurt

2 cups fresh strawberries, chopped

4 teaspoons chocolate syrup

Directions

In a blender combine the milk, egg, egg whites, 2 teaspoons oil, vanilla, flour, sugar and salt. Process until smooth. Place the remaining 2 teaspoons of oil in a small bowl. Heat an 8-inch nonstick skillet over medium heat and lightly brush the pan with a little oil.

When the skillet is hot, pour ¼ cup of the batter into pan, tilting to completely coat the surface of the pan. Cook 2 to 5 minutes, turning once, until golden. Repeat with remaining batter to make 8 crêpes in total, lightly brushing pan with oil before cooking each crêpe if needed. Fill each crêpe with 3 tablespoons low-fat vanilla yogurt and ¼ cup chopped strawberries. Roll crêpe to enclose the filling and drizzle the top of each crêpe with chocolate syrup. One serving consists of 2 stuffed crêpes drizzled with 1 teaspoon chocolate syrup.

Test Kitchen Tip

These crêpes keep several days in the refrigerator, or you can freeze them with a sheet of wax paper in between each and store in a freezer bag.

Nutritional info (per serving)

Calories........................ 311
    From fat................20%
Fat .... 7 g
    Saturated .... 2 g
    Trans .... 0 g
Carbohydrates ....48 g
Protein .... 13 g
Sodium .... 197 mg
Cholesterol .... 59 mg
Calcium .... 256 mg
Fiber .... 2 g
Food exchanges
    1 starch, 1 fruit, 1 milk, 1 fat

Sunshine Muffins

These muffins where given a thumbs up by a group of 8- and 9-year-olds. So they are kid-tested, kid-approved and easy to whip up.

 15 45 mins total

Ingredients

15 (2 ½-inch) foil baking cups or vegetable oil cooking spray

3 tablespoons trans fat-free margarine

3 tablespoons (1 ½ ounces) reduced-fat cream cheese

1 cup sugar

1 tablespoon orange zest

1 large egg

1 teaspoon vanilla or orange extract

1 cup all-purpose flour

1 cup white whole-wheat flour (such as King Arthur white whole-wheat flour)

2 teaspoons baking powder

½ teaspoon baking soda

⅛ teaspoon salt

1 cup (about one 15-ounce can) mandarin oranges packed in juice, drained

½ cup skim milk

Directions

Preheat oven to 400 degrees.

Line a muffin cup tin with foil liners or coat with vegetable oil cooking spray and set aside. In a large mixing bowl with a mixer on medium speed, beat margarine, cream cheese, sugar and orange zest until light and fluffy. Beat in egg and extract. In a separate bowl, combine all-purpose flour, white whole-wheat flour, baking powder, baking soda and salt. Add flour mixture to the sugar mixture alternately with oranges and milk, mixing after each addition. Spoon batter into prepared muffin cups and bake for 12 to 14 minutes or until a wooden pick inserted in the center comes out clean. Allow muffins to cool on a wire rack and serve.

Nutritional info (per serving)

Calories........................142
    From fat.................13%
Fat ....2 g
    Saturated.................1 g
    Trans ....0 g
Carbohydrates .... 27 g
Protein ....3 g
Sodium .... 126 mg
Cholesterol ....16 mg
Calcium ....31 mg
Fiber ....1 g
Food exchanges
    1 starch, 1 fruit

 Test Kitchen Tip
Use the leftover juice from mandarin oranges in marinades and vinaigrettes.

Vegetable Frittata

One large egg yolk contains about 210 milligrams of cholesterol. All of the cholesterol, as well as all of the fat, is packed in the yolk, while most of the protein is in the egg white. If you're cutting back on cholesterol, try using an egg substitute.

 6   1 hour total

Ingredients

1 tablespoon canola oil

½ cup diced onion

2 cloves garlic, peeled minced

1 cup sliced mushrooms

1 cup diced zucchini

½ cup diced red bell pepper

¼ teaspoon salt

¼ teaspoon black pepper

2 cups fat-free egg substitute

¾ cup skim milk

Vegetable oil cooking spray

⅔ cup (2 ½ ounces) shredded reduced-fat sharp cheddar cheese

4 tablespoons grated Parmesan cheese

Directions

Preheat oven to 375 degrees. In a large nonstick skillet, heat canola oil over medium heat and sauté onion and garlic until onion is soft, about 5 minutes. Add mushrooms, zucchini and red bell pepper and sauté 5 to 8 minutes. While vegetables are sautéing, season them with salt and black pepper.

Coat a 9- or 10-inch pie plate with vegetable oil cooking spray.

In a large bowl combine egg substitute and milk. Using an electric hand mixer, beat egg mixture on medium-high speed until it becomes frothy, about 3 minutes. Pour egg mixture over vegetables in the pie plate and add shredded cheddar cheese. Using a spatula or spoon, gently stir to distribute cheese and vegetables. Sprinkle the top of the frittata mixture with Parmesan cheese. Bake for 25 to 30 minutes or until center is set. Let stand about 5 minutes before serving.

Nutritional info (per serving)

Calories	140	Sodium	402 mg
From fat	39%	Cholesterol	12 mg
Fat	6 g	Calcium	196 mg
Saturated	2 g	Fiber	1 g
Trans	0 g		
Carbohydrates	7 g		
Protein	14 g		

Food exchanges
1 vegetable, 2 lean meat, 1 fat

 Test Kitchen Tip

In most recipes substitute two egg whites or ¼ cup of egg substitute to replace one large egg.

Zucchini Bread

This recipe gets a fiber boost by using a combination of whole-wheat and all-purpose flour. A general rule of thumb when you want to incorporate some whole-wheat flour for the all-purpose is to use half whole-wheat flour and half all-purpose flour. For example, if the recipe calls for 2 cups all-purpose flour, use 1 cup all-purpose and 1 cup whole-wheat.

 24 slices   **1 hour 30 mins total**

Ingredients

Floured baking spray

1 container (7 ounces) low-fat Greek-style yogurt

¼ cup canola oil

1 ¾ cup granulated sugar

1 large egg

3 egg whites

1 tablespoon vanilla extract

1 ½ cups all-purpose flour

1 ½ cups white whole-wheat flour (such as King Arthur white whole-wheat flour)

1 tablespoon ground cinnamon

2 teaspoons baking powder

1 teaspoon baking soda

¼ teaspoon salt

3 cups shredded zucchini, patted dry

2 teaspoons orange zest

Glaze

½ cup powdered sugar

2 tablespoons fresh orange juice

1 tablespoon melted trans fat-free margarine

Directions

Preheat oven to 350 degrees. Spray two 9-by-5-inch loaf pans (or you can use several mini loaf pans) with the floured baking spray. In a large bowl, beat together yogurt, oil, sugar, egg, egg whites and vanilla.

In a separate bowl, combine all-purpose flour, white whole-wheat flour, cinnamon, baking powder, baking soda and salt. Add the yogurt mixture to flour mixture and gently combine until just moistened, being careful not to over mix. Add zucchini and orange zest and stir to combine.

Pour batter into the prepared loaf pans and bake for 45 to 55 minutes or until a wooden pick inserted in the center comes out clean.

To prepare glaze, combine powdered sugar, orange juice and melted margarine; stir until smooth. Spread glaze over top of bread while it is still warm. Allow bread to cool in pans on a wire rack for 20 minutes. (You can omit glaze if desired.)

Remove bread from pans and cool completely on the wire rack. Each loaf yields 12 slices. One slice equals one serving.

Test Kitchen Tip
Zucchini freezes well. It's a good idea to freeze shredded zucchini in one or 2 cups portions sizes so it's handy to use for recipes such as this one.

Nutritional info (per serving)

Calories...................... 157	Sodium .... 110 mg
From fat................. 17%	Cholesterol .... 9 mg
Fat .... 3 g	Calcium .... 24 mg
Saturated.............. 0 g	Fiber .... 1 g
Trans .... 0 g	Food exchanges
Carbohydrates .... 29 g	2 starch
Protein .... 3 g	

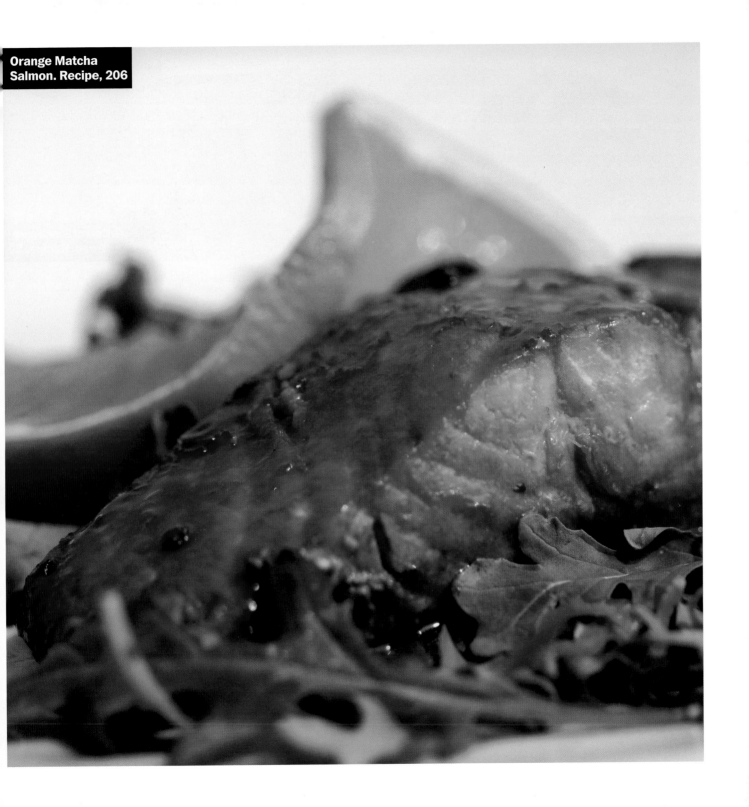

Orange Matcha
Salmon. Recipe, 206

Kung Pau Pork. Recipe, 167

Carrot Pineapple Bread. Recipe, 50

Shrimp Enchiladas. Recipe, 210

Lemon Rice Florentine.
Recipe, 113

Braised Balsamic Chicken
with Artichokes. Recipe, 178

Quinoa Tabbouleh.
Recipe, 119

Raspberry Sour Cream Coffee Cake. Recipe, 252

Roasted Rosemary Potatoes. Recipe, 148

Spaghetti with Creamy Sun-Dried Tomato Sauce. Recipe, 122

Mandarin Orange and Kiwi Cornmeal Cake. Recipe, 246

Roasted Brussel
Sprouts. Recipe, 146

Pork Medallions in Brandy
Cream Sauce. Recipe, 171

Chicken with Cherry Balsamic Glaze. Recipe, 183

Roasted Pumpkin Soup. Recipe, 93

Teriyaki Beef Stir-Fry. Recipe, 161

Spinach and Mushroom Stromboli. Recipe, 100

Tuscan Bean Salad. Recipe, 80

Apple Walnut Cookies. Recipe, 235

Pizza Pinwheels.
Recipe, 40

White Bean Spread.
Recipe, 45

Michigan Apple Salsa.
Recipe, 39

Ricotta Cheese Pancakes with Strawberry Rhubarb Compote. Recipe, 60

Ultimate Heart Smart® Chocolate Chip Cookies. Recipe, 239

Tomato Florentine Pasta Bake. Recipe, 127

Crab Cakes with Remoulade Sauce. Recipe, 203

Spicy Cornmeal Cod with Tarter Sauce. Recipe 211

Heart Smart® Fattoush Recipe, 73

Almond Strawberry Smoothie. Recipe, 47

Antipasto Salad. Recipe, 67

Mushroom Bolognese with Whole-Wheat Pasta. Recipe, 116

Salads

Salads

There is a growing consensus among nutrition researchers that the most powerful disease fighting foods can be found in the produce section of the grocery store. They say the single most important thing you can do to improve your diet is to eat more fruits and vegetables.

The nutritional advantages to filling half your plate at every meal with fruits and vegetables are endless. They supply vitamins, minerals and fiber, all of which seem to work together to protect against a host of chronic diseases, including heart disease, high blood pressure and diabetes. Plus, most fruits and vegetables are naturally low in calories, fat and sodium.

Fruits and vegetables supply a laundry list of antioxidants and phytochemicals, both of which are essential to good health.

Antioxidants help protect cells in the body from destructive molecules called free radicals. While it's normal that the body produces free radicals, an overproduction can cause cell damage that may lead to a variety of health problems including cancer, cataracts and arthritis. Antioxidants mop up free radicals before they do damage. Two well-known antioxidants are beta-carotene and vitamin C.

While phytochemicals offer no nutritional value, research suggests that they work together with other nutrients in food to protect us against disease. Some phytochemicals may inhibit the growth of cancer cells while others may lower blood cholesterol levels. These friendly chemicals have tongue-twisting names such as allyl sulfides found in onions, garlic and leeks; isothiocyanates found in broccoli and cabbage; limonene found in citrus fruits and ellagic acid found in strawberries, raspberries, apples, grapes and pears.

The easiest way to load up on antioxidants and phytochemicals is to enjoy a variety of brightly colored fruits and vegetables. The more brilliant and intense a food's color, the greater the food's disease-fighting properties. The latest Dietary Guidelines for Americans encourages adults to consume at least 2 cups of fruit and 2 1/2 cups of vegetables every day.

The recipes that follow, such as our Chinese Cabbage Salad with Asian Dressing, Heart Smart® Fattoush or Spicy Thai Slaw, show how easy it is to add more fruits and vegetables to your day.

Antipasto Salad

Research has shown that a healthy eating plan called DASH (Dietary Approaches to Stop Hypertension) can lower your blood pressure or reduce your chances of developing high blood pressure. The plan emphasizes fruits, vegetables, whole grains and low-fat dairy products. You can enjoy this Antipasto Salad for dinner, which provides two vegetable servings.

 14 (¾-cup servings)   55 mins total

Ingredients

- 3 cups 2-inch sliced asparagus (about ¾ pound)
- 3 cups quartered mushrooms (about ¾ pound)
- 1 cup red bell pepper strips
- 1 cup diced cucumbers
- ½ cup pitted black olives
- 3 ounces part-skim mozzarella cheese, cubed
- 1 can (15 ounces) chickpeas,
- drained and rinsed
- ½ cup diced red onion
- ⅓ cup cider vinegar
- ¼ cup fresh chopped parsley
- 2 tablespoons olive oil
- 2 teaspoons dried oregano
- 1 teaspoon sugar
- ¼ teaspoon salt
- ¼ teaspoon black pepper
- 3 cloves garlic, peeled, minced

Directions

Steam asparagus, covered, for 2 minutes. Drain and plunge into an ice-water bath; drain well.

In a large bowl, combine asparagus, mushrooms, red bell pepper, cucumber, olives, cheese, chickpeas and red onion.

In a small bowl, whisk together vinegar, parsley, olive oil, oregano, sugar, salt, black pepper and garlic. Pour vinaigrette over vegetables, tossing gently to coat. Cover and marinate in refrigerator 2 hours; stir occasionally.

Test Kitchen Tip

Some fresh mushrooms have more dirt on them than others. Use a damp paper towel to wipe off any dirt. If you must rinse them under cold water, do so quickly because mushrooms are like sponges and will soak up additional water.

Nutritional info (per serving)

Calories..........................84
    From fat.................43%
Fat..................................4 g
    Saturated.................1 g
    Trans......................0 g
Carbohydrates.............9 g
Protein..........................4 g
Sodium..................177 mg
Cholesterol..............4 mg
Calcium...................74 mg
Fiber............................2 g
Food exchanges
    2 vegetable, 1 fat

Watch This!

Scan this QR code with your smartphone to watch the Heart Smart® video.

Baby Spinach and Strawberries with Honey Balsamic Vinaigrette

Traditional dressings can easily add 20 grams of fat and 300 calories to healthy, low-fat salad greens. You can lower that considerably by making your own. Most homemade dressings call for a ratio of three parts oil to one part vinegar. Try three parts vinegar to one part oil. You can substitute orange juice, apple cider, balsamic vinegar or herb vinegars for wine vinegars. These ingredients are less acidic, so it takes less oil to achieve a pleasant flavor. Adding Dijon mustard in place of some oil to vinaigrette dressings not only enhances flavor and body but also reduces the fat content.

8 **15 mins total**

Ingredients

1 tablespoon olive oil

1 tablespoon balsamic vinegar

1 tablespoon honey

1 tablespoon water

2 teaspoons Dijon mustard

⅛ teaspoon salt

⅛ teaspoon freshly ground black pepper

1 package (5 ounces) baby spinach, cleaned and trimmed

1 cup sliced strawberries

2 tablespoons toasted slivered almonds

Directions

In a jar with a tight-fitting lid, combine olive oil, balsamic vinegar, honey, water, mustard, salt and pepper. Cover and shake to combine. In a large bowl, combine spinach and strawberries. Add the dressing and toss to coat. Sprinkle almonds on top of the salad greens and serve immediately.

Test Kitchen Tip

Hang on to almost-empty Dijon mustard containers. Add your dressing ingredients to the container and shake well. Not only have you used up all of the mustard in the container, but you have a great dressing dispenser.

Nutritional info (per serving)

Calories...........................46	Sodium ....75 mg
From fat.................59%	Cholesterol ....0 mg
Fat ....3 g	Calcium .... 25 mg
Saturated ....0 g	Fiber ....1 g
Trans ....0 g	Food exchanges
Carbohydrates ....5 g	1 vegetable, ½ fat
Protein ....1 g	

Celery Slaw with Edamame

Edamame (eh-dah-MAH-meh) is the Japanese name for fresh soybeans. Edamame, which are usually bright to dark green, are available fresh in the produce section in some grocery stores or in Asian markets. They're also available frozen as whole pods or shelled beans. Enjoy edamame as a snack, vegetable or addition to soups, stews and salads.

 4 **30 mins total**

Ingredients

4 large celery ribs

1 carrot, peeled

1 cup cooked sweet green soybeans (edamame)

2 green onions, thinly sliced

¼ cup chopped cilantro leaves,

2 tablespoons coarsely chopped celery leaves

1 ½ tablespoons rice vinegar

2 teaspoons canola oil

½ teaspoon celery seed

Directions

In a food processor or with a sharp knife, slice celery and carrot as thinly as possible.

Put celery and carrot in a bowl of ice water and crisp them for 15 minutes. Drain and pat them dry. Wipe out the bowl and return the celery and carrot to it.

Add soybeans, green onions, cilantro and celery leaves to the celery and carrots and toss well.

In another bowl, whisk rice vinegar with the oil and celery seed. Pour the dressing over the vegetables; toss and serve.

Nutritional info (per serving)

Calories......................104	Sodium ....72 mg
From fat................44%	Cholesterol ....0 mg
Fat ....5 g	Calcium .... 123 mg
Saturated ....1 g	Fiber ....4 g
Trans ....0 g	Food exchanges
Carbohydrates ....9 g	2 vegetable, 1 fat
Protein ....6 g	

 Test Kitchen Tip

If you buy edamame frozen and uncooked, cook them in a medium saucepan of boiling water for 5 minutes. Drain and refresh them under cold water.

Chinese Cabbage Salad with Asian Dressing

Napa cabbage, also called Chinese or Peking cabbage, celery cabbage or wong bok, is a great addition to salads, slaws and stir-fries. It has a mild and mellow flavor and can be eaten raw or cooked. At most grocery stores, you will likely find the large and barrel-shaped variety with tightly packed leaves, resembling a bunch of wide-stalked celery. The white to light-green leaves are crinkly and have thick veins. And like other cabbages and cruciferous vegetables, such as broccoli and cauliflower, napa cabbage contains compounds called indoles that may help reduce the risk of cancer.

 7 (1-cup servings) **25 mins total**

Ingredients

3 tablespoons rice vinegar

1 tablespoon canola oil

1 tablespoon honey

1 tablespoon reduced-sodium soy sauce

1 tablespoon water

½ teaspoon grated gingerroot

⅛ teaspoon salt

⅛ teaspoon red pepper flakes, optional

6 cups finely shredded napa cabbage

1 cup diced red bell pepper

½ cup coarsely shredded carrots

⅓ cup sliced green onions, green part only

1 can (15 ounces) mandarin oranges packed in juice, drained

¼ cup chopped unsalted peanuts

Directions

In a jar with a tight-fitting lid, combine rice vinegar, oil, honey, soy sauce, water, gingerroot, salt and red pepper flakes. Cover and shake to combine. In a large bowl, combine cabbage, red bell pepper, carrots and green onions. Add the dressing and toss to coat. Add oranges and peanuts, gently toss again and serve.

Nutritional info (per serving)

Calories.........................95
   From fat.................47%

Fat ....5 g
   Saturated ....1 g
   Trans ....0 g

Carbohydrates ....12 g

Protein ....3 g

Sodium .... 125 mg

Cholesterol ....0 mg

Calcium .... 66 mg

Fiber ....2 g

Food exchanges
   2 vegetable, 1 fat

 Test Kitchen Tip

You can reserve the juice from the mandarin oranges to make other citrus dressings. When selecting napa cabbage, choose firm, tightly packed heads with crisp, green-tipped leaves that are free of brown spots. Refrigerate and use within four days.

Classic Macaroni Salad

Cooking tricks can turn an unhealthy recipe into a delicious, nutritious one. This Classic Macaroni Salad begins with a fiber boost — whole-wheat pasta instead of refined. Using reduced-fat versions of mayonnaise and sour cream cut the fat. What we didn't cut was flavor. Adding dry mustard, horseradish and cider vinegar provides the zip to this family favorite. Extra vegetables in this salad add color and crunch as well as nutrition.

 8 (¾-cup servings)   30 mins total

Ingredients

8 ounces (2 cups) dry whole-wheat macaroni

½ cup diced celery

½ cup diced red pepper

½ cup peeled and diced cucumber

½ cup diced red onion

¼ cup reduced-fat mayonnaise

¼ cup reduced-fat sour cream

1 teaspoon dry mustard

1 teaspoon horseradish

1 tablespoon cider vinegar

½ teaspoon salt

¼ teaspoon ground white pepper

Directions

Cook macaroni according to package directions, omitting the salt. When done, rinse pasta under cold water and drain well.

In a large bowl, combine macaroni, celery, red pepper, cucumber and red onion. In a small bowl combine mayonnaise, sour cream, dry mustard, horseradish, cider vinegar, salt and white pepper. Add dressing mixture to macaroni mixture and toss to coat.

Chill at least 2 hours before serving.

 Test Kitchen Tip

Use any whole-wheat pasta, such as shell macaroni, in this recipe.

Nutritional info (per serving)

Calories........................137
    From fat.................26%

Fat................................4 g
    Saturated.................1 g
    Trans.......................0 g

Carbohydrates...........22 g

Protein.........................4 g

Sodium.................195 mg

Cholesterol..............7 mg

Calcium..................30 mg

Fiber............................3 g

Food exchanges
    1 starch, 1 vegetable, ½ fat

Heart Smart® Chopped Salad

Legumes (dried beans and peas) provide a healthy dose of soluble fiber, which may help reduce the risk of heart disease by lowering LDL (bad) cholesterol levels. Beans are also low in fat, cholesterol-free and rich in protein, folate, iron and zinc. This chopped salad recipe features chickpeas — also known as garbanzo beans and ceci beans. This pale, round, cream-colored legume has a firm texture and mild, nutty flavor. Chickpeas are great in soups, stews, casseroles, salads and pasta dishes.

 6 (1-cup servings)  30 mins total

Ingredients

1 tablespoon olive oil

3 tablespoons red wine vinegar

2 tablespoons grated Parmesan cheese

1 teaspoon sugar

1 clove garlic, peeled, minced

½ teaspoon dried oregano

¼ teaspoon ground black pepper

¼ teaspoon salt

3 cups Bibb lettuce, chopped

1 cup julienned red pepper

1 cup chopped cucumber

1 cup canned chickpeas, drained and rinsed

½ cup sliced radishes

¼ cup sliced red onion

Directions

In a small bowl or measuring cup, combine olive oil, red wine vinegar, Parmesan cheese, sugar, garlic, oregano, black pepper and salt and whisk until combined.

In a large bowl, place Bibb lettuce, red pepper, cucumber, chickpeas, radishes and onion.

Pour vinaigrette over the vegetables and toss gently to coat.

Test Kitchen Tip

To reduce the gas-producing properties of beans, presoak dried beans for at least 6 hours before cooking them, and discard the soaking water.

Nutritional info (per serving)

Calories..........................85	Sodium .... 194 mg
From fat.................42%	Cholesterol .... 1 mg
Fat .... 4 g	Calcium .... 56 mg
Saturated.................1 g	Fiber .... 3 g
Trans ....0 g	Food exchanges
Carbohydrates .... 10 g	2 vegetable, 1 fat
Protein .... 3 g	

Heart Smart® Fattoush

Fattoush is a traditional Lebanese salad made from toasted or fried pieces of pita bread mixed with fresh greens and a variety of seasonal vegetables and topped with a tart vinaigrette dressing. To boost the fiber content of this Heart Smart® Fattoush, whole-wheat pita bread is used and the bread is toasted — not fried — to keep a lid on the fat content. The vinaigrette gets its tartness from lemon juice and sumac.

Look for sumac at Greek and Middle Eastern markets or in the ethnic aisle of some grocery stores. Sumac is sold as coarsely ground powder or as whole berries.

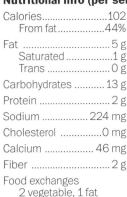

 6 (about 1 ⅓-cup servings)  **15 mins total**

Ingredients

¼ cup lemon juice

2 tablespoons olive oil

1 teaspoon sugar

2 cloves garlic, peeled, minced

½ teaspoon salt

½ teaspoon ground black pepper

2 teaspoons ground sumac

3 cups chopped romaine lettuce

2 cups chopped tomatoes

2 cups diced English cucumber

½ cup sliced red onion

½ cup chopped fresh parsley

¼ cup chopped fresh mint

1 round whole-wheat pita bread (9-inch), toasted and torn into bite-size pieces

Nutritional info (per serving)

Calories	102
From fat	44%
Fat	5 g
Saturated	1 g
Trans	0 g
Carbohydrates	13 g
Protein	2 g
Sodium	224 mg
Cholesterol	0 mg
Calcium	46 mg
Fiber	2 g

Food exchanges
2 vegetable, 1 fat

Directions

In a small bowl or measuring cup, combine lemon juice, olive oil, sugar, garlic, salt, black pepper and sumac and whisk until combined. Place romaine lettuce, tomatoes, cucumber, onion, parsley and mint in a large bowl. Pour the dressing over vegetables and toss gently to coat. Add toasted pita pieces and toss to coat.

Jicama and Black Bean Salad

Jicama (pronounced HEE-kah-mah) is a large, bulbous root vegetable with a thin, brown skin and white, crisp, juicy flesh similar to that of a Fuji apple. Often called the Mexican potato, it is a legume, a relative of the bean family. Jicama also is a good source of vitamin C, an excellent source of fiber and low in calories. One cup of cubed jicama contains just 45 calories.

 6 (²⁄₃-cup servings)   20 mins total

Ingredients

2 cups peeled and julienned jicama

1 can (15 ounces) black beans, drained and rinsed

1 cup diced cucumber

½ cup diced red pepper

¼ cup sliced green onions

3 tablespoons lime juice

1 tablespoon canola oil

1 tablespoon sugar

1 teaspoon Dijon mustard

½ teaspoon ground ginger

¼ teaspoon ground cumin

¼ teaspoon salt

Directions

In a large bowl gently combine jicama, black beans, cucumber, red pepper and green onions.

In a small jar, place lime juice, oil, sugar, Dijon mustard, ginger, cumin and salt. Seal tightly with a lid and shake vigorously to combine. Pour dressing over vegetable mixture, gently toss to combine; chill before serving.

Test Kitchen Tip

Look for hard, unblemished jicama tubers that are heavy for their size and free of cracks and bruises. Peel the skin with a paring knife just before using. A 1-pound jicama yields about 3 cups chopped.

Nutritional info (per serving)

Calories.......................122
    From fat.................22%
Fat ....3 g
    Saturated ....0 g
    Trans ....0 g
Carbohydrates ....20 g
Protein ....5 g
Sodium ....231 mg
Cholesterol ....0 mg
Calcium ....42 mg
Fiber ....5 g
Food exchanges
    1 starch, 1 vegetable,
    ½ fat

Mediterranean Potato Salad

This salad has an added sweet flavor from sun-dried tomatoes. These tomatoes are vine-ripened tomatoes dried in the sun or mechanically dried to remove the water. They have a rich and intense flavor, so a little goes a long way. Use sun-dried tomatoes to enhance pasta and vegetable dishes, breads and soups, stews and sauces. Sun-dried tomatoes are sold packed dry, in oil or ready to use.

Dry-packed tomatoes should be rehydrated before use, so soak them in warm water for 30 minutes. Oil-packed sun-dried tomatoes do not need to be rehydrated but do add fat to the recipe. Sun-dried tomatoes also can be purchased ready to eat straight from the package.

 8 (¾-cup servings)   50 mins total

Ingredients

- 2 pounds red-skin potatoes, cooked, cooled and cut into cubes
- ¼ cup fresh lemon juice
- 2 tablespoons olive oil
- 1 clove garlic, peeled, minced
- ½ teaspoon dried oregano
- ¼ teaspoon salt
- ¼ teaspoon ground black pepper
- ¼ cup sun-dried tomatoes, thinly sliced
- ⅓ cup crumbled feta cheese
- ¼ cup pitted kalamata olives, quartered
- 3 green onions, washed, thinly sliced

Directions

Place the cooked, cubed potatoes in a large bowl.

In a measuring cup, whisk together the lemon juice, olive oil, garlic, oregano, salt and pepper. Pour the dressing mixture over the potatoes and stir gently. Add the sun-dried tomatoes, feta cheese, olives and green onions and gently stir to combine. Cover and refrigerate at least 4 hours to allow flavors to blend.

 Test Kitchen Tip

To soften the ready-to-eat sun-dried tomatoes in this recipe, place them in the bottom of the colander and drain the cooked potatoes over them. Slice the sun-dried tomatoes using kitchen scissors.

Watch This!

Scan this QR code with your smartphone to watch the Heart Smart® video.

Nutritional info (per serving)

Calories........................ 137	Sodium ....218 mg
From fat.................33%	Cholesterol ....2 mg
Fat................................5 g	Calcium .... 40 mg
Saturated.................1 g	Fiber ....3 g
Trans ....0 g	Food exchanges
Carbohydrates ....21 g	1 starch, 1 vegetable, 1 fat
Protein ....4 g	

My Big, Not So Fat, Greek Pasta Salad

This salad packs a lot of flavor from the feta cheese and kalamata olives. It's easily put together and is finished off with a lemony dressing. You can serve this as a side salad or pack it for lunch.

6   30 mins total

Ingredients

SALAD

1 ½ cups uncooked farfalle (bow-tie pasta)

1 cup diced cucumber

1 can (15 ounces) chickpeas (garbanzo beans), drained and rinsed

1 ounce crumbled feta cheese

¼ cup chopped red onion

¼ cup kalamata olives, pitted, halved

DRESSING

3 tablespoons fresh lemon juice

1 tablespoon olive oil

½ teaspoon dried oregano

¼ teaspoon salt

¼ teaspoon ground black pepper

Test Kitchen Tip

You can use about 1 tablespoon of fresh oregano in place of dried oregano in this recipe.

Nutritional info (per serving)

Calories........................130
    From fat.................35%
Fat ....5 g
    Saturated ....1 g
    Trans ....0 g
Carbohydrates ....18 g
Protein ....4 g
Sodium ....222 mg
Cholesterol ....3 mg
Calcium .... 39 mg
Fiber ....3 g
Food exchanges
    1 starch, 1 fat

Directions

To prepare salad, cook pasta according to package directions, omitting the salt. When done, rinse pasta under cold water and drain well. Place the pasta, cucumber, chickpeas, feta cheese, red onion and olives in a large bowl.

To prepare the dressing, combine lemon juice, olive oil, oregano, salt and pepper in a small jar with a tight-fitting lid and shake well. Drizzle the dressing over salad and toss gently to coat. Serve or refrigerate until ready to serve.

Romaine and Cucumber Salad with Avocado Dressing

The dressing in this recipe gets some of its creaminess from buttermilk and mashed avocado. Despite its name and creamy consistency, buttermilk actually is low in fat. Buttermilk is made by adding cultures or friendly bacteria to fat-free or 1% milk in the same way that yogurt and sour cream are made. The result is a slightly thickened milk with a tart, tangy flavor.

 6 (1-cup servings) 20 mins total

Ingredients

¼ cup low-fat buttermilk

1 tablespoon reduced-fat sour cream

½ of a ripe avocado, diced

1 tablespoon fresh lime juice

1 clove garlic, peeled, coarsely chopped

¼ teaspoon salt

⅛ teaspoon ground red pepper

5 cups chopped romaine lettuce

1 cup diced cucumber

⅓ cup sliced red onion

Directions

Place buttermilk, sour cream, avocado, lime juice, garlic, salt and ground red pepper in a blender and process until smooth, scraping the sides as needed. Combine lettuce, cucumber and red onion in a large bowl; add the dressing and toss gently to coat. The salad dressing is very thick. If you prefer a thinner dressing, add an additional tablespoon of lime juice or 1 tablespoon of skim milk.

Test Kitchen Tip

If you don't have buttermilk on hand, mix equal parts of nonfat yogurt and skim milk. You also can place 1 tablespoon of vinegar or lemon juice in a measuring cup, fill to the 1-cup mark with skim milk and let stand for about 10 minutes or until the milk thickens and begins to curdle. Dry, powdered buttermilk also is available. To dice an avocado, cut it in half, running a knife along the pit. Separate the halves. Slice the avocado, still in the skin, lengthwise and then crosswise. Use a spoon to scoop out the diced avocado pieces.

Nutritional info (per serving)

Calories...........................43
    From fat................63%
Fat ....3 g
    Saturated.................1 g
    Trans ....0 g
Carbohydrates ....4 g
Protein ....1 g
Sodium ....96 mg
Cholesterol ....2 mg
Calcium ....37 mg
Fiber ....2 g
Food exchanges
    1 vegetable, ½ fat

Singapore Black Bean Salad

This salad is easy to make and terrific tasting with a dressing made with a blend of picante sauce and peanut butter. It also has a nice crunch from the romaine lettuce. Kids will like the flavor and can lend a hand in making this. Serve this salad as a side dish.

 8   15 mins total

Ingredients

½ cup picante sauce

⅓ cup rice vinegar

3 tablespoons peanut butter

1 clove garlic, peeled

6 cups romaine lettuce, torn in bite-size pieces

1 can (16 ounces) black beans, drained and rinsed

½ cup sliced red onion

1 large red pepper, cut into ¼-inch thick rings

Directions

In a blender place picante sauce, rice vinegar, peanut butter and garlic. Cover and blend until smooth. Toss romaine lettuce, black beans and onions with dressing until evenly coated. Arrange red pepper rings over salad and serve.

Nutritional info (per serving)

Calories.........................117
        From fat.................30%

Fat .... 4 g
        Saturated ....1 g
        Trans ....0 g

Carbohydrates .... 15 g

Protein .... 6 g

Sodium ....211 mg

Cholesterol ....0 mg

Calcium ....41 mg

Fiber .... 4 g

Food exchanges
        3 vegetable, 1 fat

Spicy Thai Slaw

Cruciferous vegetables, such as broccoli, cauliflower, red and green cabbage, Brussels sprouts, collard and mustard greens, kale and bok choy contain nutrients and phytochemicals that seem to be effective in warding off certain forms of cancers. It's important to enjoy cruciferous vegetables often. This slaw recipe is made with red cabbage tossed with a peanut-soy dressing.

 8 35 mins total

Ingredients

½ cup water

3 tablespoons rice wine vinegar

1 tablespoon reduced-sodium soy sauce

1 ½ teaspoons cornstarch

1 teaspoon sugar

1 tablespoon creamy peanut butter

1 large garlic clove, peeled, minced

1 tablespoon freshly chopped cilantro

½ teaspoon crushed red pepper

4 cups finely shredded red cabbage

½ cup shredded carrot

½ cup sliced green onion

Test Kitchen Tip

The amount of sodium in soy sauce can vary by brand, so be sure check the labels. Many well known brands of lower-sodium soy sauce have about 50% less sodium than the original.

Directions

In a small saucepan, combine the water, rice wine vinegar, soy sauce, cornstarch and sugar. Bring the liquid to a boil and cook 1 minute, stirring constantly. Remove the pan from the heat and whisk in the peanut butter until the mixture is smooth.

Stir in the garlic, cilantro and red pepper. Cover the dressing and chill it while preparing the slaw ingredients.

In a large bowl, place the red cabbage, carrot and green onion; add the dressing, tossing gently to coat.

Cover and chill before serving.

Nutritional info (per serving)

Calories	38
From fat	25%
Fat	1 g
Saturated	0 g
Trans	0 g
Carbohydrates	6 g
Protein	1 g
Sodium	144 mg
Cholesterol	0 mg
Calcium	27 mg
Fiber	2 g

Food exchanges
1 vegetable, ½ fat

Tuscan Bean Salad

Beans are a great source of fiber. In this salad, navy beans are paired with penne pasta and vegetables in a vinaigrette. Up the fiber even more by using whole-wheat penne pasta.

 8 (½-cup servings)   25 mins total

Ingredients

1 cup cooked penne pasta

1 can (15 ounces) navy beans, drained and rinsed

⅔ cup diced green pepper

⅔ cup diced celery

⅓ cup diced red onion

2 tablespoons red wine vinegar

2 tablespoons olive oil

1 tablespoon water

1 teaspoon Dijon mustard

1 teaspoon sugar

2 tablespoons chopped fresh parsley

½ teaspoon dried oregano

½ teaspoon dried thyme

¼ teaspoon salt

¼ teaspoon black pepper

1 clove garlic, peeled, minced

Directions

Place cooked pasta in a large bowl.

Add navy beans, green pepper, celery and red onion. In a small jar with a tight-fitting lid, combine red wine vinegar, olive oil, water, Dijon mustard, sugar, parsley, oregano, thyme, salt, black pepper and garlic; shake well. Pour the vinaigrette over bean mixture, tossing gently to coat. Refrigerate at least 2 hours before serving to allow flavors to blend.

Test Kitchen Tip

Many canned beans are high in sodium. Rinse them before using to remove excess sodium.

Nutritional info (per serving)

Calories	122
From fat	30%
Fat	4 g
Saturated	1 g
Trans	0 g
Carbohydrates	17 g
Protein	5 g
Sodium	230 mg
Cholesterol	0 mg
Calcium	32 mg
Fiber	3 g

Food exchanges
1 starch, 1 fat

Watermelon and Grilled Peach Salad with Strawberry Yogurt Dressing

This salad, from the recipe file of chef Frank Turner, director of Culinary Wellness at Henry Ford West Bloomfield Hospital, makes a great salad starter presentation. Each serving has a nutrient boost from the spinach and watermelon. You can slice the watermelon as you like, but triangular pieces fit nicely between the grilled peaches. The dressing makes more than you need but can be used as a fruit dip or with other salads.

 4 60 mins total

Ingredients

4 large seedless watermelon slices at least 1-inch thick

1 cup strawberries, washed and hulled

½ cup low-fat plain yogurt

1 tablespoon Agave syrup or honey

1 tablespoon cider vinegar

2 ripe peaches, quartered

2 teaspoons canola oil

3 cups baby spinach

1 cup thinly sliced red onion

Directions

Preheat or prepare grill for medium heat.

For each serving, cut each watermelon slice into 4 triangular pieces or slice them in wedges wide or narrow enough to fit on a salad serving plate.

To prepare the dressing, combine the strawberries, yogurt, Agave syrup and vinegar in the blender and purée until smooth. Refrigerate until ready to use.

Brush peach quarters with oil and grill on each cut side until grill marks appear, being careful not to overcook.

Toss the spinach with ½ cup of the dressing and arrange on a plate. Slice the grilled peach quarters and arrange around spinach with the watermelon slices and red onion.

Nutritional info (per serving)

Calories........................ 167
    From fat................. 16%

Fat .... 3 g
    Saturated .... 0 g
    Trans .... 0 g

Carbohydrates ....35 g

Protein .... 4 g

Sodium .... 38 mg

Cholesterol .... 1 mg

Calcium .... 90 mg

Fiber .... 3 g

Food exchanges
    2 fruit, 1 vegetable, ½ fat

Watch This!

Scan this QR code with your smartphone to watch the Heart Smart® video.

Soups, Sandwiches and Slices

Soups, Sandwiches and Slices

Tossing salt over your shoulder instead of on your baked potato may do more than spare you some bad luck. It may help prevent health problems such as heart disease, kidney disease and high blood pressure.

Government guidelines recommend that people consume less than 2,300 milligrams of sodium per day. That's the amount of sodium in one teaspoon of salt or three dill pickles. A further reduction to no more than 1,500 milligrams sodium a day is encouraged for anyone 51 and older, for African Americans and those with hypertension, diabetes and chronic kidney disease. The average American adult consumes 3,000 to 4,500 milligrams of sodium each day.

Most of us don't have much wiggle room in our sodium budget, especially if we rely on processed foods. It is estimated that 75% of the sodium we eat is hidden in prepared and processed foods, such as lunch meats, canned soups, condiments, restaurant meals and frozen dinners.

To get serious about reducing your sodium intake, start reading food labels and spend more time in your kitchen with this cookbook preparing meals. Our Corn Chowder recipe is less than 450 milligrams of sodium compared to the soup can version and our Turkey and Feta Wrap with Tzatziki Sauce spares you an additional 1,000 milligrams of sodium compared to the deli version. Here are some things you can do to reduce your sodium consumption.

• Use less salt or no salt at the table and in cooking. If a favorite recipe calls for salt, start by cutting the amount you add in half.

• Buy fresh poultry, fish and lean meat rather than canned, smoked or processed varieties.

• Season foods with herbs and spices, garlic, lemon juice and flavored vinegars.

• Drain and rinse canned vegetables and legumes. This rids them of some added sodium.

• Shop for low-sodium and no-added salt versions of foods and be cautious with products labeled reduced-sodium. Look for less familiar terms that mean salt — baking soda (sodium bicarbonate), baking powder, brine, monosodium glutamate (MSG), sodium benzoate, sodium caseinate, sodium citrate and sodium nitrite.

Butternut Squash Soup

Focusing on whole grains, fruits, vegetables and healthy fats are part of a Heart Smart® way of eating. This Butternut Squash Soup includes apples too. One cup is a delicious way to sneak in a fruit and vegetable serving.

Nutritional info (per serving)

Calories........................157	Sodium ....43 mg
From fat..................17%	Cholesterol ....0 mg
Fat...................................3 g	Calcium ....78 mg
Saturated.................1 g	Fiber ....2 g
Trans ....0 g	Food exchanges
Carbohydrates ....34 g	1 starch, 1 fruit,
Protein ....2 g	1 vegetable

 9 (1-cup servings) **1 hour total**

Ingredients

- 2 tablespoons trans fat-free margarine
- 1 cup diced onion
- 2 large Granny Smith apples, cored, peeled and chopped
- 1 tablespoon gingerroot, minced
- 2 teaspoons curry powder
- ½ teaspoon ground cinnamon
- 8 cups (about 2 medium) butternut squash, peeled, seeded and cut into chunks
- 3 cups unsweetened apple juice
- 1 tablespoon brown sugar

Directions

In a large stockpot, over medium-high heat, melt margarine and cook onion until tender; about 5 minutes.

Add the apples, ginger, curry powder and cinnamon; cook for 1 minute. Add the butternut squash, apple juice and brown sugar. Heat to a boil. Cover and reduce heat. Simmer for 30 minutes or until squash is tender.

Remove from the heat. In a blender or food processor, purée soup in batches, until smooth.

Return soup to stockpot and heat through. Serve hot or chilled.

Test Kitchen Tip

Squash has tough skin that is hard to cut through. To soften the skin, use a fork to poke several holes in the skin. Microwave the squash for 2 to 3 minutes to make the skin soft enough to easily cut through.

Chicken Soup with Orzo

This is an easy-to-make ultimate feel-good soup and a great way to use leftover chicken and vegetables.

The addition of orzo, a rice-shaped pasta, is an alternative to noodles and gives it a hearty texture.

 12 45 mins total

Ingredients

1 tablespoon olive oil

½ cup diced onion

2 ribs celery, thinly sliced

3 cups thinly sliced carrots

8 cups fat-free, less-sodium chicken broth or homemade chicken stock

3 cups shredded cooked chicken breast

1 cup uncooked orzo or small pasta such as ditalini

2 cups frozen cut green beans

¼ teaspoon sea salt and freshly ground black pepper to taste

½ cup chopped fresh parsley

Nutritional info (per 1-cup serving)

Calories.......................155	Sodium .... 467 mg
From fat.................17%	Cholesterol .... 30 mg
Fat .... 3 g	Calcium .... 43 mg
Saturated ....1 g	Fiber .... 2 g
Trans .... 0 g	Food exchanges
Carbohydrates .... 16 g	½ starch, 1 vegetable,
Protein .... 16 g	2 lean meat

Directions

In a medium soup pot, heat the olive oil over medium heat. Add the onions, celery and carrots. Stir until evenly coated with oil. Cover and reduce the heat to medium-low. Cook, stirring occasionally, until the vegetables are soft; about 15 minutes.

Watch carefully so the vegetables don't burn. Add some water or broth if the pan gets too dry.

Add the chicken broth and shredded chicken. Cook uncovered for 10 minutes over medium heat.

Add the orzo, cover and cook about 6 minutes or until orzo is al dente. Add the green beans and cook for another 5 minutes. Season to taste with salt and black pepper. Stir in the parsley and serve.

Chilled Mango Melon Soup

If you're tired of eating salads for dinner, try this cool and refreshing Chilled Mango Melon Soup. Cold soups are easy to make and a great start to a summer luncheon or family dinner. Best of all, it's a good way to sneak in a few fruit or vegetable servings. One portion of this soup provides two fruit servings. Many nutrition experts say the most important thing we can do to improve our diets is to eat more fruits and vegetables. The National Cancer Institute recommends eating at least five to nine servings each day.

  5 (1-cup servings)   2 hours 20 mins total

Ingredients

3 mangoes, peeled, seeded and cubed

½ cantaloupe, peeled, seeded and cubed

2 tablespoons sugar

Juice from 1 lime

Zest from 1 lime

1 ½ cups fat-free half-and-half (such as Land O' Lakes)

5 to 10 fresh mint leaves, optional

Directions

Place mango cubes, cantaloupe cubes, sugar, lime juice, lime zest and half- and-half in a blender or food processor. Cover and process until smooth and creamy. Chill at least 2 hours before serving. Serve soup chilled and garnish with mint leaves.

Nutritional info (per serving)

Calories..........................171
 From fat 0%
Fat ....0 g
 Saturated................0 g
 Trans ....0 g
Carbohydrates ....39 g
Protein ....4 g
Sodium ....84 mg
Cholesterol ....0 mg
Calcium ....91 mg
Fiber ....3 g
Food exchanges
 2 fruit, ½ milk

Test Kitchen Tip

To get more juice from the lime, roll it around on the counter pressing down on it with the heel of your hand. This breaks down the cells. You also can microwave the lime for 15 seconds. Mangos have a long, flat seed that runs the length of the fruit, making it hard to cut in half. Peel the fruit using a paring knife, and locate the seed by cutting a piece off the bottom of the mango so you can see where the seed is. Cut the mango lengthwise from top to bottom on one side as close to the seed as possible. Do the same on the other side.

Corn Chowder

Many canned soups are high in sodium. Buy canned soups that contain no more than 480 milligrams of sodium per serving. This Corn Chowder is easy to make, tastes great and has less than 480 milligrams of sodium per serving.

 8 (1-cup servings)   45 mins total

Ingredients

2 tablespoons trans fat-free margarine

1 cup diced onion

1 cup finely diced carrots

3 tablespoons all-purpose flour

5 cups skim milk

1 package (10 ounces) frozen kernel corn

1 can (15 ounces) cream-style corn

2 ½ teaspoons instant bouillon chicken granules

1 teaspoon dried thyme leaves

½ teaspoon black pepper

3 tablespoons real bacon bits (such as Oscar Mayer real bacon bits)

Directions

In a large stock pot, melt margarine over medium-high heat. Add onion and carrots; sauté 5 minutes or until carrots are soft.

Sprinkle the sautéed vegetables with flour, stirring to coat. Add the milk, frozen corn, cream-style corn, bouillon granules, thyme and black pepper. Simmer over medium heat for 3 minutes.

Reduce heat to low, cover and cook 10 to 20 minutes. While the soup is heating, toast the bacon bits in a small nonstick sauté pan until crisp and add them to the soup at serving time.

Watch This!

Scan this QR code with your smartphone to watch the Heart Smart® video.

Nutritional info (per serving)

Calories........................ 181
    From fat................20%
Fat .... 4 g
    Saturated ....1 g
    Trans .... 0 g
Carbohydrates ....29 g
Protein .... 9 g
Sodium ....445 mg
Cholesterol ....5 mg
Calcium ....206 mg
Fiber .... 2 g
Food exchanges
    1 starch, 1 milk,
    ½ fat

French Onion Soup

Cheese is a good source of nutrients such as calcium, protein and riboflavin, but it's also high in saturated fat. To enjoy cheese without wreaking havoc on your health, choose lower-fat and fat-free cheeses. If you must use full-fat cheeses, shred them to limit the amount you use and keep the saturated fat intake to a minimum. This recipe calls for Gruyere (groo-YEHR or gree-YEHR), a firm cheese with a rich, sweet, nutty flavor. Just one tablespoon of cheese is sprinkled on top.

 8   1 hour 30 mins total

Ingredients

Vegetable oil cooking spray

2 ½ pounds onions, peeled, thinly sliced

4 cans (14.5 ounces each), low-sodium beef broth, divided

1 bay leaf

1 sprig fresh parsley

1 large sprig fresh thyme

2 tablespoons Madeira wine or sherry

Freshly ground black pepper to taste

½ teaspoon salt

½ pound French bread, cut into 8 slices

½ cup grated Gruyere cheese, divided

Directions

Spray a large soup pot with vegetable oil cooking spray and place it over medium heat. Add the onions and stir until they are softened and golden brown, about 35 minutes.

Increase the heat to high and pour in ½ cup of the broth, stirring until most of the broth is absorbed. Continue until you have used up 2 cups of the broth.

Then pour in the remaining broth. Wrap the bay leaf, parsley and thyme in a piece of cheesecloth. Add the wrapped herbs to the soup, reduce the heat to low and simmer, covered, for 15 minutes.

Preheat oven to 400 degrees.

Remove and discard the cheesecloth with its herbs. Season the soup with the Madeira wine, salt and black pepper to taste.

Toast the bread in the oven on a baking sheet, about 5 minutes.

Divide the soup among 8 ovenproof bowls. Top each cup of soup with a slice of the bread. Then sprinkle each bowl with 1 tablespoon of Gruyere cheese. Place the bowls on a baking sheet and bake until the cheese bubbles, about 10 minutes.

Nutritional info (per serving)

Calories......................193	Sodium ....354 mg
From fat.................22%	Cholesterol ....8 mg
Fat ....4 g	Calcium ....114 mg
Saturated ....2 g	Fiber ....2 g
Trans ....0 g	Food exchanges
Carbohydrates ....30 g	1 starch, 2 vegetable,
Protein ....10 g	½ meat, ½ fat

Garden Gazpacho

When it's too hot to cook or when you're awash in fresh tomatoes from the garden, try this Gazpacho. This cold refreshing soup can be made in a snap and is a good way to get in several vegetable servings.

 8 **30 mins total**

Ingredients

2 pounds tomatoes, seeded

1 red bell pepper

1 green or yellow bell pepper

3 salad cucumbers

1 large shallot, peeled

2 cloves garlic, peeled

2 tablespoons olive oil

2 tablespoons red wine vinegar or sherry vinegar

1 tablespoon hot red pepper sauce

1 ¾ cup low-sodium or no-salt added tomato juice or vegetable juice

1 ear fresh corn, kernels removed

Fresh basil leaves, sliced

¼ to ½ teaspoon salt

Freshly ground black pepper to taste

2 teaspoons sugar

4 to 6 green onions, green and white parts thinly sliced

Nutritional info (per serving)

Calories........................118	Sodium .... 156 mg
From fat.................31%	Cholesterol ....0 mg
Fat ....4 g	Calcium ....51 mg
Saturated.................1 g	Fiber ....4 g
Trans ....0 g	Food exchanges
Carbohydrates ....20 g	3 vegetable, 1 fat
Protein ....3 g	

Test Kitchen Tip

Since a food processor (or blender) is used to purée the mixture, you need to only roughly chop a portion of the vegetables and dice the other portion for garnish. Adding sugar to tomatoes enhances their flavor.

Directions

Roughly chop about three-fourths of the tomatoes. Place in a food processor fitted with the metal blade or a blender. Dice the remaining tomatoes and set aside.

For the red and green bell peppers, roughly chop half of each one and add to the food processor. Dice the remaining bell peppers and set aside.

Peel, seed and roughly chop two of the cucumbers and add to the food processor. Leave the peel on the remaining cucumber, slice in half lengthwise, scoop out the seeds and dice; set aside. Add the shallot, garlic cloves, olive oil, red wine vinegar and hot pepper sauce to the food processor. Process until smooth, about 1 minute.

Transfer to a glass bowl (or leave in the blender jar). Stir in the tomato juice, corn, basil, remaining diced tomatoes, salt. pepper to taste, sugar and half of the green onions. Adjust seasoning as necessary.

Chill for 2 hours. Serve in cups, bowls and garnished with a bit of the diced bell peppers, diced cucumbers and green onion slices.

Hearty Minestrone

Health experts agree that eating a variety of fruits and vegetables is essential for good health. These foods provide nutrients that may help fight heart disease, high blood pressure and cancer. Aim for a daily intake of at least five servings of fruits and vegetables. Just one cup of this soup provides two vegetable servings.

 8   1 hour 20 mins total

Ingredients

1 tablespoon olive oil

1 cup chopped onions

1 cup sliced carrots

1 cup sliced celery

2 cloves garlic, peeled, minced

2 cups water, divided

2 cans (14.5 ounces each) fat-free, less-sodium chicken broth

1 can (14 ounces) no-salt-added chopped stewed tomatoes with juice

1 can (15 ounces) cannellini beans, drained and rinsed

2 cups zucchini (about 1 medium), halved and sliced

1 package (10 ounces) frozen, chopped spinach, thawed and drained

½ teaspoon ground black pepper

1 teaspoon Italian seasoning

¼ cup white wine vinegar

½ cup small seashell pasta, uncooked

Nutritional info (per serving)

Calories..........................146
    From fat 12%

Fat ....2 g
    Saturated................0 g
    Trans ....0 g

Carbohydrates ....25 g

Protein ....8 g

Sodium ....347 mg

Cholesterol ....0 mg

Calcium ....106 mg

Fiber ....6 g

Food exchanges
    1 starch, 2 vegetable,
    ½ fat

Directions

In a large stock pot heat the olive oil over medium-high heat. Add the onions, carrots, celery and garlic. Cook and stir until onions are tender, about 6 minutes. Add 1 cup water, chicken broth, stewed tomatoes with juice, cannellini beans, zucchini, spinach, ground black pepper and Italian seasoning.

Bring to a boil, then reduce the heat.

Cover and simmer about 20 minutes. Add the remaining 1 cup of water, white wine vinegar and pasta. Return to a boil, and then reduce heat. Cover and simmer about 15 minutes or until pasta is tender but firm.

Hearty Turkey Soup

It's often said that the best part of Thanksgiving is all the yummy leftovers. This easy-to-make soup makes good use of onions, carrots, and celery that you might have leftover from Thanksgiving. And, of course, it also makes good use of leftover turkey breast.

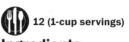 12 (1-cup servings)   30 mins total

Ingredients

2 tablespoons olive oil

1 ½ cups chopped onions

1 ½ cups chopped carrots

1 ½ cups chopped celery with leaves

8 cups turkey stock or fat-free less-sodium chicken or vegetable broth

4 cups shredded leftover turkey breast

5 cups chopped spinach

1 cup uncooked ditalini or other small-shaped pasta

Black pepper to taste

¼ teaspoon favorite all-purpose seasoning to taste

Croutons made from leftover rolls for serving, optional

Test Kitchen Tip

When storing a soup after it's made, do not leave it out on the counter to cool more than 2 hours. Divide the soup among several containers so it cools quickly. Once cool, cover and refrigerate. This soup also freezes well.

Nutritional info (per serving)

Calories........................164
   From fat.................27%

Fat ....5 g
   Saturated ....1 g
   Trans ....0 g

Carbohydrates ....12 g

Protein ....18 g

Sodium ....466 mg

Cholesterol ....35 mg

Calcium ....53 mg

Fiber ....1 g

Food exchanges
   2 vegetable,
   2 lean meat

Directions

In a large soup pot, heat the olive oil. Add the onions, carrots and celery with leaves and sauté until just tender. Stir in the stock or broth and bring to just a boil. Reduce the heat and stir in the turkey, spinach and pasta. Cook until the pasta is tender. Taste and adjust seasonings, adding black pepper and all-purpose seasoning to taste. Serve topped with croutons.

Roasted Pumpkin Soup

The pumpkin's big claim to nutrient fame is the carotenoids it contains. Carotenoids such as beta-carotene and lutein are pigments that make pumpkins orange. Carotenoids might protect against chronic diseases like heart disease and cancer and also might help ward off age-related vision loss such as macular degeneration. Pumpkin also provides a healthy dose of fiber, potassium, vitamin C, vitamin E and iron.

Nutritional info (per serving)

Calories.........................150	Sodium ....333 mg
From fat.................30%	Cholesterol ....0 mg
Fat..................................5 g	Calcium ....93 mg
Saturated................0 g	Fiber ....3 g
Trans ....0 g	Food exchanges
Carbohydrates...........23 g	1 starch, 2 vegetable,
Protein ....6 g	1 fat

Test Kitchen Tip

When buying a pumpkin for this recipe choose sugar or pie pumpkins that are blemish-free, feel heavy and have a tough skin. To easily cut the pumpkin, position a meat cleaver or heavy duty knife to the side of the stem, and hit it with a meat mallet to cut through the pumpkin. (Never cook a pumpkin that has been carved for decoration; the cut flesh could harbor bacteria.) Cooked pumpkin will keep in the refrigerator for up to five days, or you can freeze for up to six months.

 6 (1-cup servings)   1 hour 15 mins total

Ingredients

Vegetable oil cooking spray or parchment paper

1 ½ pounds sugar pumpkin, peeled, seeded and cubed

2 large carrots, peeled, cut into 1-inch pieces

1 large onion, cut into wedges

3 cloves garlic, peeled

2 tablespoons canola oil

1 can (14 ounces) fat-free, less-sodium chicken broth

1 cup fat-free half-and-half

3 tablespoons brown sugar

1 ½ teaspoons pumpkin pie spice

½ teaspoon salt

Directions

Preheat oven to 375 degrees. Line a baking sheet with parchment paper or coat with vegetable oil cooking spray. Place the pumpkin, carrots, onion wedges and garlic cloves on the baking sheet, and drizzle with the canola oil. Stir until all vegetables are coated with oil.

Bake vegetables for 40 to 50 minutes, until softened but not blackened. Place roasted vegetables in a large stockpot and add chicken broth. Heat vegetables and broth over medium heat until heated through. Working in batches if necessary, purée vegetables and broth until smooth in a blender, food processor or use an immersion blender. If using a blender or food processor, return soup to the pot and continue to heat on low. Whisk in the half-and-half, brown sugar, pumpkin pie spice and salt. Heat gently, being careful not to boil, and serve.

Asian Lettuce Wraps

Hoisin sauce is the key to a more authentic flavor in this Asian Lettuce Wrap recipe. Pronounced hoy-SIHN, this thick, reddish-brown sauce is also called Peking sauce because it's a featured ingredient in Peking duck. Hoisin sauce is sweet and spicy, has a consistency similar to a thick barbecue sauce and is mainly used as a table condiment and flavoring agent for many meat, poultry and seafood dishes. It's also used in stir-fry recipes and in marinades.

 6 45 mins total

Ingredients

WRAPS

18 Bibb or butter lettuce leaves

2 tablespoons canola oil

⅛ teaspoon red pepper flakes

1 teaspoon ground ginger

1 cup chopped onion

3 cloves garlic, peeled, minced

½ cup diced celery

¾ cup shredded carrot

1 can (8 ounces) sliced water chestnuts, drained and diced

1 pound ground chicken or turkey breast

¼ cup hoisin sauce

2 tablespoons rice vinegar

1 tablespoon reduced-sodium soy sauce

¼ teaspoon black pepper

4 sliced green onions, green part only

SAUCE

2 tablespoons chunky peanut butter

1 tablespoon hoisin sauce

1 tablespoon honey

1 tablespoon reduced-sodium soy sauce

1 tablespoon sweet chili sauce (such as Kame Sweet Chili Sauce)

1 tablespoon rice vinegar

2 tablespoons hot water

Directions

Rinse whole lettuce leaves and pat dry, being careful not to tear. Set aside.

In a large nonstick skillet, heat the oil over medium heat. Add the red pepper flakes and ground ginger; sauté 1 minute. Add the onion and continue to sauté until softened, about 6 to 8 minutes. Add the garlic, celery, carrots and water chestnuts and continue to cook, stirring constantly, about 2 to 4 minutes. Add the ground chicken and continue to cook, incorporating it into the sautéed vegetables. Add the hoisin sauce, rice vinegar, soy sauce and black pepper.

Cook, stirring every minute until most of the liquid has evaporated and the chicken is cooked through, about 8 to 10 minutes. Add the green onions and continue cooking until the onion just begins to wilt.

To prepare the sauce, combine the peanut butter, hoisin sauce, honey, soy sauce, sweet chili sauce, rice vinegar and hot water until smooth.

Serve ¾ cup of the chicken filling distributed between 3 lettuce leaves and topped with 4 teaspoons of sauce.

Nutritional info (per serving)

Calories	257	Sodium	515 mg
From fat	35%	Cholesterol	49 mg
Fat	10 g	Calcium	48 mg
Saturated	1 g	Fiber	3 g
Trans	0 g		
Carbohydrates	20 g	Food exchanges	
Protein	21 g	3 vegetable, 3 lean meat, 1 fat	

 Test Kitchen Tip

Hoisin sauce can be found in the ethnic aisle of most grocery stores or at Asian specialty stores. Once opened, store sauce in the refrigerator.

Barbecue Chicken Sandwiches

These chicken sandwiches are flavorful and super-easy to make. By serving them on whole-wheat buns you get a dose of fiber. Each sandwich contains 5 grams of fiber.

  6   45 mins total

Ingredients

½ cup chopped onion

½ cup chopped red bell pepper

1 clove garlic, peeled, minced

1 tablespoon trans fat-free margarine

½ cup salsa

½ cup ketchup

2 tablespoons brown sugar

2 tablespoons cider vinegar

1 tablespoon Worcestershire sauce

½ teaspoon chili powder

⅛ teaspoon black pepper

2 cups shredded cooked chicken breast

6 whole-wheat hamburger buns

Directions

In a saucepan, sauté the onion, red bell pepper and garlic in margarine until tender. Stir in the salsa, ketchup, brown sugar, vinegar, Worcestershire sauce, chili powder and black pepper. Add the chicken; stir to coat. Bring to a boil. Reduce heat; cover and simmer for 15 minutes.

Serve about ⅓ cup chicken mixture on each bun.

Nutritional info (per serving)

Calories...................... 290
    From fat 22%

Fat ....7 g
    Saturated.................1 g
    Trans ....0 g

Carbohydrates ....38 g

Protein ....20 g

Sodium .... 617 mg

Cholesterol .... 36 mg

Calcium .... 141 mg

Fiber ....5 g

Food exchanges
    2 starch, 1 vegetable,
    2 lean meat

 Test Kitchen Tip

When choosing whole-grain hamburger buns for this recipe, check the ingredient list on the package. Choose one that list whole-wheat as the first ingredient.

Black Bean Burger Wraps

Panko — pronouced PAN-koh — is a type of bread crumb. Also referred to as Japanese-style bread crumbs, panko crumbs are typically white because they are made from white bread without crust. Look for panko in Asian markets, speciality stores and supermarkets.

Nutritional info (per serving)

Calories......................305	Sodium ....513 mg
From fat.................30%	Cholesterol .... 39 mg
Fat ....10 g	Calcium ....113 mg
Saturated ....2 g	Fiber ....5 g
Trans ....0 g	Food exchanges
Carbohydrates ....43 g	2 starch, 2 vegetable,
Protein ....11 g	1 lean meat, 1 fat

Test Kitchen Tip

Chilling the bean mixture makes it easier to form into patties. To warm tortillas, place them on a microwave-safe dish, cover with paper towel and microwave-safe plastic wrap. Microwave on high for 1 minute.

 6   40 mins total

Ingredients

- 1 can (15 ounces) black beans, drained and rinsed
- ½ cup cooked brown rice
- ½ cup chopped red onion
- 1 egg, slightly beaten
- 2 egg whites
- 2 cloves garlic, peeled, coarsely chopped
- ¼ cup plus 1 tablespoon salsa, divided
- ¼ teaspoon salt
- ½ cup panko bread crumbs
- ¼ cup cornmeal
- 2 tablespoons canola oil, divided
- 3 tablespoons reduced-fat sour cream
- 6 (6-inches each) flour tortillas, warmed
- 1 ½ cups shredded romaine lettuce
- ¾ cup diced red tomato

Directions

Place the black beans, cooked brown rice, chopped red onion, egg, egg whites, garlic, 2 tablespoons salsa and salt in the bowl of a food processor. Pulse five times or until the mixture is evenly mixed but not puréed. Transfer bean mixture to a medium-sized bowl and stir in the bread crumbs. Refrigerate bean burger mixture for 30 minutes before forming into patties.

To form the patties, use a ⅓ cup measure for each one, dividing the bean burger mixture into six patties. Because the mixture will be quite sticky, form each patty in the palm of your hand and sprinkle both sides with the cornmeal. Add 1 tablespoon of canola oil to a nonstick skillet. Over medium heat, cook three burgers for 4 to 5 minutes on each side or until firm and browned. Use the remaining tablespoon of oil to cook the remaining three burgers. In a small bowl combine the remaining salsa and sour cream.

To assemble each wrap, cut cooked bean burger in half and place both halves in the center of a warmed tortilla. Top each burger with 1 tablespoon of salsa and sour cream sauce, ¼ cup shredded lettuce and 2 tablespoons diced tomatoes. Roll up and serve immediately.

Leftover Turkey Salad

This super-easy recipe is great for using up leftover turkey. The celery and walnuts give it a good crunch. Toasting walnuts intensifies the flavor.

 6    25 mins total

Ingredients

⅓ cup fat-free French dressing

¼ cup reduced-fat mayonnaise

¼ teaspoon black pepper

3 cups cooked turkey breast meat, cubed

1 cup red or green grapes, cut in half

¾ cup chopped celery

¼ cup chopped onion

¼ cup walnuts, toasted, chopped

Directions

In a large bowl, combine the French dressing, mayonnaise and black pepper.

Add turkey breast, grapes, celery, onion and walnuts to the dressing mixture and mix until well combined.

Test Kitchen Tip

To toast the walnuts, preheat oven to 350 degrees. Spread the walnuts on a sided baking sheet and bake for 8 minutes or until fragrant. Watch carefully because walnuts can burn easily.

Nutritional info (per serving)

Calories........................213
    From fat.................30%
Fat ....7 g
    Saturated................1 g
    Trans ....0 g
Carbohydrates ....13 g
Protein ....24 g
Sodium ....246 mg
Cholesterol ....66 mg
Calcium ....250 mg
Fiber ....1 g
Food exchanges
    3 lean meat, 1 fruit

Pulled Pork Wraps

The pork in this recipe becomes nice and tender because it's cooked for several hours in a slow cooker. It's an ideal dish that requires very little hands-on prep work. The added bonus to this recipe is sweet red peppers that are packed with nutrients, such as beta-carotene and vitamin C. One large red bell pepper provides twice the amount of vitamin C needed each day.

 6   4 hours 40 mins total

Ingredients

16 ounces boneless pork loin chops or sirloin pork cutlets

½ cup sliced onion

½ cup sliced (1-inch pieces) red bell pepper

4 cloves garlic, peeled, minced

½ cup salsa

½ cup ketchup

2 tablespoons brown sugar

1 tablespoon cider vinegar

½ teaspoon dried sage

½ teaspoon dried oregano

6 (6 inches each flour tortillas

Nutritional info (per serving)

Calories...................... 259	
From fat.................28%	
Fat................................. 8 g	
Saturated............... 2 g	
Trans .... 0 g	
Carbohydrates ....28 g	
Protein .... 19 g	

Sodium .... 488 mg	
Cholesterol .... 46 mg	
Calcium .... 65 mg	
Fiber .... 2 g	

Food exchanges
2 starch, 1 vegetable, 2 lean meat

Directions

Place pork in the bottom of a 5- to 6-quart slow cooker and top with onion, red bell pepper and garlic. In a small bowl combine the salsa, ketchup, brown sugar, cider vinegar, sage and oregano. Pour over the pork and vegetables. Cover and cook on high until meat is tender and easy to pull apart, about 3 ½ to 4 hours.

Using two forks, pull the meat apart until shredded, being careful not to touch the sides of the slow cooker. Continue cooking until the mixture has reached a desired consistency, about 1 additional hour. Place ½ cup pulled pork in the center of each tortilla. Wrap the tortilla around the meat mixture and serve.

Test Kitchen Tip

When selecting red peppers choose firm, richly colored peppers with shiny skin. They should feel heavy for their size. Store peppers in a plastic bag in the refrigerator for up to a week.

Sloppy Joes

These Sloppy Joes get a kick from horseradish. According to the Horseradish Information Council, an estimated 24 million pounds of horseradish roots are ground and processed each year to produce approximately 6 million gallons of prepared, ready-to-eat horseradish. Horseradish is grown mainly for its large, white, spicy roots. The aroma of the root are virtually nonexistent until it is grated or ground. Crushing the root cells releases the volatile oils that give horseradish its familiar kick.

 6   **35 mins total**

Ingredients

1 tablespoon canola oil

1 pound ground turkey breast

⅓ cup diced onion

⅓ cup diced green pepper

⅓ cup diced celery

1 teaspoon chili powder

1 teaspoon garlic powder

½ teaspoon celery seeds

¼ teaspoon black pepper

3 tablespoons brown sugar

3 tablespoons Worcestershire sauce

1 tablespoon cider vinegar

1 tablespoon horseradish

1 can (6 ounces) tomato paste

1 cup water

6 whole-wheat hamburger buns (2 ounces each)

Nutritional info (per serving)

Calories	308
From fat	15%
Fat	5 g
Saturated	1 g
Trans	0 g
Carbohydrates	42 g
Protein	24 g
Sodium	436 mg
Cholesterol	47 mg
Calcium	80 mg
Fiber	6 g

Food exchanges
2 starch, 2 vegetable

Directions

In a large nonstick skillet, heat the oil over medium heat. Add the ground turkey, onion, green pepper and celery. Cook, stirring frequently, until vegetables are softened and meat is broken into crumbles and cooked through, about 6 to 8 minutes. Stir in the chili powder, garlic powder, celery seeds, black pepper, brown sugar, Worcestershire sauce, vinegar and horseradish. Continue to cook until all the liquid is absorbed, about 5 to 7 minutes. Add the tomato paste and water and cook until combined and heated through. Top each bun with ½ cup of Sloppy Joe mixture and serve.

Test Kitchen Tip

Horseradish is a fat-free, low-sodium root that adds distinctive, pungent flavor to a host of dishes. You can buy it as a fresh, whole root or grated and bottled. Bottled horseradish is white if preserved in vinegar or red if preserved in beet juice.

Spinach and Mushroom Stromboli

The most important thing parents can do to produce healthy kids is to be role models for healthy behaviors. A good way is to get kids involved with food preparation. With this Spinach and Mushroom Stromboli recipe, kids can help shape the dough and add the filling ingredients.

Watch This!

Scan this QR code with your smartphone to watch the Heart Smart® video.

Nutritional info (per serving)

Calories	325
From fat	22%
Fat	8 g
Saturated	4 g
Trans	0 g
Carbohydrates	45 g
Protein	18 g
Sodium	544 mg
Cholesterol	23 mg
Calcium	288 mg
Fiber	1 g

Food exchanges
3 starch, 1 vegetable, 1 meat

5 **1 hour total**

Ingredients

1 pound pizza dough, thawed if frozen

All-purpose flour for work surface

½ cup plus 2 tablespoons pizza sauce

1 ¼ cups baby leaf spinach

1 ¼ cups sliced mushrooms

½ cup plus 2 tablespoons thinly sliced red onion

1 ¼ cups (5 ounces) shredded part-skim mozzarella cheese

5 tablespoons grated Parmesan cheese

Directions

Preheat oven to 400 degrees.

Line a large rimmed baking sheet with parchment paper or foil. Divide dough into 5 equal portions. On a clean, lightly floured work surface, stretch out each piece of dough to about a 6-by-8-inch oval. Allow the dough to rest briefly if it becomes too elastic to work with.

Top each section of dough with 2 tablespoons of pizza sauce, ¼ cup spinach leaves, ¼ cup mushrooms, 2 tablespoons red onion, ¼ cup mozzarella cheese and 1 tablespoon Parmesan cheese, leaving a ½-inch border. Starting at one end, roll up each stromboli and place seam side down on the baking sheet. Cut two slits in the top of each stromboli.

Bake until golden brown, about 25 to 30 minutes. Remove from oven and serve.

Sun-Dried Tomato Pizza Pie

If you've been thinking about experimenting with fresh herbs, this Sun-Dried Tomato Pizza Pie is a great place to start. It features fresh basil, oregano and marjoram. When it comes to using fresh herbs, start small, adding 1 teaspoon of fresh herbs for every four servings. Too much of any herb can overwhelm a food or make it bitter. Be sure to use fresh herbs in this recipe — dried ingredients just won't do.

Nutritional info (per serving)

Calories	157	Sodium	537 mg
From fat	29%	Cholesterol	10 mg
Fat	5 g	Calcium	125 mg
Saturated	2 g	Fiber	1 g
Trans	0 g		
Carbohydrates	21 g		
Protein	8 g		

Food exchanges
1 starch, 1 vegetable,
½ meat, ½ fat

  8 slices 1 hour total

Ingredients

1 package (10 ounces) refrigerated pizza dough

⅓ cup low-fat mayonnaise

1 tablespoon real bacon bits

⅛ teaspoon black pepper

1 clove garlic, pressed

1 cup (4 ounces) reduced-fat shredded mozzarella cheese

1 teaspoon snipped fresh basil

1 teaspoon snipped fresh marjoram

1 teaspoon snipped fresh oregano

½ cup sun-dried tomatoes, julienned

½ cup diced green pepper, diced

1 tablespoon finely shredded Parmesan cheese

Directions

Preheat oven to 400 degrees.

Press pizza dough into a 12-inch circle on a pizza pan.

In a small bowl, combine mayonnaise, bacon bits, pepper and garlic. Mix well. Stir in mozzarella cheese, basil, marjoram and oregano.

Spread the mixture on the pizza dough. (The cheese mixture will be spread very thin.) Top with sun-dried tomatoes and green pepper. Sprinkle with Parmesan cheese.

Bake until the crust is golden brown, 15 to 20 minutes. Serve hot or cool.

 Test Kitchen Tip

Choose fresh herbs with evenly colored leaves and have a clean, fresh fragrance. To store fresh herbs, trim about ¼-inch from the stem, rinse them with cold water and loosely wrap them in paper towels. Place them in the refrigerator in a sealed airtight plastic bag for up to five days. Just before using, wash the herbs and blot them dry with a paper towel.

Fresh herbs are not as strong or concentrated as their dried counterparts. To substitute dried herbs for fresh, use a one-to-three ratio. For example, one teaspoon of dried oregano would be equivalent to one tablespoon of fresh oregano.

Turkey and Feta Wrap with Tzatziki Sauce

Tzatziki (dza-DZEE-kee) is a creamy, white Greek sauce often served as a dip, spread or condiment or simply eaten alone. Made with strained yogurt, diced cucumbers, lemon juice, garlic, salt, pepper and a variety of herbs including dill, parsley or mint, tzatziki is commonly paired with an array of Mediterranean dishes. One of the latest trends in the yogurt aisle is Greek or Greek-style low-fat and fat-free yogurt. Thicker and creamier than traditional yogurt, Greek yogurt resembles sour cream in taste and texture but is loaded with protein.

 4   30 mins total

Ingredients

1 container (7 ounces) low-fat, Greek-style yogurt

2 tablespoons lemon juice

1 clove garlic, peeled, minced

2 teaspoons dill weed

¼ teaspoon black pepper

⅛ teaspoon salt

8 ounces (about 1 ⅔ cup) cooked, diced turkey breast meat

½ cup diced cucumbers

½ cup canned chickpeas, drained and rinsed

⅓ cup crumbled feta cheese

¼ cup thinly sliced red onion

4 flour tortillas (6 inches each)

Directions

To make the tzatziki sauce, in a medium bowl combine the yogurt, lemon juice, garlic, dill weed, black pepper and salt in a medium bowl. Stir in the turkey breast, cucumbers, garbanzo beans, feta cheese and red onion. Spoon one quarter of the turkey mixture on top of each tortilla. Fold opposite sides of wrap over the filling and roll tightly into a cylinder.

 Test Kitchen Tip
In many recipes, especially dips, Greek-style yogurt can be substituted for sour cream.

Nutritional info (per serving)

Calories........................276	Sodium ....469 mg
From fat..................23%	Cholesterol ....57 mg
Fat ....7 g	Calcium ....147 mg
Saturated ....3 g	Fiber ....3 g
Trans ....0 g	Food exchanges
Carbohydrates ....26 g	1 starch, 3 lean meat,
Protein ....28 g	2 vegetable

Turkey Salad Wraps

This Turkey Salad Wrap can be part of a sensible diet that conforms to the recommendations of the American Heart Association, the American Cancer Society and the American Diabetes Association. It's a great tasting on-the-go option.

 6  20 mins total

Ingredients

⅓ cup reduced-fat mayonnaise

2 tablespoons cider vinegar

1 tablespoon chili sauce

½ teaspoon salt

¼ teaspoon ground black pepper

3 cups cooked turkey breast meat, shredded

⅓ cup diced sweet pickles

⅓ cup chopped red onion

⅓ cup chopped celery

6 (6 inches each) whole-wheat pita or favorite wrap-style bread

6 red leaf lettuce leaves, rinsed and patted dry

Directions

In a medium bowl, whisk together the mayonnaise, cider vinegar, chili sauce, salt and black pepper.

Stir in the turkey, pickles, red onion and celery.

Line each pita wrap with a lettuce leaf. Spoon the turkey mixture on top.

Fold opposite sides of the wrap over the filling and roll it tightly into a cylinder.

Nutritional info (per serving)

Calories........................199
    From fat 32%
Fat ....7 g
    Saturated...............2 g
    Trans ....0 g
Carbohydrates ....12 g
Protein ....22 g
Sodium ....538 mg
Cholesterol ....53 mg
Calcium .... 20 mg
Fiber ....1 g
Food exchanges
    2 lean meat, 1 starch

Beans, Grains and Pasta

Beans, Grains and Pasta

A fiber-rich diet rich offers many health benefits, possibly reducing the risk of heart disease, obesity and type 2 diabetes.

Dietary fiber, the part of plant foods our bodies can't digest, comes in two forms — soluble and insoluble. Soluble fiber provides heart-health benefits by soaking up cholesterol while it's still in the digestive tract and sending it out of the body, instead of allowing it to be absorbed into the bloodstream. Oats, barley, prunes, raisins, apples, oranges, carrots, and legumes provide soluble fiber. Insoluble fiber promotes regularity and helps prevent constipation. Whole-wheat foods, such as brown rice and whole-wheat pasta, bran, and many vegetables provide insoluble fiber.

Three pantry staples — legumes, whole-wheat pasta and brown rice — are featured in many recipes in this chapter. These ingredients can help you reach the recommended daily dietary fiber goal of 25 to 38 grams and provide you with both types of fiber.

Legumes. Legumes (dried beans, peas and lentils) are great sources of fiber, providing four to eight grams in every half-cup serving. Give soup, salad, casserole and chili recipes a fiber boost by tossing in a variety of legumes. The Mexican Bean Salad features black beans, garbanzo beans and dark red kidney beans has a whopping seven grams of fiber per serving. When using canned beans, drain and rinse them well to eliminate an estimated 30% of sodium.

Whole-Wheat Pasta. Increase the nutritional value of pasta by choosing those made with whole-wheat flour. Whole-wheat pasta provides three times the fiber of pastas made from refined flour. Thanks to improved technology, whole-wheat pastas have a smoother, less grainy texture and milder taste. Try the Spaghetti and Meatballs recipe which features whole-wheat angel hair pasta.

Brown Rice. The difference between brown rice and white rice is the milling process. Milling or whitening removes the outer bran layer of the rice kernel, leaving white rice. It is the fiber-rich bran coating that gives brown rice its light tan color and chewy texture. Brown rice retains an impressive array of vitamins and minerals, including vitamin B6, folate, vitamin E, potassium and magnesium. You'll find brown rice in the Curried Rice with Raisins and Almonds recipe, as well as the Gingered Fried Rice recipe.

Asian Brown Rice Salad

The flavor of this rice dish is enhanced by five-spice powder. Used extensively in Chinese cooking, the traditional mixture combines fennel seed, cloves, cinnamon, star anise and Szechuan peppercorns. Some brands of five-spice powder also contain ginger, nutmeg or licorice. Five-spice powder should be sodium-free, but check the ingredient list to make sure.

 7 (²/₃-cup serving)   25 mins total

Ingredients

3 cups cooked brown rice

½ cup diced celery

½ cup diced carrot

½ cup diced red bell pepper

¼ cup sliced green onions (green and white parts)

¼ cup rice vinegar

1 tablespoon sugar

2 tablespoons canola oil

2 tablespoons minced fresh parsley

1 tablespoon water

1 tablespoon reduced-sodium soy sauce

1 teaspoon grated gingerroot

1 clove garlic, peeled, minced

½ teaspoon Chinese five-spice powder

½ teaspoon mustard powder

¼ teaspoon salt

¼ teaspoon black pepper

Directions

Prepare rice according to package directions, omitting the salt, to yield 3 cups cooked. In a large bowl, combine the cooked rice, celery, carrot, red pepper and green onions. In a jar with a tight-fitting lid, combine the vinegar, sugar, oil, parsley, water, soy sauce, gingerroot, garlic, five-spice powder, mustard powder, salt and black pepper; shake well. Pour dressing over rice mixture and gently toss.

 Test Kitchen Tip

Five-spice powder is available at most grocery stores. Store the five-spice powder in a closed jar in a dry place. It is a pungent spice, so use it sparingly.

Nutritional info (per serving)

Calories.......................148	Sodium ....161 mg
From fat.................30%	Cholesterol ....0 mg
Fat................................5 g	Calcium .... 23 mg
Saturated...............0 g	Fiber ....2 g
Trans ....0 g	Food exchanges
Carbohydrates ....23 g	1 starch, 1 vegetable,
Protein ....3 g	1 fat

Asian Rice Cakes

If you're looking for healthy and different hors d'oeuvres to serve during the holidays try these rice cakes. These Asian Rice Cakes are low-fat and a healthy alternative to many high-fat hors d'oeuvres. A cool, yet sweet and tart cucumber is served on top of rice cakes.

 4   1 hour 15 mins total

Ingredients

¼ cup rice wine vinegar, divided

2 tablespoons sugar, divided

1 teaspoon reduced-sodium soy sauce

½ teaspoon grated gingerroot

1 ½ cups seeded and diced cucumber

½ cup uncooked short-grain rice

1 ½ cups water

3 tablespoons minced carrot

3 tablespoons minced red bell pepper

2 tablespoons minced green onion

1 to 2 egg whites, divided

2 teaspoons canola oil

Directions

In a small bowl, combine 2 tablespoons of rice wine vinegar, 1 tablespoon of sugar, soy sauce and gingerroot; add the cucumbers and toss to mix well. Cover and refrigerate at least 1 hour.

Meanwhile, wash the rice in several changes of cold water until the water is nearly clear. In a medium saucepan, bring 1 ½ cups water to a boil; stir in the rice and return to a boil. Reduce the heat to low; cook for 20 minutes, until the rice is tender and sticky. Set it aside and cool completely.

In a small saucepan, combine the remaining 2 tablespoons rice wine vinegar and remaining 1 tablespoon sugar. Cook over low heat, stirring occasionally, about 1 minute, until the sugar dissolves.

Pour the vinegar mixture into the cooked rice; stir to mix well. Stir in the carrots, red bell peppers and green onions; let the dish cool to room temperature.

Add 1 egg white to the rice mixture; stir to mix well. Shape into 8 equal patties, each about ½-inch thick. If the mixture seems as if it is not holding together, add the additional egg white.

In a large nonstick skillet, heat 1 teaspoon oil and add 4 patties. Cook over medium-high heat about 3 minutes on each side. Repeat the procedure with the remaining teaspoon of oil and 4 patties.

To serve, top the rice cakes with the cucumber mixture and serve immediately.

Nutritional info (per serving)

Calories........................ 167
    From fat 11%

Fat .... 2 g
    Saturated................ 0 g
    Trans .... 0 g

Carbohydrates .... 31 g

Protein .... 3 g

Sodium .... 68 mg

Cholesterol .... 0 mg

Calcium ....14 mg

Fiber .... 2 g

Food exchanges
    2 starch

Test Kitchen Tip

Be sure to use short or medium grain rice, or rice labeled for sushi. If you ever have leftover rice, it freezes for several months. Reheat the rice in the microwave when you're ready to eat.

Best Ever Turkey Lasagna

Many lasagna recipes are fat-loaded and sodium-soaked, some with 20 grams of fat and more than 850 milligrams of sodium per serving. This Heart Smart® lasagna — which uses lean ground turkey breast, low-fat ricotta cheese and part-skim mozzarella cheese — has just 7 grams of fat and 277 calories per serving. To keep the sodium in check, we used a jarred pasta sauce that contained less than 400 milligrams of sodium per half-cup serving.

 12   2 hours total

Ingredients

10 lasagna noodles

2 tablespoons trans fat-free margarine

1 cup chopped onion

3 cloves garlic, peeled, minced

1 ¼ pounds ground turkey breast

1 can (28 ounces) crushed tomatoes

1 can (6 ounces) tomato paste

1 jar (12 ounces) pasta sauce (such as Di Sorrento Classico Roasted Garlic)

½ cup water

2 tablespoons sugar

1 teaspoon dried basil

1 teaspoon fennel seed

1 teaspoon Italian seasoning

¼ teaspoon ground black pepper

4 tablespoons chopped fresh parsley, divided

½ teaspoon ground nutmeg, divided

1 container (15 ounces) low-fat ricotta cheese

1 egg

8 ounces shredded part-skim mozzarella cheese, divided

¼ cup grated Parmesan cheese

Directions

Fill a 9-by-13-inch baking dish half full with hot tap water and soak the noodles for 20 minutes.

Meanwhile, in a Dutch oven or large stockpot, melt the margarine. Cook the onion and garlic over medium heat until onions soften, about 3 to 5 minutes. Add the ground turkey; cook until browned, about 10 minutes. Stir in the crushed tomatoes, tomato paste, pasta sauce and water. Add the sugar, basil, fennel seed, Italian seasoning, black pepper, 2 tablespoons of the parsley and ¼ teaspoon of the nutmeg. Simmer, covered, while preparing the remainder of the recipe, stirring occasionally.

Preheat oven to 375 degrees.

Drain the water from noodles, and set noodles aside.

In a mixing bowl, combine the ricotta cheese, egg, remaining 2 tablespoons of parsley and remaining ¼ teaspoon of nutmeg; set aside.

To assemble the lasagna, place one-third of the meat sauce evenly across the bottom of the prepared baking dish. Place 4 noodles lengthwise in pan, overlapping slightly. Place 1 noodle widthwise across the center, and adjust size to fit in pan. Spread half of the ricotta cheese mixture in a thin layer across the noodles. Sprinkle ½ cup of the mozzarella cheese over the ricotta mixture. Spoon one-third of the meat sauce over the cheese. Place the remaining noodles over the meat sauce in the same pattern. Spread the remaining ricotta cheese mixture over the noodles. Sprinkle ½ cup of mozzarella cheese over the ricotta mixture. Spoon the remaining meat sauce over the cheese. Cover with foil and bake for 25 minutes. Remove the foil, sprinkle the remaining 1 cup mozzarella cheese and Parmesan cheese over the top and cook uncovered for 25 minutes. Cool for 15 minutes before serving.

Nutritional info (per serving)

Calories	277
From fat	23%
Fat	7 g
Saturated	4 g
Trans	0 g
Carbohydrates	28 g
Protein	24 g
Sodium	501 mg
Cholesterol	69 mg
Calcium	284 mg
Fiber	3 g

Food exchanges
1 starch, 2 vegetable, 3 lean meat

Black Bean and Pineapple Relish

This colorful, sweet and spicy relish goes well with any type of grilled chicken, pork or seafood. Fresh cilantro gives this relish a distinct taste. Cilantro is traditionally used in Middle Eastern, Mexican, Indian and Asian cooking. Its taste is a pungent mix of parsley, citrus and anise.

 8 (²/₃-cup servings)   15 mins total

Ingredients

1 ¼ cups diced fresh pineapple or canned pineapple tidbits packed in juice

1 can (15 ounces) black beans, drained and rinsed

1 cup frozen corn kernels

½ cup diced red bell pepper

½ cup seeded and diced cucumber

½ cup finely chopped red onion

2 tablespoons minced jalapeño pepper

¼ cup chopped fresh cilantro

3 tablespoons lime juice

1 tablespoon olive oil

1 tablespoon sugar

1 clove garlic, peeled, minced

½ teaspoon ground cumin

½ teaspoon chili powder

¼ teaspoon salt

¼ teaspoon ground black pepper

Test Kitchen Tip

Choose cilantro bunches with bright green leaves and no sign of wilting. It should be well-rinsed and patted dry with paper towel before using. Cilantro may be stored for up to one week in a plastic bag in the refrigerator. It can also be placed, stems down, in a glass of water and covered with a plastic bag. Refrigerate and change the water every two days.

Nutritional info (per serving)

Calories..........................99
   From fat.................18%
Fat ....2 g
   Saturated ....0 g
   Trans ....0 g
Carbohydrates ....19 g
Protein ....3 g
Sodium ....82 mg
Cholesterol ....0 mg
Calcium ....26 mg
Fiber ....3 g
Food exchanges
  ½ starch, 2 vegetable

Directions

In a large bowl, combine the pineapple, black beans, corn, red bell pepper, cucumber, red onion, jalapeño pepper and cilantro and gently toss to combine. In a small bowl or measuring cup, whisk together the lime juice, olive oil, sugar, garlic, cumin, chili powder, salt and black pepper. Pour the dressing over the black bean mixture and toss to coat. Refrigerate at least 2 hours to allow flavors to blend. Stir well before serving.

Curried Rice with Raisins and Almonds

This dish makes a terrific side dish. The addition of curry powder is a good match for the golden raisins and almonds.

 6 (¹/₂-cup servings)   **15 mins total**

Ingredients

1 cup uncooked instant brown rice

2 tablespoons trans fat-free margarine

¹/₄ cup finely chopped onion

1 teaspoon curry powder

¹/₂ teaspoon salt

¹/₄ teaspoon black pepper

¹/₃ cup golden raisins

2 tablespoons slivered almonds, toasted

Directions

Prepare rice according to package directions, omitting the salt and butter. In a large skillet, melt the margarine over medium heat. Cook onion in the margarine about 2 minutes, stirring occasionally until tender. Stir in curry powder, salt and black pepper and continue to sauté for 1 minute. Add raisins and cooked brown rice and stir to combine. Sprinkle with almonds and serve.

 Test Kitchen Tip

Foods that are already prepped for use or prepackaged often cost more. This recipe uses instant brown rice to reduce cooking time. However, purchasing regular brown rice could be cheaper.

Nutritional info (per serving)

Calories...................... 175	Sodium ....189 mg
From fat................. 21%	Cholesterol ....0 mg
Fat .... 4 g	Calcium .... 20 mg
Saturated.................1 g	Fiber ....2 g
Trans ....0 g	Food exchanges
Carbohydrates .... 31 g	2 starch, ¹/₂ fat
Protein ....3 g	

Watch This!

Scan this QR code with your smartphone to watch the Heart Smart® video.

Gingered Fried Rice

This recipe offers an excellent, albeit sneaky, way to introduce your family to brown rice. Given the tan color of fried rice, those enjoying this dish aren't likely to question that brown rice, a healthy whole grain, was used. In keeping this fried rice heart-healthy egg whites are used to keep the cholesterol in check and reduced-sodium soy sauce is used to limit the sodium. This Gingered Fried Rice is designed to use any leftover vegetables you have on hand or you can add leftover cooked chicken for a main dish meal.

 6 (½-cup servings) **35 mins total**

Ingredients

2 tablespoons trans fat-free margarine, divided

½ cup diced onion

1 clove garlic, peeled, minced

1 tablespoon minced gingerroot

¾ cup broccoli florets cut into small, ½-inch pieces

½ cup grated carrots

½ cup diced celery

2 egg whites

2 cups cooked brown rice

2 tablespoons reduced-sodium soy sauce

1 teaspoon brown sugar

½ teaspoon ground mustard

⅛ teaspoon ground ginger

⅛ teaspoon garlic powder

⅛ teaspoon ground black pepper

⅓ cup thinly sliced green onion

Directions

In a large nonstick skillet over medium heat, melt 1 table-spoon plus 2 teaspoons margarine and sauté the onion, garlic and gingerroot until fragrant, about 3 minutes. Add the broccoli, carrots and celery and continue to sauté an additional 5 to 8 minutes. Remove vegetable mixture from skillet and set aside.

In the same skillet, add the remaining 1 teaspoon of margarine and cook and stir the egg whites over medium heat until completely set. Add vegetable mixture back to the skillet along with the cooked rice. In a small bowl, whisk together the soy sauce, brown sugar, mustard, ginger, garlic powder and black pepper. Add the sauce to the skillet and combine until heated through. Serve topped with green onion.

Nutritional info (per serving)

Calories	126	Sodium	241 mg
From fat	21%	Cholesterol	0 mg
Fat	3 g	Calcium	31 mg
Saturated	0 g	Fiber	2 g
Trans	0 g		
Carbohydrates	20 g		
Protein	4 g		

Food exchanges
1 starch, 1 vegetable, ½ fat

Test Kitchen Tip

Using day-old rice allows the grains to dry out and become firm. Freshly prepared hot rice contains too much moisture, which results in fried mush instead of fried rice.

Lemon Rice Florentine

Aromatic rice is an umbrella term for rice varieties that have a toasty, nutty fragrance and a flavor similar to popcorn or roasted nuts. Basmati and jasmine are popular types of aromatic rice. You can use either in this recipe that pairs the aromatic rice with lemon and spinach.

 6 (½-cup servings)    40 mins total

Ingredients

1 tablespoon canola oil

¾ cup chopped onion

1 cup uncooked jasmine or basmati rice

2 cups water

2 cups fresh spinach, chopped

2 tablespoons lemon juice

1 teaspoon lemon zest

½ teaspoon salt

¼ teaspoon black pepper

Directions

In a large saucepan, heat the oil over medium heat. Add the onion and sauté for 2 to 3 minutes. Add the rice and continue to cook for 2 minutes, stirring constantly. Add the water and heat to boiling. Reduce heat to low, cover and simmer until rice is tender, about 20 minutes. Remove from heat and add the spinach. Cover for 3 to 5 minutes, allowing the spinach to soften. Add the lemon juice, lemon zest, salt and black pepper and stir to combine.

Nutritional info (per serving)

Calories.........................139
    From fat 13%

Fat ....2 g
    Saturated................0 g
    Trans ....0 g

Carbohydrates ....27 g

Protein ....2 g

Sodium ....171 mg

Cholesterol ....0 mg

Calcium ....17 mg

Fiber ....1 g

Food exchanges
    1 ½ starch, ½ fat

Test Kitchen Tip

For the best flavor, aromatic rice should be used within six months of purchase. Old rice tends to develop a woody flavor and will lose its aromatic scent if allowed to age too long.

Macaroni and Cheese

If you're new to trying whole-wheat pastas, try this Macaroni and Cheese. Using whole-wheat elbow macaroni gives this classic comfort food added fiber.

 8  1 hour 15 mins total

Ingredients

4 cups cooked whole-wheat elbow macaroni (about 2 cups uncooked)

2 cups (8 ounces) shredded reduced-fat sharp cheddar cheese

1 cup low-fat cottage cheese

¾ cup reduced-fat sour cream

½ cup skim milk

2 tablespoons grated fresh onion

½ teaspoon salt

¼ teaspoon black pepper

¼ cup fat-free egg substitute, lightly beaten

Vegetable oil cooking spray

¼ cup plain bread crumbs

1 tablespoon trans fat-free margarine, melted

¼ teaspoon paprika

Directions

Preheat oven to 350 degrees.

In a large bowl combine cooked macaroni, cheddar cheese, cottage cheese, sour cream, skim milk, onion, salt, pepper and egg substitute. Spoon the mixture into a 2-quart casserole coated with vegetable oil cooking spray.

In a small bowl, mix bread crumbs, margarine and paprika. Sprinkle over the casserole. Cover and bake for 30 minutes. Uncover and bake 5 minutes or until set.

Nutritional info (per serving)

Calories...................... 265
    From fat.................34%
Fat ....10 g
    Saturated ....5 g
    Trans ....0 g
Carbohydrates ....25 g
Protein ....17 g
Sodium ....560 mg
Cholesterol .... 29 mg
Calcium ....305 mg
Fiber ....2 g
Food exchanges
    1 ½ starch, 2 meat

Mexican Bean Salad

This bean salad goes together in a snap and is a great dish to bring to a potluck. It also provides 7 grams of fiber per serving.

 8 (¾-cup servings)    **20 mins total**

Ingredients

1 can (14.5 ounces) black beans, drained and rinsed

1 can (14.5 ounces) garbanzo beans, drained and rinsed

1 can (14.5 ounces) dark red kidney beans, drained and rinsed

¾ cup chopped red bell pepper

¾ cup chopped green pepper

½ cup diced red onion

2 tablespoons olive oil

2 tablespoons lime juice

2 tablespoons cider vinegar

¼ cup chopped fresh cilantro

2 teaspoons sugar

1 teaspoon ground cumin

1 teaspoon chili powder

1 garlic, peeled, minced

½ teaspoon salt

¼ teaspoon ground black pepper

Nutritional info (per serving)

Calories..........................166	Sodium ....267 mg
From fat..................22%	Cholesterol ....0 mg
Fat..................................4 g	Calcium ....53 mg
Saturated................0 g	Fiber ....7 g
Trans ....0 g	Food exchanges
Carbohydrates ....25 g	1 starch, 2 vegetable,
Protein ....8 g	½ fat

Directions

In a large bowl, combine black beans, garbanzo beans, kidney beans, red bell pepper, green pepper and red onion. In a small container or jar, combine olive oil, lime juice, cider vinegar, cilantro, sugar, cumin, chili powder, garlic, salt and black pepper. Seal the container and shake vigorously. Pour the dressing mixture over the bean mixture and gently stir to combine all ingredients. Chill at least 2 hours before serving to allow flavors to blend.

 Test Kitchen Tip

The liquid in canned beans contains sodium. Rinsing the drained beans can reduce the sodium.

Mushroom Bolognese with Whole-Wheat Penne

An authentic Bolognese begins with a mixture of finely chopped onions, carrots, garlic and celery sautéed in diced pancetta (an Italian rolled bacon), butter or olive oil. Ground beef and tomatoes (or tomato paste) also are added. This Heart Smart® version gets its hearty flavor from mushrooms. Served over whole-wheat penne, it's an excellent source of fiber.

 6   1 hour total

Ingredients

2 tablespoons olive oil

1 medium red onion, peeled, finely chopped

3 carrots, peeled, finely chopped

2 celery ribs, finely chopped

3 cloves garlic, peeled, minced

1 package (8 ounces) mushrooms, wiped clean, coarsely chopped

¾ cup dry red wine

1 can (6 ounces) tomato paste

1 can (14 ounces) fat-free, less-sodium chicken broth

½ cup fat-free half-and-half

½ teaspoon salt

6 cups cooked whole-wheat penne pasta

½ cup plus 1 tablespoon grated Parmesan cheese

Directions

In a large, heavy pot, heat olive oil over medium heat and sauté the red onion, carrots, celery and garlic, stirring occasionally, until vegetables are tender, 8 to 10 minutes. Add mushrooms and red wine and cook until the wine has almost evaporated, 12 to 15 minutes. Add tomato paste, stirring occasionally until the mixture is lightly browned, 8 to 10 minutes. Add chicken broth to loosen pan renderings. Add half-and-half and salt and allow sauce to simmer until it is thick and creamy, 10 to 15 minutes. While sauce is cooking, prepare pasta according to package directions, omitting the fat and salt. To serve, top 1 cup cooked pasta with ¾ cup Bolognese and sprinkle with 1 ½ tablespoons grated Parmesan cheese.

 Test Kitchen Tip

To clean mushrooms, wipe the dirt away with a damp paper towel. Mushrooms are like sponges so don't soak them in water to clean them.

Nutritional info (per serving)

Calories	355
From fat	20%
Fat	8 g
Saturated	2 g
Trans	0 g
Carbohydrates	54 g
Protein	16 g
Sodium	510 mg
Cholesterol	7 mg
Calcium	157 mg
Fiber	7 g

Food exchanges
2 starch, 4 vegetable, 2 fat

Pasta Puttanesca

This pasta is a terrific source of fiber, with 10 grams per serving. It's easy enough to make for a weeknight meal. The sun-dried tomatoes in this recipe give the sauce a slightly sweet flavor.

  10   30 mins total

Ingredients

2 tablespoons olive oil

1 ½ cups diced onion

¼ cup sliced ready-to-eat sun-dried tomatoes (not packed in oil)

6 cloves garlic, peeled, minced

2 anchovy fillets, chopped

¼ teaspoon red pepper flakes

1 can (28 ounces) diced tomatoes

1 can (28 ounces) crushed tomatoes

10 black olives, pitted, chopped

2 tablespoons sugar

1 teaspoon dried oregano

1 teaspoon dried basil

10 cups hot cooked whole-wheat spaghetti noodles

Directions

In a large stockpot, heat olive oil over medium heat; add onions, sun-dried tomatoes, garlic, anchovy fillets and red pepper flakes. Sauté until onion is tender and translucent, about 5 minutes.

Stir in diced tomatoes, crushed tomatoes, black olives, sugar, oregano and basil.

Reduce heat to medium and cook 15 to 20 minutes or until the sauce is slightly reduced and the flavors are blended.

While sauce is cooking, prepare the pasta according to the package directions, omitting salt.

Toss the sauce with the cooked pasta and serve.

Nutritional info (per serving)

Calories	271
From fat	13%
Fat	4 g
Saturated	1 g
Trans	0 g
Carbohydrates	53 g
Protein	10 g
Sodium	363 mg
Cholesterol	1 mg
Calcium	81 mg
Fiber	10 g

Food exchanges
3 starch, 2 vegetable

Test Kitchen Tip

Slice the sun-dried tomatoes using kitchen scissors. To rehydrate sun-dried tomatoes that are not ready-to-eat, place them in hot water for about 20 to 30 minutes.

Quinoa and Black Bean Salad

Quinoa, pronounced KEEN-wah, is a grain with a delicate taste and light flavor. You can use it in soup, salad and pilaf recipes, as well as in other dishes. It is often called the mother grain because it contains all of the essential amino acids and is high in protein.

 6 (²/₃-cup servings)   25 mins total

Ingredients

½ cup quinoa, rinsed

1 can (15 ounces) black beans, drained and rinsed

½ cup diced celery

½ cup diced green pepper

¼ cup diced red onion

2 tablespoons red wine vinegar

1 tablespoon lemon juice

1 ½ tablespoons olive oil

1 clove garlic, peeled, crushed

½ teaspoon dried thyme leaves

½ teaspoon ground cumin

¼ teaspoon salt

¼ teaspoon black pepper

Directions

Prepare the quinoa according to package directions, omitting salt. Drain and cool the quinoa.

In a large bowl gently combine the cooled quinoa, black beans, celery, green pepper and red onion.

In a small jar place the red wine vinegar, lemon juice, olive oil, garlic, thyme, cumin, salt and black pepper. Shake vigorously to combine.

Pour the dressing over the quinoa mixture and chill before serving.

Test Kitchen Tip

Most grocery stores carry quinoa. You also can look for it at health food and specialty stores. Always rinse quinoa before using.

Nutritional info (per serving)

Calories........................138
    From fat.................26%
Fat ....4 g
    Saturated.................1 g
    Trans ....0 g
Carbohydrates ....20 g
Protein ....5 g
Sodium ....243 mg
Cholesterol ....0 mg
Calcium ....40 mg
Fiber ....4 g
Food exchanges
    1 starch, 1 vegetable,
    1 fat

Quinoa Tabbouleh Salad

Tabbouleh is a Middle Eastern salad made with bulgur, chopped tomatoes, parsley and other ingredients. This Heart Smart® version, created by chef Frank Turner, director of Culinary Wellness at Henry Ford West Bloomfield Hospital, features quinoa for a twist.

 7 (¹/₂-cup servings)    25 mins total

Ingredients

1 ½ cups cooked quinoa (about 1 cup raw), rinsed

2 cups water

2 tablespoons chopped fresh mint

2 tablespoons olive oil

1 tablespoon fresh lemon juice

1 tablespoon minced red onion

2 teaspoons sherry vinegar

1 teaspoon ground black pepper

¹/₂ teaspoon salt

¹/₄ cup finely diced seedless cucumber, peel included

¹/₃ cup finely diced red bell pepper

1 cup chopped flat-leaf parsley

Directions

Cook the quinoa in 2 cups water at a medium-high simmer for 12 to 15 minutes, stirring often. Drain the quinoa and chill. In a small jar with a tight-fighting lid, combine the mint, olive oil, lemon juice, red onion, sherry vinegar, black pepper and salt; shake to combine. Add cucumber, red bell pepper and parsley to the quinoa, drizzle with the dressing and thoroughly toss to combine.

 Test Kitchen Tip

If you don't have sherry vinegar on hand, cider vinegar or red wine vinegar work well in this recipe.

Nutritional info (per serving)

Calories........................132
    From fat.................34%

Fat....................................5 g
    Saturated.................1 g
    Trans.......................0 g

Carbohydrates...........18 g

Protein..........................4 g

Sodium.................150 mg

Cholesterol..............0 mg

Calcium..................33 mg

Fiber.............................2 g

Food exchanges
    1 starch, 1 fat

Slow-Cooked Mushroom Marinara

This recipe develops a hearty flavor from long and low cooking in the slow cooker. It takes only 20 minutes to put all the ingredients together, and one serving of this recipe is a good source of fiber.

 8 5 hours 30 mins total (Not all active time)

Ingredients

1 can (28 ounces) diced tomatoes

1 can (15 ounces) tomato sauce

1 can (6 ounces) tomato paste

¼ cup red wine

2 tablespoons olive oil

2 cups sliced mushrooms

1 cup diced onion

½ cup grated carrots

¼ cup freshly grated Parmesan cheese

3 cloves garlic, peeled, chopped

2 tablespoons sugar

1 teaspoon dried oregano

1 teaspoon dried basil

2 whole bay leaves

Pinch of red pepper flakes

¼ teaspoon salt

8 cups hot, cooked angel hair pasta

Directions

In a 5-quart slow cooker, combine the diced tomatoes, tomato sauce, tomato paste, red wine, olive oil, mushrooms, onion, carrots, Parmesan cheese, garlic, sugar, oregano, basil, bay leaves and red pepper flakes. Stir to combine the ingredients.

Cover and cook on the low setting for 5 hours.

Once the cooking is complete, add the salt to the sauce.

Prepare the pasta according to package directions, omitting the salt.

Remove bay leaves. Toss the sauce with the cooked pasta and serve.

Test Kitchen Tip

By using freshly grated Parmesan cheese, only a small amount is used. Keep Parmesan handy in the freezer, well wrapped in foil and in a freezer bag. You can grate it directly from the freezer.

Nutritional info (per serving)

Calories	333
From fat	16%
Fat	6 g
Saturated	1 g
Trans	0 g
Carbohydrates	57 g
Protein	11 g
Sodium	528 mg
Cholesterol	2 mg
Calcium	103 mg
Fiber	5 g
Food exchanges	3 starch, 2 vegetable, 1 fat

Spaghetti Pie

While bright, colorful fruits and vegetables often are in the spotlight for their nutritional attributes, less colorful produce such as mushrooms also supply many essential nutrients, including copper and B vitamins niacin and riboflavin, as well as iron, potassium, selenium and even vitamin D. One serving of mushrooms has only 20 calories and zero grams of fat.

 6   1 hour total

Ingredients

4 ounces dry whole-wheat angel hair pasta

1 ½ tablespoons trans fat-free margarine

1 egg, beaten

⅓ cup plus 1 tablespoon grated Parmesan cheese, divided

8 ounces ground beef sirloin

½ cup chopped onion

1 cup sliced mushrooms

2 cloves garlic, peeled, minced

¼ teaspoon fennel seed, crushed

1 can (8 ounces) tomato sauce

2 teaspoons sugar

1 teaspoon dried oregano, crushed

Vegetable oil cooking spray

1 cup low-fat ricotta cheese

¾ cup (3 ounces) shredded part-skim mozzarella cheese, divided

Directions

Cook pasta according to package directions, omitting the salt, and drain.

Return spaghetti to the warm saucepan. Stir margarine into hot pasta until melted. Stir in the egg and ⅓ cup Parmesan cheese; set aside.

In a medium nonstick skillet, cook ground beef until brown. Once cooked, place beef crumbles between a few layers of paper towel to remove fat; remove any fat from skillet. Return beef crumbles to skillet and add onion, mushrooms, garlic and fennel seeds that have been crushed between your fingers. Continue to cook until onions and mushrooms are tender, about 5 minutes. Stir in the tomato sauce, sugar and oregano; heat through.

Preheat oven to 350 degrees. Spray a 9-inch pie plate with vegetable oil cooking spray. Press pasta mixture onto the bottom and sides of the pie plate, forming a crust. In a small bowl, combine ricotta cheese and ½ cup mozzarella. Spread cheese mixture over pasta crust. Spread meat mixture over cheese mixture. Sprinkle with remaining ¼ cup mozzarella cheese and 1 tablespoon Parmesan cheese on top of the meat mixture. Bake for 30 to 35 minutes.

Allow spaghetti pie to set for about 10 minutes before cutting into servings.

Nutritional info (per serving)

Calories	285
From fat	38%
Fat	12 g
Saturated	5 g
Trans	0 g
Carbohydrates	23 g
Protein	22 g
Sodium	443 mg
Cholesterol	84 mg
Calcium	256 mg
Fiber	1 g

Food exchanges
1 starch, 1 vegetable,
2 lean meat, 1 fat

Test Kitchen Tip

Refrigerate mushrooms in their original packaging for up to one week. Once opened, store mushrooms in a loosely closed paper bag in the refrigerator and use within a couple of days. Avoid storing mushrooms in airtight containers because they can spoil.

Spaghetti with Creamy Sun-Dried Tomato Sauce

Sliced sun-dried tomatoes give this easy pasta dish a sweet flavor. Using fat-free half-and-half in place of heavy cream trims the fat and calories in this recipe. This recipe is a good source of fiber with 7 grams per serving.

5 · **45 mins total**

Ingredients

- 2 tablespoons olive oil
- 1 cup finely diced onion
- 3 tablespoons real bacon bits (such as Oscar Mayer)
- 2 cloves garlic, peeled, minced
- ¼ teaspoon salt
- ¼ teaspoon black pepper
- ⅔ cup fat-free half-and-half
- ⅓ cup sun-dried tomatoes, sliced
- ¼ cup red wine
- 1 can (15 ounces) no-salt-added tomato puree
- ½ teaspoon dried basil
- 5 cups hot, cooked whole-wheat spaghetti

Directions

In a large stock pot, heat the olive oil over medium heat; add the onion, bacon bits, garlic, salt and black pepper and cook, stirring occasionally, until the onion is softened, about 5 minutes.

Add the half-and-half, sun-dried tomatoes, red wine, tomato puree and basil. Reduce the heat to medium-low and simmer until the sauce is slightly thickened, 5 to 10 minutes. Remove the sauce from the heat.

While the sauce is cooking, prepare the pasta according package directions, omitting the salt.

Toss the sauce with the cooked pasta and serve.

Test Kitchen Tip

Sun-dried tomatoes can be hard to slice with a knife because of the chewy texture; try using scissors.

Watch This!

Scan this QR code with your smartphone to watch the Heart Smart® video.

Nutritional info (per serving)

Calories	325
From fat	19%
Fat	7 g
Saturated	1 g
Trans	0 g
Carbohydrates	54 g
Protein	13 g
Sodium	390 mg
Cholesterol	3 mg
Calcium	94 mg
Fiber	7 g

Food exchanges
3 starch, 2 vegetable, 1 fat

Spaghetti with Meatballs

Making your own sauce means you can control the seasonings, especially the amount of salt. Serving these meatballs atop whole-wheat angel hair pasta adds fiber.

  8   1 hour 30 mins total

Ingredients

8 ounces ground beef sirloin

1 egg

¼ cup panko bread crumbs

3 cloves garlic, peeled, minced

2 tablespoons finely diced onion

1 ¼ teaspoons dried oregano, divided

¼ teaspoon fennel seed

¾ teaspoon salt, divided

½ teaspoon black pepper, divided

2 tablespoons olive oil

1 cup chopped onion

½ cup shredded carrots

¼ cup finely diced celery

⅛ teaspoon crushed red pepper flakes

1 can (28 ounces) no-salt-added crushed tomatoes

1 can (6 ounces) tomato paste

1 ½ cups water

1 teaspoon dried basil

1 teaspoon sugar

1 bay leaf

1 cup grated Parmesan cheese, divided

12 ounces dry whole-wheat angel hair pasta

Directions

Preheat oven to 350 degrees.

To prepare meatballs: In a large bowl, combine the ground sirloin, egg, panko, 1 minced garlic clove, 2 tablespoons diced onion, ¼ teaspoon dried oregano, fennel seed, ¼ teaspoon salt and ¼ teaspoon black pepper. Mix well and shape into 24 miniature (about 1-inch in diameter) meatballs. Arrange meatballs on a 15-by-10-by-1-inch baking pan. Bake for 15 to 20 minutes.

To prepare the sauce: Heat the olive oil in a large Dutch oven or stockpot. Add chopped onion, carrots, celery, remaining garlic and crushed red pepper and sauté until vegetables are tender, about 5 minutes. Stir in the crushed tomatoes, tomato paste, water, remaining teaspoon oregano, basil, sugar, remaining ½ teaspoon salt, and ¼ teaspoon black pepper and bay leaf. Allow sauce to bubble slightly, and then reduce heat. Cover and simmer for 30 minutes. Uncover and add ½ cup Parmesan cheese and cooked meatballs. Remove bay leaf.

Cook the angel hair pasta according to package directions, omitting the salt, and drain. Serve sauce over pasta, and sprinkle with remaining ½ cup Parmesan cheese. One serving consists of 1 cup cooked pasta, ¾ cup sauce and 4 miniature meatballs.

Nutritional info (per serving)

Calories 355
    From fat 25%

Fat .... 10 g
    Saturated .... 3 g
    Trans .... 0 g

Carbohydrates .... 49 g

Protein .... 19 g

Sodium .... 585 mg

Cholesterol .... 53 mg

Calcium .... 149 mg

Fiber .... 3 g

Food exchanges
    2 starch, 3 vegetable,
    2 lean meat, ½ fat

Test Kitchen Tip

Panko is a a bigger flaked bread crumb with a coarse texture. It's used as a coating for many fried foods because it produces a crunchy texture or for binding together a mixture, such as the meatballs in this recipe.

Spanish Rice

While onions may not be a powerhouse of nutrients, they do contain flavonoids. Some studies suggest that flavonoids may protect arteries against cholesterol damage and help prevent blood clots. The powerful sulfuric compounds in onions are responsible for their pungent odor and eye-irritating qualities.

Onions can be grouped into two categories: spring/summer onions and storage onions. Use either one in this easy Spanish Rice recipe.

 7 (²/₃-cup servings)   45 mins total

Ingredients

2 tablespoons canola oil

1 cup chopped onion

½ cup chopped green pepper

1 clove garlic, peeled, minced

1 teaspoon chili powder

¼ teaspoon ground cumin

1 can (28 ounces) diced tomatoes, undrained

¾ cup instant brown rice

1 ½ cups water

¼ teaspoon salt

⅛ teaspoon ground black pepper

Directions

In a large skillet, heat oil and sauté onion, green pepper and garlic until tender, about 4 minutes. Add chili powder and cumin; cook 1 minute more. Stir in the undrained diced tomatoes, rice, water, salt and black pepper.

Bring to a boil, then reduce heat. Simmer, covered, for about 25 to 30 minutes or until the rice is tender and most of the liquid is absorbed.

Nutritional info (per serving)

Calories	111
From fat	32%
Fat	4 g
Saturated	0 g
Trans	0 g
Carbohydrates	18 g
Protein	2 g
Sodium	304 mg
Cholesterol	18 mg
Calcium	27 mg
Fiber	3 g

Food exchanges
1 starch, 1 vegetable, ½ fat

 Test Kitchen Tip
Choose onions that feel heavy for their size with dry, papery skin. It's best to store onions in a cool, dry place.

Spicy Corn and Black Bean Salad

When it comes to salad greens the darker green the leaves, the more nutritious the lettuce. Romaine lettuce has six times as much vitamin C and five to 10 times as much beta-carotene as iceberg. Romaine lettuce is the featured green in this Heart Smart® Spicy Corn and Black Bean Salad for an added crunch.

 6 10 mins total

Ingredients

¼ cup favorite hot salsa

¼ cup reduced-fat mayonnaise

6 cups romaine lettuce, shredded

1 package (10 ounces) frozen corn kernels, thawed

1 can (15 ounces) black beans, drained and rinsed

½ cup sliced red onion

1 ounce tortilla chips, broken

Directions

In a measuring cup or small bowl, whisk together salsa and mayonnaise until combined.

In a large salad bowl, gently toss together lettuce, corn kernels, black beans and red onion. Add dressing and toss salad until evenly coated. Top with broken tortilla chips and serve.

Nutritional info (per serving)

Calories........................190
    From fat 24%

Fat ....5 g
    Saturated.................1 g
    Trans ....0 g

Carbohydrates ....29 g

Protein ....7 g

Sodium ....295 mg

Cholesterol ....4 mg

Calcium ....57 mg

Fiber ....6 g

Food exchanges
    1 starch, 2 ½ vegetable, 1 fat

Test Kitchen Tip

Store salad greens in a plastic bag in the refrigerator crisper. Romaine should keep for about 10 days. Avoid storing salad greens near fruits such as apples and bananas. As fruits ripen, they give off ethylene gas. This gas causes the greens to develop brown spots and decay rapidly.

Three Bean Salad

This Three Bean Salad is colorful and provides 4 grams of fiber per serving. It's a good dish to make ahead and ideal to take to a potluck.

 8 | 30 mins total

Ingredients

SALAD

1 can (14.5 ounces) no-salt-added green beans, drained

1 can (14.5 ounces) wax beans, drained

1 can (15 ounces) dark red kidney beans, drained and rinsed

½ cup chopped celery

¼ cup diced onion

¼ cup sweet pickles, diced

DRESSING

¼ cup cider vinegar

3 tablespoons sugar

2 tablespoons canola oil

1 tablespoon horseradish

½ teaspoon celery seed

¼ teaspoon ground black pepper

Test Kitchen Tip

Always rinse canned vegetables and beans to rid them of excess sodium.

Nutritional info (per serving)

Calories.........................117
    From fat.................23%
Fat ....3 g
    Saturated ....0 g
    Trans ....0 g
Carbohydrates ....18 g
Protein ....4 g
Sodium ....234 mg
Cholesterol ....0 mg
Calcium ....50 mg
Fiber ....4 g
Food exchanges
    ½ starch, 2 vegetable,
    ½ fat

Directions

In a large container with a sealable lid, combine green beans, wax beans, kidney beans, celery, onion and sweet pickles. Gently shake and roll the container to mix ingredients.

In a small container or jar, combine the vinegar, sugar, oil, horseradish, celery seed and black pepper. Seal the container with the lid and shake it vigorously.

Pour dressing mixture over bean mixture and gently shake to combine all ingredients.

Chill at least 2 hours before serving to allow flavors to blend.

Tomato Florentine Pasta Bake

Low in fat and rich in carbohydrates, pasta seems to fall in and out of favor based on the latest diet trend. But it can be ~~~~~~~~ althy diet if you watch whole-grain varie whole-grain flour germ during proc skin of the whole embryo of the gra protein, antioxida fiber.

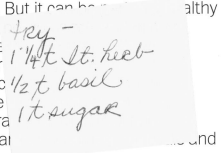

*try –
1 1/4 t. It. herb
1/2 t basil
1 t sugar*

 8 (1-cup servings)    40 mins total

Ingredients

1 tablespoon olive oil

2 cups diced onion

3 cloves garlic, peeled, minced

1/8 teaspoon red pepper flakes

1 teaspoon dried oregano

1 teaspoon dried basil

1/4 teaspoon black pepper

1 can (15 ounces) no-added-salt diced tomatoes, undrained

1 can (6 ounces) tomato paste

3/4 cup red wine

1 tablespoon sugar

1 package (10 ounces) frozen spinach, thawed and squeezed dry

5 ounces part-skim, shredded mozzarella cheese

3/4 teaspoon salt

6 ounces uncooked whole-wheat penne

Vegetable oil cooking spray

1/3 to 1/2 cup grated Parmesan cheese

Directions

Preheat oven to 350 degrees.

In a large saucepan, heat the olive oil over medium heat. Add the onion and garlic and sauté until the onion becomes soft; about 5 minutes. Add the red pepper flakes, oregano, basil and black pepper and sauté an additional 2 to 3 minutes. Add the diced tomatoes, tomato paste, red wine and sugar and stir to combine. Add the spinach, mozzarella cheese and salt and stir to incorporate. Cook the pasta according to the package directions, omitting the salt. Add the cooked, well-drained pasta to the tomato mixture and combine. Place the pasta mixture in a 2-quart baking dish coated with cooking spray and sprinkle evenly with the Parmesan cheese. Bake for 15 minutes or until heated through.

Nutritional info (per serving)

Calories	228	Sodium	394 mg
From fat	24%	Cholesterol	14 mg
Fat	6 g	Calcium	228 mg
Saturated	3 g	Fiber	6 g
Trans	0 g	Food exchanges	
Carbohydrates	29 g	1 starch, 2 vegetable,	
Protein	12 g	1 meat	

 Test Kitchen Tip
Most packages list 2 ounces of dry pasta as the serving size, which equates to about 1 cup of cooked pasta.

Wild Rice and Cranberry Salad

If you're looking for a different side dish for Thanksgiving that doesn't take up oven space, try this Wild Rice and Cranberry Salad. Wild rice is dark brown in color, has a nutty, herblike flavor and is slightly chewy when cooked. In this recipe a less expensive rice blend containing brown and wild rice is used.

 6   **1 hour 10 mins total**

Ingredients

1 cup uncooked wild and brown rice blend (such as Lundberg Wild Blend, wild and whole-grain brown rice)

2 cups water

1 cup diced apple (Fuji or Honeycrisp work well)

½ cup orange juice

2 tablespoons cider vinegar

1 tablespoon canola oil

2 teaspoons sugar

½ teaspoon salt

⅛ teaspoon fresh ground black pepper

½ cup dried cranberries

2 thinly sliced green onions

Directions

Prepare rice blend according to the package directions, omitting salt and oil. Once rice has cooked, plunge it immediately into an ice bath. Drain the rice blend well.

In a medium-size bowl, combine diced apple and orange juice, allowing apple to soak for 2 minutes. Remove apples from juice and add cider vinegar, canola oil, sugar, salt and black pepper to juice; whisk to combine. Place drained rice in a large bowl and add apples, cranberries, green onions and orange juice dressing. Gently toss to combine. Refrigerate at least 4 hours before serving.

Nutritional info (per serving)

Calories	187
From fat	14%
Fat	3 g
Saturated	0 g
Trans	0 g
Carbohydrates	37 g
Protein	3 g
Sodium	199 mg
Cholesterol	0 mg
Calcium	16 mg
Fiber	0 g

Food exchanges
1 starch, 1 ½ fruit, ½ fat

Test Kitchen Tip

When using wild rice, be sure to clean it thoroughly before cooking. Place the rice in a bowl, fill it with cold water and allow the rice to soak for a few minutes. Discard water and any debris that floats to the surface.

Ziti with Escarole

Escarole is a variety of endive that has broad leaves and is not as bitter. It can be used as a salad green or in a cooked dish. In this dish, the escarole is cooked briefly by draining the hot pasta over it. One serving of this recipe is an excellent source of fiber with 5 grams.

 7 30 mins total

Ingredients

8 ounces ziti pasta or favorite tubular pasta

6 cups escarole leaves, thinly sliced

1 cup sun-dried tomatoes (not packed in oil), thinly sliced

2 tablespoons olive oil

½ cup diced onion

3 cloves garlic, peeled, finely chopped

1 can (14 ounces) fat-free, less-sodium chicken broth

2 ½ tablespoons all-purpose flour

1 can (15.5 ounces) garbanzo beans, drained and rinsed

½ cup grated Parmesan cheese

½ teaspoon salt

¼ teaspoon coarsely ground black pepper

Directions

Cook the pasta in a large saucepot according to package directions, omitting the salt.

Place the escarole and sun-dried tomatoes in a colander and drain the pasta over them. Return the cooked pasta and escarole-tomato mixture to the saucepot.

In a large nonstick skillet, heat the olive oil over medium heat and sauté the onion and garlic until they are tender, about 5 minutes.

In a separate bowl or measuring cup, blend the chicken broth with the flour and pour it into the skillet with the onion and garlic. Add the garbanzo beans and cook, stirring occasionally, until the mixture boils and thickens.

Add the broth mixture to the pasta, tossing well. Season with Parmesan cheese, salt and black pepper and serve.

Nutritional info (per serving)

Calories...................... 271
    From fat 23%
Fat ....7 g
    Saturated................ 2 g
    Trans .... 0 g
Carbohydrates .... 41 g
Protein ....11 g
Sodium ....515 mg
Cholesterol ....5 mg
Calcium .... 129 mg
Fiber .... 5 g
Food exchanges
    2 starch, 2 vegetable,
    1 fat

Vegetables

Vegetables

The term organic is becoming more common especially on vegetables found in the produce aisle. But does organic really mean anything and are organic foods safer or more nutritious?

The U.S. Department of Agriculture (USDA) has established an organic certification program. Foods bearing the official green organic seal are required to be grown, harvested and processed according to national standards that include restrictions on pesticides, hormones and antibiotics.

The following regulated terms can be found on food packages:
• Foods labeled "100% organic" must have no synthetic ingredients and can use the USDA organic seal.
• Foods labeled "organic" have a minimum of 95% organic ingredients and can use the USDA organic seal.
• Foods labeled "made with organic ingredients" must contain at least 70% organic ingredients, but the USDA organic seal cannot be used.
• Meat, eggs, poultry and dairy labeled "organic" must come from animals that have never received antibiotics or growth hormones. The USDA has not set standards for organic seafood.

According to the USDA, pesticides on organically grown fresh vegetables and fruits, have fewer pesticide residues than conventionally grown produce. However, pesticide residues on almost all conventionally and organically grown produce sold in the U.S. are well below government-determined levels for safe consumption. The USDA makes no claims that organic foods are safer or healthier than conventional foods.

Also, there is no definitive evidence that organic food is more nutritious than conventionally grown food. What matters is eating plenty of vegetables and fruits regardless of whether they are organic. The health benefits of enjoying these nutritional staples far outweigh any potential risks from pesticide exposure. If you do go the organic route, expect to pay 10 to 100% more. More expensive farming practices and lower crop yields drive up prices.

Apple-Stuffed Acorn Squash

While squash varies widely in size, color and shape, most types have a sweet, mellow flavor. Most winter squash is rich in beta-carotene (the form of vitamin A found in plant foods) and are fairly good sources of vitamin C. Beta-carotene and vitamin C are two antioxidants that may protect us from chronic diseases such as heart disease and cancer.

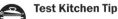 4   1 hour 15 mins total

Ingredients

1 acorn squash

1 ½ cups diced tart apple

2 tablespoons apricot jam

2 tablespoons brown sugar

2 tablespoons toasted pecan pieces

½ teaspoon ground cinnamon

⅛ teaspoon salt, divided

1 tablespoon trans fat-free margarine, divided

Directions

Preheat oven to 400 degrees. Cut the squash in half and remove seeds and strings. Place squash halves, cut sides down, in a shallow pan with ¼-inch water. Bake for 35 minutes. While the squash is baking, combine the diced apple, apricot jam, brown sugar, pecan pieces and cinnamon. Remove the squash from the oven and turn cut side up in the pan. Season each half with the salt. Place ½ tablespoon of margarine in each half and spoon apple mixture into each squash half. Bake an additional 30 minutes or until tender. If apples begin to brown, loosely place a foil tent over the top of the pan.

Nutritional info (per serving)

Calories......................144	Sodium .... 88 mg
From fat.................25%	Cholesterol ....0 mg
Fat ....4 g	Calcium .... 46 mg
Saturated ....1 g	Fiber ....3 g
Trans ....0 g	Food exchanges
Carbohydrates ....28 g	1 starch, 1 fruit
Protein ....1 g	

Test Kitchen Tip

The tastiest winter squash is solid and heavy for its size. The stem should be full, firm and have a corky feel. The skin should be hard, deep-colored and free of blemishes, cracks, soft spots and mold. The only time winter squash should be refrigerated is after it has been cut and wrapped in plastic.

Baked Onion Rings

A typical restaurant serving of onion rings — battered rings of raw onion deep-fried in fat — has more than 600 calories, 30 grams of fat and more than 1,000 milligrams of sodium. With these Heart Smart® Baked Onions Rings, we slashed more than 460 calories, 26 grams of fat and 700 milligrams of sodium from each serving with simple changes. The coated rings are sprayed with vegetable oil cooking spray and baked on a lightly oiled pan. Relying on seasonings like garlic powder, onion powder, dry mustard, black pepper and just a little salt reduced the sodium.

 6 🍽 35 mins total

Ingredients

1 large sweet onion (such as Vidalia), peeled

3 tablespoons all-purpose flour

¼ teaspoon garlic powder

¼ teaspoon onion powder

¼ teaspoon dry mustard

¼ teaspoon ground black pepper

⅛ teaspoon plus ¼ teaspoon salt, divided

¾ cup low-fat buttermilk

1 cup plain bread crumbs

1 tablespoon olive oil

Vegetable oil cooking spray

Nutritional info (per 5 ring serving)

Calories.........................136	Sodium .... 289 mg
From fat.................26%	Cholesterol .... 1 mg
Fat .... 4 g	Calcium .... 81 mg
Saturated.................1 g	Fiber ....1 g
Trans .... 0 g	Food exchanges
Carbohydrates ....22 g	2 vegetable, 1 fat
Protein .... 4 g	

Directions

Preheat oven to 450 degrees. Slice the onion into ¼-inch-thick rounds and separate into rings, discarding the smallest center rings. The separated rings should yield about 6 cups or about 30 rings of varying sizes.

In a small bowl or measuring cup, combine the flour, garlic powder, onion powder, dry mustard, black pepper and ⅛ teaspoon salt. Place flour mixture in a large, resealable plastic bag. Add sliced onions and toss to coat.

Place the buttermilk in a medium-sized bowl and the bread crumbs in a separate medium-sized bowl. Dip the floured onion rings in the buttermilk, then dredge in the bread crumbs and place on a large plate or cutting board.

Pour the olive oil onto a large, rimmed baking sheet. Place the baking sheet in the oven and heat for 2 minutes. Carefully remove the sheet from the oven and tilt to coat the pan evenly with the oil. Arrange onion rings on the sheet and spray lightly with vegetable oil cooking spray. Bake about 16 minutes, turning once during cooking. Remove from the oven and season with the remaining ¼ teaspoon salt.

Test Kitchen Tip

Drizzling the oil on the baking sheet and placing it in the oven for several minutes to heat helps set the coating on the onions and makes it crunchy.

Baked Sweet Potatoes with Brown Sugar

Eating a variety of vegetables year-round is one key to maintaining a healthy diet. In the fall when sweet potatoes are in abundance in the produce aisle, turn to this root vegetable for a healthy dose of beta-carotene.

 4   **1 hour 10 mins total**

Ingredients

4 small (4 ounces each) sweet
   potatoes, washed and scrubbed

½ cup reduced-fat sour cream

2 tablespoons packed brown sugar

½ teaspoon ground cinnamon

Directions

Preheat oven to 375 degrees. Line a baking sheet with aluminum foil. Pierce the potatoes all over with a fork. Arrange potatoes on the baking sheet and bake for 50 to 60 minutes, or until soft.

Remove from oven and when cool enough to handle, carefully cut a deep slit in each potato and push ends together to open.

In a small bowl or measuring cup combine the sour cream, brown sugar and cinnamon. Top each sweet potato with 2 tablespoons of sour cream mixture and serve.

Nutritional info (per serving)

Calories......................162
   From fat 22%

Fat ....4 g
   Saturated................2 g
   Trans ....0 g

Carbohydrates ....29 g

Protein ....3 g

Sodium ....82 mg

Cholesterol ....16 mg

Calcium .... 88 mg

Fiber ....3 g

Food exchanges
   2 starch, ½ fat

Test Kitchen Tip

When selecting sweet potatoes choose ones that are smooth, hard and heavy for their size. Avoid those with black spots, or decay that can appear as a shriveled area. Store sweet potatoes in a cool, dry place and never in the refrigerator where they can develop an odd taste.

Braised Greens

This Braised Greens recipe is from chef Frank Turner, director of Culinary Wellness at Henry Ford West Bloomfield Hospital. Dark leafy greens are an excellent source of fiber. Each serving of this side dish (about 1 cup) has 10 grams of fiber.

 6   1 hour 40 mins total

Ingredients

1 jumbo yellow onion, peeled, sliced (about 4 cups)

2 tablespoons minced garlic

1 tablespoon canola oil or grape seed oil

14 cups (1 large bunch) collard greens, cleaned and cut

14 cups (2 bunches) mustard greens, cleaned and cut

2 tablespoons red wine vinegar

1 tablespoon hot red pepper sauce (such as Frank's Red Hot Sauce)

Water, as needed to cover greens

Ground black pepper to taste

Directions

In a large stockpot, sauté the onions and garlic in oil for 2 to 3 minutes or until tender. Add collard and mustard greens and simmer over medium heat until the greens have lost their firmness and the onion and garlic is thoroughly incorporated, about 7 to 10 minutes. Add the red wine vinegar, hot sauce and enough water to cover half the greens. Cover and cook until the greens are tender, at least 30 minutes. Season to taste with black pepper.

Test Kitchen Tip

To clean the greens, trim stem ends. Rinse the greens with water and then fill a clean sink with cold water. Submerge the greens in water and swish them around to remove the grit. Remove from water, pat dry with paper towel. To cut or slice the greens, fold a leaf over on top of the other leaf so the stem and ribs are along the side. Trim off the tough stems. Roll up the leaves.

Nutritional info (per serving)

Calories.......................143
   From fat.................19%

Fat ....3 g
   Saturated ....0 g
   Trans ....0 g

Carbohydrates ....27 g

Protein ....7 g

Sodium ....153 mg

Cholesterol ....0 mg

Calcium ....409 mg

Fiber ....10 g

Food exchanges
   5 vegetable, ½ fat

Braised Red Cabbage

This recipe by chef Frank Turner, director of Culinary Wellness at Henry Ford West Bloomfield Hospital, features red cabbage and apples. It's a simple side dish to prepare with a sweet and tangy taste.

 8   1 hour total

Ingredients

2 tablespoons vegetable oil

⅓ cup diced onion

1 apple, cored, sliced with peel

6 tablespoons water

2 tablespoons red wine (Cabernet works well)

4 tablespoons cider vinegar

4 ½ tablespoons sugar

8 cups red cabbage, cored, shredded

½ teaspoon salt

½ teaspoon black pepper, or to taste

Directions

In a large saucepan, heat the oil over low-medium heat. Slowly cook the onions and apples in the oil, avoiding any browning, about 5 to 10 minutes. Add the water, red wine, cider vinegar, sugar and cabbage. Simmer the mixture until the liquid has evaporated, about 15 to 30 minutes. Add the salt and black pepper.

Nutritional info (per serving)

Calories........................162	Sodium ....82 mg
From fat.................22%	Cholesterol ....16 mg
Fat ....4 g	Calcium ....88 mg
Saturated ....2 g	Fiber ....3 g
Trans ....0 g	Food exchanges
Carbohydrates ....29 g	2 starch, ½ fat
Protein ....3 g	

Watch This!

Scan this QR code with your smartphone to watch the Heart Smart® video.

Broccoli Casserole

The crunchy topping gets a rich taste from reduced-fat buttery crackers. This tasty side dish recipe is a good way to sneak a vegetable serving. Vegetables supply dietary fiber, are low in fat and sodium and are cholesterol-free.

 8 45 mins total

Ingredients

Vegetable oil cooking spray

1 package (16 ounces) frozen broccoli cuts, thawed and drained

½ cup chopped red onion

½ cup reduced-fat sour cream

½ cup fat-free mayonnaise

2 ounces (about ¾ cup) shredded reduced-fat sharp cheddar cheese

¼ teaspoon salt

⅛ teaspoon ground black pepper

5 reduced-fat round buttery crackers (such as reduced-fat Ritz crackers)

2 teaspoons trans fat-free margarine, melted

Directions

Preheat oven to 350 degrees. Spray a round 9- or 10-inch oven-safe quiche dish with vegetable oil cooking spray.

In a large mixing bowl combine broccoli, onion, sour cream, mayonnaise, cheddar cheese, salt and pepper. Mix well and spread in prepared pan.

Place crackers in a sealable bag and crush into crumbs. In a small bowl, combine melted margarine and cracker crumbs. Sprinkle crumb mixture over broccoli mixture and bake for 30 to 35 minutes or until edges are lightly browned.

Nutritional info (per serving)

Calories	92
From fat	49%
Fat	5 g
Saturated	2 g
Trans	0 g
Carbohydrates	8 g
Protein	4 g
Sodium	297 mg
Cholesterol	13 mg
Calcium	112 mg
Fiber	2 g
Food exchanges	
1 vegetable, 1 fat	

Test Kitchen Tip

To easily crush crackers to use for a crumb topping, place them flat in a plastic sealable bag. Seal bag and use a rolling pin to crush the crackers.

Broccoli Rice Casserole

When you have leftover cooked brown rice, this Broccoli Rice Casserole is a way to use it up. Using brown rice, which is a whole grain, adds fiber to this casserole. The crusty cheese topping gets a flavor boost from using Italian-seasoned bread crumbs.

   10 1 hour 10 mins total

Ingredients

Vegetable oil cooking spray

1 bag (16 ounces) frozen broccoli pieces

1 cup chopped onion

1 cup fat-free, less-sodium chicken broth

2 cups cooked brown rice

¾ cup reduced-fat sour cream

1 cup (4 ounces) shredded reduced-fat sharp cheddar cheese

¼ cup grated Parmesan cheese, divided

¼ cup Italian-seasoned bread crumbs

½ teaspoon salt

¼ teaspoon black pepper

¼ cup fat-free egg substitute

Directions

Preheat oven to 350 degrees.

Coat a 1 ½- to 2-quart casserole dish or other baking dish with vegetable oil cooking spray.

In a large saucepan, combine the broccoli, onion and chicken broth; bring to a boil. Cover, reduce heat and simmer 20 minutes or until vegetables are tender. Drain.

In a large bowl, combine broccoli mixture, brown rice, sour cream, cheddar cheese, 2 tablespoons Parmesan cheese, bread crumbs, salt, black pepper and egg substitute; stir gently.

Spoon the mixture into the prepared baking dish. Sprinkle with the remaining 2 tablespoons of Parmesan cheese. Bake for 30 minutes or until bubbly; then broil 1 minute or until lightly browned.

Nutritional info (per serving)

Calories.........................148
   From fat 30%
Fat ....5 g
   Saturated...............3 g
   Trans ....0 g
Carbohydrates ....16 g
Protein ....9 g
Sodium ....384 mg
Cholesterol ....16 mg
Calcium ....186 mg
Fiber ....2.5 g
Food exchanges
   1 starch, 1 meat

Test Kitchen Tip

Brown rice can take about an hour to cook so it's a good idea to cook ahead of time and freeze. Portion the cooked rice in the amounts you will use, and place in freezer bags, squeeze out the air and freeze.

Creamy Confetti Corn

This recipe calls for frozen corn. But when homegrown Michigan corn starts coming in, try substituting it.

 8   45 mins total

Ingredients

Vegetable oil cooking spray

1 tablespoon trans fat-free margarine

½ cup diced green pepper

½ cup diced red onion

1 clove garlic, peeled, minced

2 boxes (10 ounces each) frozen corn kernels

3 ounces reduced-fat cream cheese, softened

¼ cup skim milk

¼ teaspoon dried thyme

¼ teaspoon salt

¼ teaspoon freshly ground black pepper

¼ cup grated Parmesan cheese

Directions

Preheat oven to 350 degrees.

Coat a 9-inch broiler-safe quiche dish or pie plate with vegetable oil cooking spray; set aside.

In a large nonstick skillet, heat margarine over medium heat and cook the green pepper, onion and garlic until slightly tender, about 3 minutes. Add the corn kernels and continue to cook for 3 to 5 minutes.

In a small bowl or measuring cup, combine the cream cheese and milk until smooth. Add the thyme, salt and pepper. Pour the cream cheese mixture over the corn mixture and gently stir to combine. Spoon the corn mixture into the prepared dish and sprinkle the top with Parmesan cheese.

Bake uncovered for 30 minutes. Place the oven on broil and continue cooking until the cheese topping is golden brown, about 2 to 4 minutes.

Nutritional info (per serving)

Calories...................... 116	Sodium ....159 mg
From fat................. 31%	Cholesterol ....10 mg
Fat ....4 g	Calcium ....52 mg
Saturated .... 2 g	Fiber .... 2 g
Trans .... 0 g	Food exchanges
Carbohydrates ....17 g	1 starch, 1 fat
Protein ....5 g	

Test Kitchen Tip

To easily cut fresh corn from the cob, first break the cob in half. Stand one half up with the cut side on the work surface. Use a sharp knife to remove the kernels from the cob.

Fried Cabbage

Cabbage is in the cruciferous vegetable family that also includes, collards, kohlrabi, radishes and turnips. Researchers have been focusing on the potential cancer-fighting ability of these vegetables. Studies suggest that cruciferous vegetables may help ward off certain forms of cancer, especially cancer of the mouth, throat and stomach. Many experts say they contain substances that seem to stimulate the release of anticancer enzymes and promote the destruction of cancer cells. As researchers learn more about the cancer-fighting properties of these vegetables, it's important to enjoy cruciferous vegetables often.

 6   30 mins total

Ingredients

2 tablespoons trans fat-free margarine

⅛ teaspoon red pepper flakes, optional

2 tablespoons real bacon bits (such as Oscar Mayer)

1 cup chopped onion

6 cups chopped cabbage

1 tablespoon water

1 tablespoon cider vinegar

1 teaspoon sugar

¼ teaspoon salt

⅛ teaspoon freshly ground black pepper

Directions

In a large skillet, melt margarine over medium heat. Add red pepper flakes, if desired, and sauté for 1 minute. Add bacon bits and onion and continue to sauté 2 to 3 minutes. Add cabbage and cook for 1 minute, stirring constantly. Add water, cider vinegar and sugar; stir to combine and cook 1 minute.

Remove from heat, add salt and pepper, and serve.

Nutritional info (per serving)

Calories..........................59
    From fat.................46%

Fat ....3 g
    Saturated.................1 g
    Trans ....0 g

Carbohydrates ....7 g

Protein ....2 g

Sodium ....192 mg

Cholesterol ....2 mg

Calcium .... 39 mg

Fiber ....2 g

Food exchanges
    1 vegetable, ½ fat

Glazed Carrots for a Crowd

This recipe is flavorful and plenty to feed a crowd. Only ½ teaspoon thyme is used in this recipe. Thyme is a strong herb and a little goes a long way.

 16 (½-cup servings)  **35 mins total**

Ingredients

10 cups (3 ½ pounds) scraped and sliced carrots

¼ cup trans fat-free margarine

½ cup finely diced onion

1 teaspoon ground ginger

¼ cup packed brown sugar

¼ cup honey

⅓ cup orange juice concentrate, thawed and undiluted

½ teaspoon dried thyme

¼ teaspoon salt

Nutritional info (per serving)

Calories	87
From fat	21%
Fat	2 g
Saturated	0 g
Trans	0 g
Carbohydrates	18 g
Protein	1 g
Sodium	103 mg
Cholesterol	0 mg
Calcium	32 mg
Fiber	2 g

Food exchanges
½ starch, 1 vegetable
½ fat

Directions

Fill a steamer-friendly saucepan with a ½-inch of water. Place steamer basket on top of the saucepan (water should not touch the bottom of the basket). Place the sliced carrots in the steamer basket (steaming in two batches may be necessary for this quantity). Cover and heat to boiling; reduce heat to low and steam for 6 to 8 minutes. Melt the margarine in a large skillet. Add the onion and ginger and cook, stirring constantly until tender, about 5 minutes. Add the brown sugar, honey and orange juice concentrate and cook until slightly thickened and bubbly. Place the carrots in the skillet, season with thyme and salt and stir to coat.

Green Beans with Dijon Vinaigrette

This recipe is a different way to season plain green beans. There are many varieties of vinegars and some flavored vinegars can contain a fair amount of sodium. For example, seasoned rice vinegar can have 250 to 350 milligrams of sodium per tablespoon. Unseasoned rice vinegar is used in this recipe. The amount of vinaigrette here may seem like not enough, but it does evenly coat the beans.

  8   20 mins total

Ingredients

2 pounds green beans (about 6 cups), trimmed

1 tablespoon olive oil

2 teaspoons rice vinegar (not seasoned)

1 teaspoon Dijon mustard

1 teaspoon sugar

¼ teaspoon salt

¼ teaspoon freshly ground black pepper

Directions

Bring 1 inch of water to a boil in a large pot fitted with a steamer basket.

Fill a large bowl with ice water; set it aside.

Place the green beans, stem ends trimmed, in the steamer basket. Cover and steam until the beans are crisp-tender, 5 to 8 minutes.

Plunge the beans in the ice water to stop the cooking.

When the beans are cool, drain and pat them dry with paper towel.

Transfer the beans to a large bowl.

In a small bowl or jar, whisk or shake the olive oil, rice vinegar, Dijon mustard, sugar, salt and pepper until they are combined. Pour the vinaigrette over the beans; toss to coat, then serve.

Nutritional info (per serving)

Calories..........................44
    From fat 41%

Fat .... 2 g
    Saturated................0 g
    Trans ....0 g

Carbohydrates .... 6 g

Protein .... 2 g

Sodium ....81 mg

Cholesterol ....0 mg

Calcium .... 32 mg

Fiber .... 3 g

Food exchanges
    1 vegetable, ½ fat

Test Kitchen Tip
Store vinegar in an airtight container and keep it in a cool, dark place. Once vinegar is opened, it will keep for about 6 months.

Mexican Corn

This easy-to-make side dish uses trans fat-free tub margarine. Trans fats are bad fats that raise the total and LDL (bad) cholesterol while lowering good HDL cholesterol. A guide for choosing a healthy margarine is to select those with no more than 1 to 2 grams of saturated fat and no trans fat per tablespoon. This recipe uses 1 tablespoon Olivio tub margarine and serves four. One tablespoon of Olivio contains 1 gram of saturated fat and no trans fat.

4   **35 mins total**

Ingredients

1 tablespoon trans fat-free margarine (such as Olivio)

½ cup diced red or green bell pepper

½ cup diced red onion

1 tablespoon minced jalapeño pepper

1 teaspoon ground cumin

1 teaspoon chili powder

¼ teaspoon salt

2 cups frozen corn, thawed

1 teaspoon lime juice

Directions

In a large nonstick skillet, over medium heat, melt margarine and sauté bell pepper, onion and jalapeño pepper for about 4 minutes. Add the cumin, chili powder and salt and continue to sauté an additional 2 minutes. Add the thawed corn and stir to combine until heated through. Drizzle with lime juice and serve.

Nutritional info (per serving)

Calories	100
From fat	18%
Fat	2 g
Saturated	0 g
Trans	0 g
Carbohydrates	20 g
Protein	3 g
Sodium	149 mg
Cholesterol	0 mg
Calcium	11 mg
Fiber	3 g
Food exchanges	1 starch, 1 vegetable

Pan-Fried Asparagus

Michigan ranks third in the nation for asparagus production, harvesting up to 25 million pounds every year. Grown mostly in counties along Lake Michigan in sandy, well-drained soil, Michigan asparagus is harvested for a six- to seven-week period from late April through mid- to late June. Asparagus provides a healthy dose of fiber, vitamin C, iron and B vitamins, especially folate. Folate is thought to help protect blood vessel walls and decrease the risk of heart disease and stroke.

 5   **20 mins total**

Ingredients

1 pound trimmed fresh asparagus

2 teaspoons trans fat-free margarine

2 teaspoons olive oil

1 clove garlic, peeled, minced

Pinch of red pepper flakes

1 teaspoon sesame seeds

1 teaspoon reduced-sodium soy sauce

$\frac{1}{8}$ teaspoon salt

$\frac{1}{8}$ teaspoon freshly ground black pepper

Directions

Trim the woody ends of asparagus spears and discard. Slice asparagus into 3-inch lengths on a diagonal slant; set aside. In a large nonstick skillet, heat the margarine and oil over medium heat.

Add the asparagus pieces and sauté about 3 minutes. Add garlic and sauté 2 to 3 minutes. Add red pepper flakes and sesame seeds and continue to sauté 3 to 4 minutes, allowing sesame seeds to toast and the asparagus to become crisp-tender or done to your liking. Add the soy sauce, salt and pepper and toss to combine.

Nutritional info (per serving)

Calories	50	Sodium	105 mg
From fat	54%	Cholesterol	0 mg
Fat	3 g	Calcium	18 mg
Saturated	0 g	Fiber	1 g
Trans	0 g		
Carbohydrates	2 g	Food exchanges	
Protein	3 g	1 vegetable, $\frac{1}{2}$ fat	

Test Kitchen Tip

When buying fresh asparagus look for firm, bright green stalks that stand straight. The tips should be deep green or purplish in color and appear closed and compact. Store fresh asparagus in the refrigerator and use within three days for best quality. To trim the woody ends, bend the spear and it should snap at its most tender point. Michigan asparagus is hand harvested and snapped at its most tender point when it's picked.

Roasted Brussels Sprouts

One cup of cooked Brussels sprouts provides all the vitamin C an adult needs for the day. They also provide a healthy dose of fiber, folate and iron. Brussels sprouts contain phytochemicals that may stimulate natural anticancer enzymes in the body.

 6   45 mins total

Ingredients

1 ½ pounds fresh Brussels sprouts

1 ½ tablespoons olive oil

½ teaspoon salt

¼ teaspoon black pepper

Parchment paper or vegetable oil cooking spray

2 tablespoons real bacon bits (such as Oscar Mayer)

4 teaspoons maple syrup

3 teaspoons balsamic vinegar

Nutritional info (per serving)

Calories......................102	Sodium ....263 mg
From fat................35%	Cholesterol ....2 mg
Fat.................................4 g	Calcium ....51 mg
Saturated.................1 g	Fiber ....4 g
Trans ....0 g	Food exchanges
Carbohydrates ....14 g	2 vegetable, 1 fat
Protein ....5 g	

Directions

Preheat oven to 375 degrees.

Trim the ends of the Brussels sprouts and remove any discolored leaves. Cut sprouts in half, wash and pat dry with paper towel. Place sprouts in a bowl, drizzle with the olive oil and toss to coat. Add the salt and pepper and toss. Place sprouts on a baking sheet lined with parchment paper or coated with cooking spray.

Roast in oven for 15 minutes. Remove baking sheet from the oven, sprinkle the bacon bits over the sprouts and return to the oven. Continue to roast for an additional 15 to 20 minutes. In a small dish or measuring cup, combine the maple syrup and balsamic vinegar. Transfer sprouts to a bowl or serving dish, drizzle with maple syrup mixture and toss to coat.

Test Kitchen Tip

When selecting Brussels sprouts, choose ones that are firm with bright green and compact heads. Yellowed or wilted leaves are a sign of age or mishandling. Old Brussels sprouts will have a strong cabbage-like odor. Store unwashed sprouts in an airtight plastic bag in the refrigerator up to three days.

Roasted Harvest Vegetables

The turnip is often snubbed as peasant fare. And that's too bad because the turnip contains cancer-fighting properties along with an ample supply of vitamin C and fiber. Young turnips have a delicate, slightly sweet taste. As they age, they become bitter and fibrous. This tasty side dish of root vegetables has just 1 gram of fat per serving and 3 grams of fiber.

 8   **1 hour 15 mins total**

Ingredients

Vegetable oil cooking spray

2 cups peeled, cubed sweet potatoes

1 ½ cups diced turnips

1 cup sliced carrots

⅓ cup pineapple juice

⅓ cup low-fat Catalina dressing

3 tablespoons maple syrup

3 cups broccoli florets

1 ½ cups red onion, cut into wedges

Directions

Preheat oven to 350 degrees. Spray a 13-by-9-inch dish with cooking spray. In a large bowl combine the sweet potatoes, turnips and carrots. In a small bowl, mix the pineapple juice, Catalina dressing and maple syrup.

Pour the syrup mixture over the sweet potato mixture; gently toss.

Cover with foil and bake for 30 minutes.

Remove the vegetables from the oven and add the broccoli and onion. Stir to coat the added vegetables with liquid.

Bake uncovered for an additional 30 minutes or until the vegetables are tender.

Nutritional info (per serving)

Calories.........................105
    From fat 9%

Fat ....1 g
    Saturated...............0 g
    Trans ....0 g

Carbohydrates ....24 g

Protein ....2 g

Sodium .... 122 mg

Cholesterol ....0 mg

Calcium .... 46 mg

Fiber ....3 g

Food exchanges
    1 starch, 1 vegetable

 **Test Kitchen Tip**

Combine turnips and potatoes for mashed potatoes, add chunks of them to soups and stews or shred them and use raw in slaw recipes.

 Watch This!

Scan this QR code with your smartphone to watch the Heart Smart® video.

Roasted Rosemary Potatoes

Nutritionally, all types of olive oil have the same amount of calories, grams of fat and all provide heart healthy monounsaturated fats. It's the cost and taste that differ. A product labeled olive oil or pure olive oil is a combination of refined olive oil and virgin olive oil. These are the least expensive and a fine choice for these Roasted Rosemary Potatoes. These roasted potatoes get a distinct flavor from dried rosemary. Because rosemary tends to be on the strong side, adjust the amount to taste.

4 · 1 hour 10 mins total

Ingredients

Vegetable oil cooking spray

1 pound red potatoes

1 tablespoon olive oil

2 tablespoons grated Parmesan cheese

2 teaspoons dried rosemary

¼ teaspoon salt

⅛ teaspoon ground black pepper

Directions

Preheat oven to 350 degrees. Coat a baking sheet with vegetable oil cooking spray.

Wash and scrub the potatoes well, but do not peel them. Cut the potatoes into 1-inch cubes.

In a large bowl combine the olive oil, Parmesan cheese, rosemary, salt and pepper. Add the potatoes and toss to coat them.

Place the potatoes on the baking sheet, arranging them in a single layer. Bake, uncovered, about 50 to 60 minutes, stirring occasionally, until the skins are crispy and the potatoes are tender.

Test Kitchen Tip

Store olive oil in a cool, dark place for up to 6 months. You can store it in the refrigerator, although it's unnecessary. Olive oil kept in the refrigerator will become cloudy and may be too thick to pour. The cloudiness will disappear once the oil comes to room temperature.

Nutritional info (per serving)

Calories	130
From fat	28%
Fat	4 g
Saturated	1 g
Trans	0 g
Carbohydrates	20 g
Protein	3 g
Sodium	191 mg
Cholesterol	2 mg
Calcium	49 mg
Fiber	3 g
Food exchanges	
1 starch, 1 fat	

Scalloped Corn

When you need a side dish that is easy to put together and hearty, try this versatile Scalloped Corn.

It has minimal prep work and the corn flakes or panko bread crumbs provide a crunchy topping.

Nutritional info (per serving)

Calories	122	Sodium	135 mg
From fat	22%	Cholesterol	30 mg
Fat	3 g	Calcium	45 mg
Saturated	1 g	Fiber	2 g
Trans	0 g	Food exchanges	
Carbohydrates	21 g	1 starch, 1 vegetable,	
Protein	5 g	½ fat	

 **7 (½-cup servings)**   **1 hour total**

Ingredients

Vegetable oil cooking spray

2 tablespoons trans fat-free margarine, divided

½ cup diced onion

¼ cup diced red bell pepper

¼ cup diced green bell pepper

2 tablespoons all-purpose flour

¼ teaspoon salt

¼ teaspoon ground mustard

⅛ teaspoon ground black pepper

¾ cup skim milk

1 package (16 ounces) frozen corn, thawed

1 egg, slightly beaten

¾ cup corn flake cereal, slightly crushed, or panko bread crumbs

Directions

Preheat oven to 350 degrees. Coat a 1-quart casserole dish with vegetable oil cooking spray.

In a nonstick skillet over medium heat, melt 1 tablespoon margarine. Add the onion, red bell pepper and green bell pepper to the skillet and cook until crisp-tender, about 3 to 5 minutes. Stir in flour, salt, ground mustard and black pepper. Cook an additional minute, stirring constantly; remove from heat. Stir in milk, return to heat and allow to boil, stirring constantly.

Boil and stir 1 minute; remove from heat. Stir in the corn and egg. Pour into prepared dish. In a small bowl or measuring cup, mix the cereal and 1 tablespoon melted margarine; sprinkle over corn mixture. Bake uncovered 40 to 45 minutes or until center is set.

Snow Peas with Apricot Mango Vinaigrette

This side dish is simple and packed with flavor. The mango vinaigrette has a little kick from the gingerroot mixed with citrus juices. When selecting a mango, look for fruit with unblemished, yellow skin blushed with red. A ripe mango will have a full, fruity aroma and is ready to eat when the fruit is slightly soft to the touch and yields to gentle pressure, like a ripe peach.

 6   20 mins total

Ingredients

- ⅓ cup apricot preserves
- 2 tablespoons cider vinegar
- 3 cups snow peas, stem ends and strings removed
- ¼ mango, peeled and seeded
- 1 tablespoon canola oil
- 2 tablespoons fresh lime juice or orange juice
- 1 tablespoon minced shallots
- 1 teaspoon minced gingerroot
- ¼ teaspoon salt
- ⅛ teaspoon ground black pepper
- ½ cup julienned radishes
- ½ cup julienned jicama
- ¼ cup diced red onion

Directions

In a medium saucepan, heat the preserves and cider vinegar for about 3 minutes or until the preserves are melted. Remove from heat and cool.

In a large pot of boiling water, cook the snow peas 1 minute, then drain. Rinse the peas under cold running water, then drain thoroughly.

In a blender, add the cooled preserve mixture, mango, canola oil, lime juice, shallots, gingerroot, salt and black pepper. Blend until smooth.

In a medium bowl combine the snow peas, radishes, jicama and red onion. Add the vinaigrette and toss gently to mix well.

Cover and refrigerate for at least 1 hour before serving.

Test Kitchen Tip

Fresh gingerroot, used in this recipe, keeps several months in the freezer. Place it in a plastic bag with the air squeezed out. To use, there's no need to thaw, break off what you need and grate, chop or mince it. You also can grate from the whole piece and return the unused portion to the freezer.

Nutritional info (per serving)

Calories	94
From fat	19%
Fat	2 g
Saturated	0 g
Trans	0 g
Carbohydrates	18 g
Protein	1 g
Sodium	110 mg
Cholesterol	0 mg
Calcium	25 mg
Fiber	2 g
Food exchanges	1 fruit, 1 vegetable

Spinach Artichoke Casserole

A growing body of research continues to support the importance of eating more fruits and vegetables to reduce the risk of heart disease, hypertension, certain types of cancer, diabetes and other diseases. People trying to lose weight also benefit from eating more fruits and vegetables because these foods are naturally low in calories and high in fiber and water. One portion of this Spinach Artichoke Casserole provides three vegetable servings.

 8   55 mins total

Ingredients

Vegetable oil cooking spray

½ cup chopped onion

1 teaspoon minced garlic

2 packages (10 ounces each) frozen spinach, thawed and squeezed dry

1 can (13.75 ounces) artichoke hearts, drained and chopped

⅛ teaspoon salt

⅛ teaspoon black pepper

1 can (12 ounces) evaporated fat-free milk, divided

6 tablespoons grated Parmesan cheese, divided

4 ounces reduced-fat cream cheese

½ cup low-fat cottage cheese

Directions

Preheat oven to 350 degrees.

Coat an 8-by-8-inch glass baking dish or 1 ½-quart casserole dish with the vegetable oil cooking spray and set aside. Spray a nonstick skillet with the cooking spray. Add the onions and garlic; cook until onions are tender.

In a bowl, combine cooked onion and garlic, spinach, artichokes, salt, black pepper, 4 ounces of evaporated skim milk and 3 tablespoons of Parmesan cheese.

In a small bowl, with an electric mixer at medium speed, beat cream cheese and cottage cheese until creamy. Reduce speed to low and gradually add remaining evaporated skim milk, mixing until well blended.

Spoon the spinach mixture into the prepared dish. Pour the cream cheese mixture evenly over spinach mixture. Sprinkle with remaining Parmesan cheese.

Bake 25 to 30 minutes or until edges bubble and top is golden.

Nutritional info (per serving)

Calories........................139
    From fat 26%
Fat ....4 g
    Saturated................2 g
    Trans ....0 g
Carbohydrates ....15 g
Protein ....12 g
Sodium ....443 mg
Cholesterol ....13 mg
Calcium ....320 mg
Fiber ....2 g
Food exchanges
    3 vegetable, 1 meat

 Test Kitchen Tip

One vegetable serving, ½ cup, is about the size of a tennis ball.

Spinach-Stuffed Baked Tomatoes

In the summer when herbs like basil and oregano and homegrown tomatoes are abundant, this is a great recipe to utilize them. Fresh herbs are a good match up for tomatoes, and this recipe is also a good one to try if you've never used fresh herbs before. The added bonus is this recipe is high in fiber with 6 grams per serving and an excellent source of calcium.

4   **50 mins total**

Ingredients

4 medium to large tomatoes (5-7 ounces each)

1 cup evaporated fat-free milk

2 tablespoons all-purpose flour

2 tablespoons real bacon bits (such as Oscar Mayer)

4 green onions, sliced

1 package (10 ounces) frozen chopped spinach, thawed and well-drained

½ cup (2 ounces) reduced-fat shredded mozzarella cheese

1 large clove garlic, peeled, crushed

1 tablespoon fresh basil or 1 teaspoon dried

1 tablespoon fresh marjoram or 1 teaspoon dried

1 tablespoon fresh oregano or 1 teaspoon dried

2 tablespoons Italian-style or regular bread crumbs

2 tablespoons finely shredded Parmesan cheese

Nutritional info (per serving)

Calories	197	Sodium	434 mg
From fat	21%	Cholesterol	12 mg
Fat	5 g	Calcium	527 mg
Saturated	2 g	Fiber	6 g
Trans	0 g		
Carbohydrates	27 g		
Protein	16 g		

Food exchanges
1 starch, 2 vegetable, 1½ meat

Directions

Preheat oven to 350 degrees. Cut a ¼-inch-thick slice from the stem end of each tomato. Cut a thin slice from the bottom of each tomato so that it stands upright. Using a spoon, carefully scoop out the core, seeds and pulp, leaving up to a ½-inch-thick shell; discard core, seeds and pulp. Place the tomatoes upside down on paper towels to drain.

In a medium saucepan, whisk together the milk and flour. Place over medium heat and cook until thickened. Stir in bacon bits, onions, spinach, mozzarella cheese, garlic, basil, marjoram, oregano and bread crumbs. Spoon spinach mixture into the tomato shells. Place stuffed tomatoes in a shallow baking dish. Cover and bake for 15 minutes. Uncover; top with shredded Parmesan cheese and bake 10 minutes more, or until heated through.

Test Kitchen Tip

When substituting dried herbs for fresh, use a 1-to-3 ratio. For example, 1 teaspoon of dried oregano would be equivalent to 1 tablespoon of fresh oregano. When buying fresh herbs, sniff them, they should have a clean, fresh fragrance. To ensure that fresh herbs stay fresh, trim about one-quarter inch from the stem, rinse with cold water and loosely wrap in paper towels. Place in the refrigerator in a sealed airtight plastic bag, up to five days. Just before using, wash herbs and blot dry with paper towel.

Steamed Asparagus with Gorgonzola and Bacon

Gorgonzola, a blue-veined cheese, has a strong, sometimes tangy bite. Its texture is crumbly and a little goes a long way. You may see some variations in color, texture and flavor which results from differences in the way the cheese is aged. Because Gorgonzola is a high-fat cheese — 8 grams of fat in a golf ball-sized serving, use it sparingly. This recipe calls for just two tablespoons of Gorgonzola but the flavor it adds is enormous.

4   **20 mins total**

Ingredients

- 1 pound fresh asparagus
- 2 tablespoons low-fat buttermilk
- 2 tablespoons reduced-fat sour cream
- 1/8 teaspoon garlic powder
- 1/8 teaspoon onion powder
- 1/8 teaspoon salt
- 1/8 teaspoon black pepper
- 1/2 teaspoon cider vinegar
- 1 teaspoon snipped fresh dill
- 1 tablespoon real bacon bits (such as Oscar Mayer)
- 2 tablespoons crumbled Gorgonzola cheese

Directions

Clean asparagus and remove woody bases. Leave spears whole or bias-slice into one-inch pieces. Place asparagus in a steamer basket, cover and steam 3 to 5 minutes.

In a small bowl or measuring cup, combine the buttermilk, sour cream, garlic powder, onion powder, salt, black pepper, vinegar and dill. Refrigerate mixture until ready to serve.

Place bacon bits in a small saucepan on the stove top and cook over medium heat until crisp. Spoon buttermilk sauce over steamed asparagus and top with crumbled Gorgonzola and crisp bacon pieces.

Test Kitchen Tip

Asparagus is versatile. Add very thinly sliced raw asparagus to salads or add to quiches and omelets. When cooking asparagus to serve on its own as a side dish, it's best to cook it al dente. If overcooked it tends to become stringy and mushy.

Nutritional info (per serving)

Calories	62
From fat	44%
Fat	3 g
Saturated	2 g
Trans	0 g
Carbohydrates	3 g
Protein	5 g
Sodium	201 mg
Cholesterol	9 mg
Calcium	57 mg
Fiber	1 g

Food exchanges
1 vegetable, 1/2 fat

Sweet Potato and Apple Bake

Apples and sweet potatoes are good pairs. In this recipe, the two also get a tart boost from dried cranberries and orange juice. This is ideal to serve as a holiday side dish.

 8   1 hour 5 mins total

Ingredients

4 cups water

3 ½ cups (½-inch) peeled, cubed sweet potatoes

3 ½ cups peeled, diced Granny Smith apples

¼ cup dried cranberries

⅓ cup orange juice

5 tablespoons packed brown sugar, divided

2 tablespoons trans fat-free margarine, divided

Vegetable oil cooking spray

3 tablespoons chopped walnuts, toasted if desired

1 tablespoon all-purpose flour

Nutritional info (per serving)

Calories..........................149	Sodium ....54 mg
From fat.................18%	Cholesterol ....0 mg
Fat................................3 g	Calcium ....29 mg
Saturated...............0 g	Fiber ....3 g
Trans ....0 g	Food exchanges
Carbohydrates ....29 g	1 starch, 1 fruit, ½ fat
Protein ....2 g	

Directions

Preheat oven to 375 degrees. Place the water in a large saucepan, add sweet potatoes and bring to a boil. Cover, reduce heat and simmer 4 minutes or until potatoes are tender. Drain well.

In a large bowl, combine cooked sweet potatoes, apples and dried cranberries.

In a small bowl, add the orange juice, 2 tablespoons brown sugar and 1 tablespoon margarine, melted; stir to combine.

Pour the orange juice mixture over the sweet potato mixture and gently stir. Spoon the sweet potato mixture into a 2-quart oven-safe casserole dish coated with vegetable oil cooking spray.

In a small bowl, combine 3 tablespoons brown sugar, 1 tablespoon margarine, walnuts and flour. Using a pastry blender or two knives combine mixture until crumbly. Spoon crumble mixture evenly over the sweet potato mixture. Bake uncovered for 25 to 35 minutes. Remove from oven and serve.

Test Kitchen Tip

Toasting nuts intensifies their flavor so you don't need to use as much. To toast the nuts, coarsely chop them or leave them whole. Spread them out on a sided baking sheet and place in a preheated 350 degree oven for 6 to 8 minutes. Watch carefully because they burn easily. Remove from oven and cool before handling or adding them to recipes.

Zucchini and Fresh Corn

Zucchini is the ubiquitous summer vegetable. You can toss it into salads, pasta dishes, casseroles and even desserts. Because this summer squash is more than 95% water, it has just 19 calories per cup. But it also provides a good source of vitamin C, fiber, potassium and magnesium — all nutrients that appear beneficial in lowering the risk of high blood pressure.

 6 **25 mins total**

Ingredients

1 tablespoon olive oil

½ cup diced red onion

4 cloves garlic, peeled, minced

½ cup fat-free, less-sodium vegetable broth

1 cup fresh corn kernels cut from cob (about 2 ears)

3 cups thinly sliced zucchini

1 tablespoon trans fat-free margarine

¼ teaspoon salt

⅛ teaspoon freshly ground black pepper

Vegetable oil cooking spray

3 tablespoons grated Parmesan cheese

Directions

In a large nonstick skillet, heat olive oil over medium heat. Add red onion and garlic and sauté until slightly tender, about 3 minutes. Add the vegetable broth and corn kernels and continue to cook until the corn is heated through, about 5 minutes. Add the zucchini, cover and continue cooking an additional 5 minutes, stirring occasionally, until vegetables are tender. Mix in the margarine, salt and black pepper. Spoon the vegetable mixture into a shallow baking dish coated with vegetable oil cooking spray and sprinkle the top with Parmesan cheese. Place in the oven and broil until the cheese topping is golden brown, about 2 to 5 minutes.

Nutritional info (per serving)

Calories.........................81
   From fat 44%

Fat ....4 g
   Saturated.................1 g
   Trans ....0 g

Carbohydrates ....8 g

Protein ....3 g

Sodium ....175 mg

Cholesterol ....2 mg

Calcium ....45 mg

Fiber ....1 g

Food exchanges
   2 vegetable, 1 fat

Test Kitchen Tip

Select zucchini no more than 6 or 7 inches long and 1 to 2 inches in diameter. Large zucchini can be slightly bitter and will have very large seeds, tough rinds and stringy, coarse flesh. The skin should be shiny and free of cuts, bruises and decay. Zucchini freezes beautifully. You can shred it in portion sizes you will use and freeze in freezer-quality plastic sealable bags.

Meats

Keeping It Lean

If you think a Heart Smart® eating plan involves eliminating meat from your diet, think again. Through advances in breeding, feeding and trimming practices, beef, pork, lamb and veal are leaner than ever. Meat provides an excellent source of iron, zinc, and vitamin B12 — nutrients that can be hard to obtain elsewhere.

By following the three simple steps below, you can feel confident about including meat in your healthy eating plan.

Select Lean. Certain cuts of meat are leaner than others. When selecting lean cuts of beef, look for the words round or loin in the name. Eye of round, top round steak, top sirloin, and tenderloin are examples of lean cuts of beef. With respect to ground beef, select those labeled at least 90% lean. Ground sirloin typically is 90% lean, ground round about 86% lean, and ground chuck about 81% lean. For pork or lamb, look for the words loin or leg. Tenderloin, boneless loin roast, center cut loin chop, loin rib chop are leaner cuts of pork. Leg of lamb and lamb loin chop are leaner cuts of lamb. When purchasing veal, look for rib or loin chop, cutlet or rib roast.

Cook Lean. Trim any visible fat from meat before cooking. Trimming before cooking prevents the fat along the edge of the cut from migrating into the meat during cooking. Broiling, grilling, roasting on a rack (allowing more fat to drip away from the meat) are preferred and sautéing or stir-frying with a small amount of oil are great runner-up cooking methods.

Portion Lean. Even with lean cuts of meat, portion size still matters. It is recommended that most adults consume no more than six ounces of lean meat, poultry or fish each day. That translates to having two, three-ounce servings. Use a deck of cards or the size of a woman's palm to visualize a three-ounce portion. For a three-ounce cooked serving, start with about four ounces of boneless raw meat.

Apricot Glazed Pork Tenderloins

Apricot jam is what gives this pork its sweetness. Chili sauce and Dijon mustard give it tangy tones. This dish is easy to put together for a weeknight dinner.

 6 — 30 mins total

Ingredients

2 pork tenderloins (about 12 ounces each), fat trimmed

1 tablespoon olive oil

½ teaspoon salt

¼ teaspoon black pepper

½ cup apricot jam

2 tablespoons Dijon mustard

1 tablespoon chili sauce

1 tablespoon apple cider vinegar

1 tablespoon brown sugar

Directions

Heat broiler; set rack 4 inches from the heat. Line a rimmed baking sheet with foil. Rub the pork with oil and season with salt and black pepper. Broil 10 minutes, turning once after 5 minutes.

Meanwhile, in a small saucepan, whisk together jam, mustard, chili sauce, cider vinegar and brown sugar. Cook over medium heat until jam melts, 3 to 4 minutes; remove from heat. Transfer half of the sauce to a small bowl for brushing. Cover pan to keep remaining sauce warm. Remove pork from broiler and brush with reserved sauce. Continue broiling until pork is browned in spots and registers 145 degrees in the center using an instant-read thermometer, about 8 to 10 minutes more.

Cover pork loosely with foil; let rest 3 to 5 minutes before slicing. The temperature will continue to rise. Serve drizzled with warm sauce from saucepan. Discard sauce from bowl.

Test Kitchen Tip

In 2011, the U.S. Department of Agriculture lowered its safe cooking temperature recommendation for pork products, such as pork loin chops and pork tenderloin, to 145 degrees from 160 degrees — the temperature found in many cookbooks. The USDA says 145 degrees plus a 3-minute resting time is enough to kill any bacteria. Use an instant read thermometer to check the center internal temperature of the pork.

Nutritional info (per serving)

Calories...................... 260	Sodium .... 369 mg
From fat................. 28%	Cholesterol .... 80 mg
Fat .... 8 g	Calcium .... 18 mg
Saturated .... 2 g	Fiber .... 0 g
Trans .... 0 g	Food exchanges
Carbohydrates .... 20 g	3 lean meat, 1 fruit,
Protein .... 26 g	1 vegetable

Beef and Chipotle Burritos

This recipe has 15 minutes prep time and the rest of the work is done using a slow cooker. The beef round steak benefits from the slow-cookers low and slow cooking method so it becomes tender. Chipotle chili peppers are dried, smoked jalapeño peppers that have a hot and smoky flavor. At most grocery stores, they are sold canned in adobo sauce — a spicy sauce made from ground chilies, herbs and vinegar. Look for them in the ethnic aisle at some grocery stores or at Hispanic specialty markets.

 6   **4 hours 45 mins total**

Ingredients

1 pound boneless beef round steak, cut ¾-inch thick

1 can (14.5 ounces) diced tomatoes, undrained

½ cup chopped onion

1 to 2 canned chipotle peppers in adobo sauce, chopped

1 tablespoon brown sugar

1 teaspoon oregano

½ teaspoon ground cumin

¼ teaspoon freshly ground black pepper

½ teaspoon salt

1 clove garlic, peeled, minced

6 (6 inch) low-fat flour tortillas, warmed

¾ cup (3 ounces) reduced-fat shredded sharp cheddar cheese

1 ½ cups romaine lettuce, shredded

Directions

Cut the meat into 4 pieces.

In a 3 ½- or 4-quart slow-cooker, place meat, undrained tomatoes, onion, chipotle peppers, brown sugar, oregano, cumin, black pepper, salt and garlic. Cover and cook on the high heat setting for 3 ½ hours.

Using 2 forks pull meat into shreds. Gently stir to combine meat and the sauce. Cover and continue cooking an additional 30 minutes.

Divide meat mixture among the warm tortillas. Top each with 2 tablespoons cheese and ¼ cup lettuce and roll up each tortilla.

Nutritional info (per serving)

Calories...................... 295
 From fat................ 31%
Fat .... 10 g
 Saturated .... 4 g
 Trans .... 0 g
Carbohydrates ....24 g
Protein .... 25 g
Sodium .... 629 mg
Cholesterol .... 42 mg
Calcium .... 182 mg
Fiber .... 3 g
Food exchanges
 1 starch, 2 medium-fat meat,
 2 vegetable

 Test Kitchen Tip
Canned chipotle chili peppers have about 5 or 6 peppers in adobo sauce. You can freeze any leftover peppers with sauce individually in ice cube trays. Once they are frozen, pop out the cubes and store them in a freezer bag. This way you can take out just what you need. To warm the tortillas, wrap a stack of them in foil. Heat them in a 350-degree oven for 10 minutes to soften or place several on a microwave-safe plate, cover with a paper towel and microwave-safe plastic wrap and microwave 1 minute, or more if needed, to warm them.

Teriyaki Beef Stir-Fry

The American Heart Association notes that the beneficial impact of soy protein on bad LDL cholesterol and other heart disease risk factors may have been overstated. But the AHA stills promotes the use of such soy products as tofu, soy nuts, soy milk and edamame, an ingredient in this stir-fry. Edamame (eh-dah-MAH-meh) or sweet soybeans have a mild, sweet, nutty flavor and firm texture. Soy products are a healthy substitute for protein sources that are higher in artery-clogging saturated fat and cholesterol, and they provide an impressive array of vitamins, minerals, phytochemicals and fiber.

 6   **35 mins total**

Ingredients

1 ¼ cups orange juice

6 tablespoons reduced-sodium teriyaki sauce

1 tablespoon ground ginger

1 teaspoon garlic powder

¼ teaspoon ground black pepper

⅛ teaspoon red pepper flakes

1 pound beef eye of round steak, cut into thin strips

3 tablespoons brown sugar

1 tablespoon cornstarch

2 tablespoons canola oil, divided

2 cups broccoli florets

1 cup julienned carrots

1 cup red, orange or yellow bell pepper strips

1 cup chopped onion

½ cup edamame

4 cups hot cooked brown rice

Nutritional info (per serving)

Calories	410	
From fat	22%	
Fat	10 g	
Saturated	2 g	
Trans	0 g	
Carbohydrates	55 g	
Protein	25 g	

Sodium	393 mg
Cholesterol	39 mg
Calcium	108 mg
Fiber	6 g

Food exchanges
2 ½ starch, 3 vegetable, 2 lean meat, 1 fat

Directions

In a small bowl or measuring cup, combine orange juice, teriyaki sauce, ginger, garlic powder, black pepper and red pepper flakes. Place the beef in a large resealable bag or glass dish. Pour ½ cup of the orange juice marinade over the beef and turn to coat well. Marinate in the refrigerator for at least 15 minutes or longer for extra flavor.

Add brown sugar and cornstarch to the remaining marinade, stirring until smooth; set aside. Heat 1 tablespoon of oil in a wok or large skillet on high heat. Remove the beef from the marinade and discard the marinade. Add beef to the wok and stir-fry 3 to 5 minutes or until beef is no longer pink. Remove beef from the skillet. Add the remaining 1 tablespoon of oil to the wok and add broccoli, carrots, bell peppers, onion and edamame; stir-fry 4 to 6 minutes or until vegetables are tender-crisp. Pour the reserved marinade over vegetable mixture. Reduce heat to medium and, stirring constantly, bring the sauce to a boil for 1 minute. Return beef to the wok and cook until heated through.

Prepare rice according to package directions, omitting the salt. Serve the stir-fry over the rice. One serving consists of approximately ¾ cup stir-fry over ⅔ cup rice.

 Test Kitchen Tip

Place the meat in the freezer for 20 minutes to make slicing easier. Add shelled edamame to casseroles, soups, stews, salads or stir-fry meals, or enjoy them straight out of the pod as a snack food. Edamame is available year-round in the frozen vegetable section as shelled beans or whole pods. The pods that house them look like large, fuzzy sugar snap peas, remove the beans from the pod before eating or adding to a recipe.

Cherry-Balsamic Glazed Pork Chops

Many cuts of pork are 30% leaner than they were 20 years ago thanks to changes in the breeding and feeding of hogs. Well-trimmed pork tenderloin is similar to skinless chicken breast in fat content. The American Heart Association and the Heart Smart® program recommend lean meat as an important source of complete protein and essential vitamins and minerals.

Choose lean cuts such as tenderloin and center loin, and trim all visible fat before cooking and eat healthy portions. One portion of these Heart Smart® Cherry-Balsamic Glazed Pork Chops is the size of a deck of cards or 3 ounces.

 4   35 mins total

Ingredients

Vegetable oil cooking spray

1 teaspoon canola oil

½ cup chopped red onion

½ teaspoon dried thyme

½ teaspoon salt, divided

4 (4 ounces) boneless pork loin chop, trimmed

⅓ cup cherry preserves

2 tablespoons balsamic vinegar

¼ teaspoon black pepper

¼ cup sliced almonds

Directions

Coat a large nonstick skillet with vegetable oil cooking spray. Add the canola oil and heat over medium-high heat until hot. Add red onion and sauté 5 minutes. Combine thyme and ¼ teaspoon salt and sprinkle both sides of pork chops. Add pork chops to the skillet; sauté 4 to 6 minutes on each side depending on the thickness or until cooked through. Remove pork chops from skillet; keep warm.

Reduce heat to medium-low. Add ¼ teaspoon salt, preserves, balsamic vinegar and black pepper to skillet. Stir constantly until preserves melt. Spoon cherry sauce over pork chops, sprinkle with almonds and serve.

Nutritional info (per serving)

Calories	310
From fat	32%
Fat	11 g
Saturated	3 g
Trans	0 g
Carbohydrates	24 g
Protein	27 g
Sodium	308 mg
Cholesterol	67 mg
Calcium	56 mg
Fiber	2 g

Food exchanges
1 ½ starch, 3 meat, ½ fat

Curried Pork with Apples and Raisins

In 2011, the United States Department of Agriculture lowered its safe cooking recommendation for pork products, such as pork loin chops to 145 degrees from 160 degrees — the temperature found in many cookbooks. The USDA says that temperature is enough to kill any bacteria. Once the pork reaches that temperature it needs to rest at least 3 minutes according to the USDA. The temperature will continue to rise another few degrees. The safe cooking temperature for ground pork remained unchanged at 165 degrees.

  4 30 mins total

Ingredients

3 cups hot cooked brown rice

4 (4 ounce) lean boneless pork chops, trimmed

¼ teaspoon salt

¼ teaspoon coarse ground black pepper

1 tablespoon canola oil

1 medium onion, peeled, chopped

1 tablespoon curry powder

1 Granny Smith apple, cored and chopped

¼ cup golden raisins

1 cup less-sodium, fat-free chicken broth

3 tablespoons chili sauce

3 tablespoons apricot preserves

2 tablespoons peanuts, chopped

Directions

Prepare rice according to package directions, omitting salt. Trim any excess fat from pork. Combine salt and black pepper in a small cup and rub the surface of pork with the mixture.

In a large nonstick skillet, heat oil over medium heat. Add pork chops and cook 3 to 4 minutes on each side. Transfer chops to a plate and keep them warm.

Drain fat from the skillet and add onions. Cook for 5 minutes or until soft. Stir in curry powder and cook 1 minute.

Return pork to the skillet; add apple, raisins, chicken broth, chili sauce and apricot preserves. Stir to combine and bring to a boil. Cover, reduce heat to medium-low and cook about 10 minutes or until done. The pork should reach an internal temperature of at least 145 degrees.

Remove from heat and serve over rice; sprinkle with chopped peanuts.

Nutritional info (per serving)

Calories	503	Sodium	477 mg
From fat	25%	Cholesterol	80 mg
Fat	14 g	Calcium	50 mg
Saturated	3 g	Fiber	5 g
Trans	0 g		
Carbohydrates	62 g		
Protein	32 g		

Food exchanges
3 starch, 3 lean meat, 1 fruit, 1 fat

Filet Mignon with Blue Cheese and Mushrooms

Blue cheese is used in this recipe even though it's high in fat (10 grams in a golf ball-size serving). The trick to making it an appropriate ingredient in a Heart Smart® recipe is using a small amount. Blue cheese has a sharp, tangy flavor, so a little goes a long way. This recipe uses ¼ cup of blue cheese for four servings or 1 tablespoon per serving.

 4   **40 mins total**

Ingredients

2 tablespoons trans fat-free margarine, divided

4 beef tenderloin steaks, about 4 ounces each

¼ cup crumbled blue cheese

1 clove garlic, peeled, minced

½ cup sliced mushrooms

½ teaspoon dried thyme

¾ cup fat-free, less-sodium beef broth

½ cup port wine

1 tablespoon Worcestershire sauce

⅛ teaspoon ground black pepper

⅛ teaspoon salt

Directions

Preheat oven to 350 degrees. Trim any fat from steaks. In a cast-iron or other oven-safe skillet, heat 1 tablespoon of margarine over high heat. Add steaks and sear quickly on both sides. Place the skillet in the oven and roast steaks for 8 to 10 minutes or to desired degree of doneness.

Remove skillet from the oven and top each steak with 1 tablespoon crumbled blue cheese. Preheat the oven's broiler and return the steaks to the oven until the cheese is bubbly and golden brown, about 3 minutes. Remove skillet from the oven and place the steaks on a plate, covering to keep them warm. Place skillet on the stovetop and over medium heat; sauté garlic, mushrooms and thyme in the skillet drippings, stirring constantly until mushrooms soften, about 3 to 5 minutes. Stir in beef broth, scraping to loosen bits from the bottom of the pan. Stir in port wine and Worcestershire sauce and cook until the sauce has reduced to about ¾ cup. Whisk in 1 tablespoon of margarine, black pepper and salt and continue to cook 2 to 3 minutes. Drizzle filets with the mushroom wine sauce and serve.

Nutritional info (per serving)

Calories........................277
    From fat.................39%
Fat...............................12 g
    Saturated................4 g
    Trans........................0 g
Carbohydrates.............6 g
Protein........................27 g
Sodium.................401 mg
Cholesterol.............73 mg
Calcium...................57 mg
Fiber.............................0 g
Food exchanges
    3 meat, 1 fat

 Test Kitchen Tip

When purchasing blue cheese, you will likely have a few choices. The French call it Roquefort; the Italians, Gorgonzola; the English, Stilton, and the Americans, Maytag. Any variety works well with this recipe.

Heart Smart® Picadillo

A popular item in many Latin countries, picadillo (pronounced pee-kah-DEE-yoh) is a ground meat dish with a sweet, sour and spicy taste. It's typically made with ground beef, pork or veal, tomatoes, onions, garlic and other regional ingredients such as raisins and pimento-stuffed green olives. This picadillo is Heart Smart® because leaner ground beef, such as ground sirloin, is used and more vegetables are added. Using no-added-salt tomatoes and fewer olives helped keep a lid on the sodium.

 5   45 mins total

Ingredients

¾ pound ground beef sirloin

1 cup diced onion

1 cup diced red bell pepper

¼ cup pimento-stuffed green olives, finely diced

½ cup dark raisins, chopped

1 teaspoon chili powder

1 teaspoon ground cumin

½ teaspoon ground cinnamon

¼ teaspoon salt

1 can (14.5 ounces) no-salt added diced tomatoes, undrained

2 ½ cups cooked brown rice

Directions

In a large stock pot over medium heat, cook ground beef until it crumbles and is no longer pink. Drain well and return to the pot. Stir in onion, red bell pepper and olives; continue cooking 5 to 8 minutes, stirring often. Add raisins, chili powder, cumin, cinnamon and salt; continue cooking 5 to 8 minutes, stirring often. Add undrained diced tomatoes and continue cooking 10 to 15 minutes, stirring often. Prepare brown rice according to package directions, omitting the salt. Serve about ¾ cup picadillo with ½ cup cooked brown rice.

Nutritional info (per serving)

Calories........................312
    From fat 23%

Fat ....8 g
    Saturated................3 g
    Trans ....0 g

Carbohydrates ....43 g

Protein .... 18 g

Sodium ....273 mg

Cholesterol .... 43 mg

Calcium ....51 mg

Fiber ....4 g

Food exchanges
    2 starch, 2 vegetable, 1 lean meat, 1 fat

 Test Kitchen Tip

Serve this picadillo stuffed into soft tacos and serve with beans and rice over pasta, on a baked potato or even as a Sloppy Joe.

Herb-Crusted Pork Roast with Sherry Glazed Onions

This pork loin roast gets a huge flavor boost from being cooked on a bed of onions. Once the pork roast is done, a sauce is made from the pan juices and onions. Roasting the onions brings out their natural sweetness which caramelizes during roasting. The caramelized onions along with the pan juices are turned into a terrific pan sauce.

 8   2 hours total

Ingredients

1 tablespoon sugar

1 teaspoon dried thyme

1 teaspoon ground sage

½ teaspoon salt

½ teaspoon garlic powder

¼ teaspoon celery seed

⅛ teaspoon ground mustard

⅛ teaspoon ground black pepper

1 tablespoon olive oil

1 boneless pork loin roast, about 2 pounds

8 cups (about 1 to 2 large onions) sliced onion

2 tablespoons sherry

1 tablespoon water

2 teaspoons cornstarch

Nutritional info (per serving)

Calories	197
From fat	24%
Fat	8 g
Saturated	2 g
Trans	0 g
Carbohydrates	5 g
Protein	25 g
Sodium	179 mg
Cholesterol	67 mg
Calcium	29 mg
Fiber	0 g
Food exchanges	1 vegetable, 3 lean meat

Directions

In a small bowl combine sugar, thyme, sage, salt, garlic powder, celery seed, ground mustard and black pepper. Rub olive oil over the entire pork roast followed by spice mixture. Cover and refrigerate at least 4 hours or overnight.

When the roast is ready to be cooked, slice onion into ¼-inch-thick slices and separate into rings and place in the bottom of a shallow roasting pan. Place the pork loin directly on top of the onion slices.

Bake uncovered at 325 degrees for 1 hour or until a meat thermometer reads 145 degrees. Remove the roast from the pan and let it rest 10 to 15 minutes before slicing.

To make glazed onions, cut onion rings into quarters. Place onions and pan juices into a nonstick skillet. In a small bowl or measuring cup, combine sherry, water and corn-starch; stir until cornstarch is dissolved. Over medium heat, add sherry sauce to onion and stir until the mixture has thickened slightly, about 3 to 5 minutes. Slice roast into 16 pieces and top with the sherry-glazed onion.

Test Kitchen Tip

It's important to let meats, such as this roast, rest after cooking and before slicing. While the meat rests, the juices flow back into the meat so it stays moist. The internal temperature also continues to rise as the meat rests.

Kung Pao Pork

Kung Pao is a classic dish in Szechuan cuisine. The Westernized version of Kung Pao dishes commonly consist of diced marinated meat such as chicken, beef, pork, shrimp or scallops, stir-fried with unsalted peanuts and vegetables, fused together in a savory sauce. This version uses bok choy, also called Chinese white cabbage, pak choy, pak choi or white mustard cabbage. Bok choy is a loose, bulbous cluster of white to light-green stems surrounded by dark green leaves. It provides a good dose of beta-carotene, iron and vitamin C.

 6   40 mins total

Ingredients

1 tablespoon sugar

3 tablespoons water

4 tablespoons reduced-sodium soy sauce, divided

2 tablespoons dry sherry

1 tablespoon white vinegar

1 tablespoon plus 1 teaspoon cornstarch, divided

1/4 teaspoon salt

16 ounces pork tenderloin

1 tablespoon peanut oil

1/8 teaspoon red pepper flakes

3 cups sliced bok choy

2 cups onion, cut into 1/2-inch pieces

1/2 cup unsalted peanuts

3 sliced green onions

4 1/2 cups cooked brown rice, prepared omitting salt and oil

Directions

Combine sugar, water, 3 tablespoons soy sauce, sherry, vinegar, 1 teaspoon cornstarch and salt in a small bowl; stir until well blended. Set aside. Trim any excess fat and silver skin from the pork tenderloin and cut into 1-inch cubes. (Place pork tenderloin in the freezer for 15 minutes so it's easier to slice into cubes.)

Combine pork, 1 tablespoon cornstarch and 1 tablespoon soy sauce in a bowl; stir well. Cover and marinate in the refrigerator 15 minutes. In a large wok, heat oil over medium-high heat.

Add red pepper flakes and stir-fry 1 minute. Add pork mixture to the wok and stir-fry 3 to 5 minutes. Add bok choy and onions and continue to stir-fry 4 to 6 minutes. Add sherry mixture and peanuts and stir-fry until sauce bubbles and thickens, about 3 to 5 minutes. Top with green onions and serve over cooked rice. Each serving consists of about 3/4 cup Kung Pao Pork over 3/4 cup of brown rice.

Nutritional info (per serving)

Calories......................415
   From fat.................28%
Fat...............................13 g
   Saturated...............3 g
   Trans.......................0 g
Carbohydrates...........49 g
Protein........................25 g

Sodium.................463 mg
Cholesterol............45 mg
Calcium...................76 mg
Fiber.............................5 g
Food exchanges
   3 lean meat, 2 1/2 starch
   2 vegetable

Test Kitchen Tip

Choose bok choy bunches that have firm white stems and crisp, dark green leaves. Use bok choy raw in salads, in a stir-fry or as a cooked vegetable. Refrigerate bok choy in an air-tight container for three to four days.

Marinated Pork Medallions with Mustard Sauce

These pan sautéed pork medallions are paired with a tangy mustard sauce. Once the pork is marinated the dish comes together quickly. To cut back on sodium, reduced-sodium soy sauce is used which has 525 milligrams of sodium per tablespoon. One tablespoon of regular soy sauce has more than 1,200 milligrams of sodium.

 8   25 mins total

Ingredients

2 pork tenderloins (16 ounces each), fat trimmed and silver removed

⅓ cup reduced-sodium soy sauce

⅓ cup bourbon

MUSTARD SAUCE

⅓ cup maple syrup

¼ cup fat-free half-and-half

⅓ cup water

2 tablespoons packed brown sugar

1 tablespoon canola oil

1 tablespoon trans fat-free margarine

2 tablespoons Dijon mustard

¼ teaspoon salt

Directions

Slice each tenderloin into 12 medallions. In a small bowl, combine soy sauce, bourbon, water and brown sugar, stirring until sugar is dissolved. Place marinade and pork medallions in a large resealable plastic bag. Marinate at least 8 hours or overnight in the refrigerator.

To prepare medallions, heat the oil and margarine in a large skillet over medium high heat. Add pork to the skillet, discarding the marinade, and cook on each side for 5 to 8 minutes or until an internal temperature of 145 degrees is reached. Remove pork from skillet and keep warm.

To prepare the mustard sauce, in a small sauce pan whisk together maple syrup, half and half, Dijon mustard and salt. Heat over medium-low heat. Do not allow sauce to boil. The sauce can be served as is or can be placed in the skillet used to cook the pork. Over low heat, stir sauce in the skillet until pan renderings are incorporated. Serve pork medallions drizzled with warm sauce.

Test Kitchen Tip

The thin silver membrane on the tenderloin is usually on one side of the tenderloin. It is very tough and should be removed before cooking. Slide a sharp knife under the silver and cut it away.

Nutritional info (per serving)

Calories	233
From fat	27%
Fat	7 g
Saturated	2 g
Trans	0 g
Carbohydrates	11 g
Protein	28 g
Sodium	311 mg
Cholesterol	80 mg
Calcium	21 mg
Fiber	0 g
Food exchanges	1 starch, 3 lean meat

Meatloaf Mediterranean Style

Feta cheese, sun-dried tomatoes and black olives give this meatloaf a Mediterranean flavor. A blend of ground turkey breast and ground sirloin is used. Ground turkey can be a leaner substitute for ground beef, provided it's made from mostly breast meat, the leanest cut. When buying ground turkey, look for packages labeled "ground turkey breast." A 3-ounce serving of ground turkey breast contains just 2 grams of total fat. Ground turkey meat, which contains light and dark meat but no skin, is also an acceptable option. It has about 5 grams of total fat in a 3-ounce serving.

 5   1 hour 5 mins total

Ingredients

Vegetable oil cooking spray

8 ounces ground turkey breast

8 ounces ground beef sirloin

⅓ cup panko bread crumbs

⅓ cup finely diced onion

⅓ cup fresh spinach, finely chopped

⅓ cup feta cheese, crumbled

¼ cup sun-dried tomatoes, finely diced

¼ cup black olives, finely diced

2 egg whites

1 clove garlic, peeled, minced

1 tablespoon Worcestershire sauce

½ teaspoon ground black pepper

¼ teaspoon ground cinnamon

Directions

Preheat oven to 375 degrees. Coat a 9-by-5-inch loaf pan with vegetable oil cooking spray.

In a large bowl, combine all the remaining ingredients. Form mixture into a loaf and place in the prepared loaf pan. Bake uncovered until the internal temperature registers 165 degrees, about 35 to 45 minutes. Let stand 10 minutes before serving.

Nutritional info (per serving)

Calories.........................184
   From fat 34%

Fat ....7 g
   Saturated.................3 g
   Trans ....0 g

Carbohydrates ....7 g

Protein ....23 g

Sodium ....333 mg

Cholesterol ....61 mg

Calcium ....47 mg

Fiber ....1 g

Food exchanges
   1 vegetable, 3 lean meat

 Test Kitchen Tip

Panko bread crumbs have been gaining in popularity over the last several years. These bread crumbs have a larger crumb and make a good binder in this recipe. Look for panko bread crumbs in the ethnic aisle of most grocery stores.

One Pot Beef Stew

Mushrooms, sherry and beef broth gives this stew a hearty flavor. Flat iron steak is used and has become a more popular cut of meat. It's a cut from the top blade or chuck roast. You might see it labeled as "top blade steak." Flat iron is very tender, and some say it's second in tenderness to beef tenderloin.

 6   2 hours 30 mins total

Ingredients

- 1 pound flat iron steak or lean beef stew meat, cut into ½-inch cubes
- 3 tablespoons all-purpose flour
- 1 tablespoon canola oil
- ¼ cup sherry
- 1 cup fat-free, less-sodium beef broth
- 2 cups onion, cut into ½-inch chunks
- 2 cloves garlic, peeled, minced
- 5 carrots, peeled, sliced
- 4 celery ribs, sliced

- 1 package (8 ounces) mushrooms, cleaned, quartered
- 1 can (14.5 ounces) no-salt-added diced tomatoes, undrained
- 2 tablespoons Worcestershire sauce
- ½ teaspoon dried thyme
- 1 teaspoon paprika
- 2 bay leaves
- ½ teaspoon ground black pepper
- 1 tablespoon cornstarch
- 2 tablespoons cold water
- ½ teaspoon salt

Nutritional info (per serving)

Calories.........................237	Sodium ....412 mg
From fat.................29%	Cholesterol ....37 mg
Fat ....7 g	Calcium ....61 mg
Saturated ....2 g	Fiber ....4 g
Trans ....0 g	Food exchanges
Carbohydrates ....22 g	1 starch, 2 vegetable,
Protein ....19 g	2 lean meat

Directions

Preheat oven to 375 degrees.

Pat the meat cubes dry with paper towel. Coat beef with flour, shaking off excess. In a large Dutch oven or other stovetop and oven-safe pot, heat the oil over medium-high heat. Add the beef and sauté until browned on all sides, about 5 minutes. Remove beef from pot.

Add the sherry and broth to the pot, loosening the bits from the bottom of the pan. Add the onion, garlic, carrots, celery, mushrooms, tomatoes, Worcestershire sauce, thyme, paprika, bay leaves and black pepper. Add browned beef.

Stir to combine, cover and place in the oven for about 2 hours or until meat and vegetables are tender. Remove from the oven and place on stovetop.

In a small bowl or measuring cup, combine the cornstarch and water until dissolved. If you want to thicken the stew, mix the cornstarch mixture into the stew and allow to thicken, stirring constantly, over medium heat. Stir in the salt and remove bay leaves. Each serving yields about 1 cup. Serve the stew on its own or with a crusty multigrain baguette, yolk-free egg noodles or brown rice.

Test Kitchen Tip

Place the flat iron steak in the freezer for 20 minutes to make it easier to cut into even cubes. Patting the meat dry with paper towel before browning helps develop a nice sear on the beef cubes, sealing in the juices.

Pork Medallions in Brandy Cream Sauce

The creamy pan sauce in this recipe gets a hearty flavor from mushrooms. It makes these easy pork medallions excellent for a weeknight dinner. Brandy provides a bit of sweet flavor, and the Dijon mustard a tangy tone to the sauce.

 4   45 min total

Ingredients

1 pound pork tenderloin

¼ cup all-purpose flour

½ teaspoon salt, divided

¼ teaspoon plus ⅛ teaspoon freshly ground black pepper, divided

1 tablespoon canola oil

1 tablespoon trans fat-free margarine

½ cup chopped onion

1 clove garlic, peeled, minced

3 cups cleaned and thinly sliced fresh mushrooms (about 8 ounces)

½ cup brandy

1 cup fat-free half-and-half

2 teaspoons cornstarch

1 teaspoon Dijon mustard

2 cups cooked angel hair pasta

1 tablespoon chopped fresh parsley

Nutritional info (per serving)

Calories.......................481
    From fat................19%
Fat...............................10 g
    Saturated...............2 g
    Trans.......................0 g
Carbohydrates...........39 g
Protein........................37 g

Sodium..................411 mg
Cholesterol............80 mg
Calcium...................73 mg
Fiber............................2 g
Food exchanges
    2 starch, 3 lean meat,
    2 vegetable, 1 ½ fat

Test Kitchen Tip

Try using cremini mushrooms in this recipe to give the sauce a hearty flavor. Cremini mushrooms are a dark brown variety of the typical white, cultivated mushrooms. To clean mushrooms, wipe them with a damp paper towel. Do not soak mushrooms in water to clean them.

Directions

Slice the tenderloin into 16 medallions.

In a shallow dish, combine the flour, ¼ teaspoon salt and ¼ teaspoon black pepper. Dredge each medallion in the flour mixture. Place canola oil in a large nonstick skillet. Over medium heat, cook medallions 4 to 5 minutes on each side, allowing a brown coat to develop. Transfer pork to a separate dish and cover to keep warm.

Add the margarine to the skillet and sauté the onion and garlic until softened, about 3 minutes.

Add the mushrooms to the skillet and sauté one additional minute. Add the brandy to the skillet and continue to sauté the vegetables an additional 3 to 4 minutes.

In a measuring cup, whisk together the half-and-half and cornstarch until dissolved; add the Dijon mustard to the cream mixture and continue to whisk. Add the half-and-half mixture to the mushroom mixture; stir in the remaining ¼ teaspoon of salt and ⅛ teaspoon black pepper. Cook over medium heat until sauce is slightly thickened, about 5 minutes. Return the pork medallions to the skillet to heat through. Serve four pork medallions over ½ cup angel hair pasta serving. Pour about ⅓ cup of the brandy cream sauce over the medallions and garnish with chopped parsley.

Slow Cooker Pepper Steak

This beef dish is flavor packed and has an antioxidant boast from the tomatoes and peppers. The seasoned tender beef is a perfect entrée served over hearty brown rice. Using a slow cooker is an easy way to put together a dinner with little effort.

 6   6 hours 30 mins total (Not all active time)

Ingredients

¼ teaspoon salt

¼ teaspoon ground black pepper

¼ teaspoon ground cumin

1 pound boneless beef round steak, cut into strips

1 tablespoon canola oil

2 cloves garlic, peeled, finely minced

1 can (14.5 ounces) Italian-style stewed tomatoes

1 tablespoon Worcestershire sauce

2 teaspoons sugar

1 tablespoon cornstarch

¼ cup cold water

1 bag (16 ounces) frozen pepper stir fry vegetables

1 can (8 ounces) water chestnuts, drained and rinsed

3 cups cooked brown rice

Nutritional info (per serving)

Calories......................293
     From fat.................18%
Fat................................6 g
     Saturated.................1 g
     Trans.......................0 g
Carbohydrates...........36 g
Protein.......................22 g

Sodium.................309 mg
Cholesterol...........48 mg
Calcium.................40 mg
Fiber............................4 g
Food exchanges
     2 starch, 1 vegetable,
     2 lean meat

Directions

In a small dish, combine salt, black pepper and cumin. Rub spice mixture over both sides of round steak and cut into strips. In a large nonstick skillet, heat the oil over medium heat. Add steak strips and quickly brown on both sides, adding the garlic to the steak as it browns. Transfer steak and its juices to a slow cooker.

In a medium-size bowl, combine stewed tomatoes with the juice, Worcestershire sauce and sugar.

In a small bowl, mix cornstarch and cold water and add to tomato mixture. Pour tomato mixture over beef and add frozen vegetables and water chestnuts. Cover and cook on high for 6 to 6 ½ hours or until meat is fork tender.

Prepare rice according to package directions, omitting the salt. Serve ¾ cup pepper steak over ½ cup cooked brown rice.

 Test Kitchen Tip

When using a slow cooker, use enough liquid to cover the ingredients and fill the slow cooker at least half way to two-thirds full.

 Watch This!

Scan this QR code with your smartphone to watch the Heart Smart® video.

Taco Braid

This recipe mixes cooked ground sirloin and vegetables with reduced-sodium taco seasoning and salsa and wraps it into a nice package made of pizza dough. It makes a nice presentation and easily serves 8. For a complete meal, serve it with a tossed mixed greens salad.

 8 1 hour total

Ingredients

1 tablespoon cornmeal

1 pound pizza dough, thawed if frozen

1 pound ground beef sirloin

½ cup chopped onion

½ cup chopped green pepper

1 jalapeño pepper, finely diced

1 clove garlic, peeled, minced

3 tablespoons 30% reduced-sodium taco seasoning mix

½ cup salsa

1 egg white, beaten

½ cup (2 ounces) shredded reduced-fat sharp cheddar cheese

Directions

Lightly coat a large jelly roll baking sheet with cornmeal. Work pizza dough into a 14-by-10-inch rectangle on the baking sheet, allowing the dough to rest briefly if it becomes to elastic to work with. In a large nonstick skillet over medium heat, cook the ground beef, onion, green pepper, jalapeño pepper and garlic until beef is brown and vegetables soften, about 10 minutes. Drain to remove excess fat. Stir in the taco seasoning mix and salsa and continue to cook until the sauce thickens, about 5 minutes. Remove from heat and allow it to cool slightly before adding egg white. Place egg white in a small bowl or measuring cup, reserving 1 tablespoon. Stir remaining egg white into beef mixture and set aside.

Preheat oven to 350 degrees. To prepare the dough, on each long side, cut 1-inch wide strips about 2 inches into the center. Spread filling lengthwise down the center of the rectangle.

Sprinkle with cheese. Starting at one end, fold alternating strips at an angle across the filling and pinch the ends to seal. Brush the dough with the reserved egg white. Bake for 25 to 30 minutes or until golden brown. Remove from oven and cool slightly before slicing.

Nutritional info (per serving)

Calories	280
From fat	26%
Fat	8 g
Saturated	3 g
Trans	0 g
Carbohydrates	30 g
Protein	20 g
Sodium	473 mg
Cholesterol	43 mg
Calcium	72 mg
Fiber	1 g

Food exchanges
2 starch,
2 medium-fat meat

Test Kitchen Tip

It's the inner seeds and ribs that give jalapeño and other chili peppers their heat and kick. Remove seeds and ribs to avoid this, if desired.

Poultry

Poultry

When it comes to buying poultry products, especially chicken, consumers now have many options to choose from. Many of the poultry products are labeled in the manner they were raised.
Here is a buyer's guide to what the terms and labeling mean.

Free Range or Free Roaming.
Producers must demonstrate that fowl have been allowed to freely roam outside cages or other confined areas. However, there are no requirements for how much time the poultry spend outdoors or the quality or size of the outdoor area.

Fresh or Frozen. The term fresh on a poultry label refers to any raw poultry product that has never been below 26 degrees. Raw poultry held at 0° degrees or below must be labeled frozen or previously frozen. No specific labeling is required on raw poultry stored at temperatures between 0 and 25 degrees.

Natural. A product containing no artificial ingredients or added color and is only minimally processed (a process which does not fundamentally alter the raw product) may be labeled natural. The label must explain the use of the term natural, such as no added color, no artificial ingredients or minimally processed.

No Hormones. Hormones are not allowed in the raising of poultry. Therefore, the claim "no hormones added" cannot be used on the labels of poultry unless it is followed by a statement that says "Federal regulations prohibit the use of hormones."

No Antibiotics Added. Antibiotics may be given to prevent disease or treat disease. A withdrawal period is required from the time antibiotics are administered before the bird can be slaughtered. This ensures that no residues are present in the bird's system. The Food Safety and Inspection Service randomly samples poultry at slaughter to test for residues. "No antibiotics added" may be used on labels for poultry products if documentation is provided demonstrating that the animals were raised without antibiotics. The term "antibiotic-free" is not USDA approved.

Whether or not any of these buzz words adorn your poultry purchases, enjoy this lean and versatile protein often. Be sure to give the Frangelico Chicken a try. It was selected as one of the Best of the Free Press Test Kitchen recipes in 2009. And our Turkey Sausage and Arroz Con Pollo are sure to become family favorites.

Arroz Con Pollo (Rice with Chicken)

This Arroz Con Pollo, which is Spanish for rice with chicken, features brown rice, a whole grain, instead of white rice. The fiber-rich bran coating is what gives brown rice its light tan color and chewy texture. With the bran layer intact, brown rice is a good whole-grain option. Brown rice has an impressive array of vitamins and minerals, including vitamin B6, folate, vitamin E, potassium, magnesium and fiber.

🍴 7   ⏱ 1 hour 15 mins total

Ingredients

1 ½ pounds boneless, skinless chicken breasts

3 tablespoons olive oil, divided

1 cup chopped onion

2 cloves garlic, peeled, minced

1 cup uncooked instant brown rice

2 teaspoons ground cumin

2 teaspoons chili powder

1 can (14.5 ounces) fat-free, less-sodium chicken broth

1 can (14.5 ounces) diced tomatoes

1 can (12 ounces) beer

½ cup salsa

¾ teaspoon salt

¼ teaspoon ground black pepper

Directions

Cut chicken breasts into large strips; set aside.

In a large stockpot, heat 2 tablespoons olive oil. Add chicken and cook uncovered about 10 minutes, turning to brown evenly. Remove chicken from pot and cover to keep warm. Add the remaining 1 tablespoon oil to the pot along with the onion and garlic. Sauté until onion is tender, about 3 minutes. Add brown rice, cumin and chili powder and continue to sauté an additional 3 to 4 minutes. Carefully stir in the chicken broth, diced tomatoes and beer.

Place chicken on top of the rice mixture. Bring to a boil; reduce heat and cover. Simmer for 45 to 50 minutes or until rice is tender. Remove from heat and gently stir in the salsa, salt and black pepper.

Nutritional info (per serving)

Calories	285	Sodium	594 mg
From fat	28%	Cholesterol	62 mg
Fat	9 g	Calcium	67 mg
Saturated	2 g	Fiber	2 g
Trans	0 g		
Carbohydrates	21 g		
Protein	25 g		

Food exchanges
1 starch, 3 lean meat
1 vegetable

Test Kitchen Tip

To cut the chicken breasts into even strips, freeze it for about 20 minutes. Because brown rice contains natural oils in the bran layer, it will stay fresh in the pantry for about six months. Extend the shelf life by storing brown rice in the refrigerator or freezer.

Braised Balsamic Chicken with Artichokes

Pairing tomatoes and artichokes in this chicken dish provides 3 vegetable servings. Tomatoes provide dietary fiber, iron, potassium and a hefty dose of vitamin C. They also contain lycopene, a phytochemical. Lycopene is a carotenoid — a plant pigment that gives the tomato its red color. Diets rich in lycopene and other carotenoids might help protect against heart disease and certain cancers. Artichokes are low in calories. Three artichoke hearts contain about 35 calories.

 5 45 mins total

Ingredients

1 teaspoon garlic powder

½ teaspoon salt, divided

¼ teaspoon black pepper

16 ounces boneless, skinless chicken breast, cubed

2 tablespoons olive oil

1 ½ cups chopped onion

2 cups diced fresh tomatoes

⅓ cup balsamic vinegar

2 tablespoons sugar

1 teaspoon dried basil

1 teaspoon dried thyme

1 teaspoon dried oregano

1 can (13.75 ounces) quartered artichoke hearts, drained and rinsed

3 ¾ cups hot, cooked couscous

Directions

In a small bowl, combine garlic powder, ¼ teaspoon salt and black pepper and rub onto the cubed chicken pieces. In a large nonstick skillet, heat olive oil over medium heat and cook the chicken about 10 minutes, turning to brown evenly.

Remove the chicken, leaving drippings in the skillet. Set the chicken aside. Add onion to the skillet and continue to sauté about 5 to 8 minutes or until it's tender. Return chicken to the skillet along with tomatoes, balsamic vinegar, sugar, basil, thyme and oregano; stir to combine. Simmer until tomatoes begin to soften, about 15 to 20 minutes. Add artichoke hearts and continue to simmer until artichokes are heated through. Season with remaining ¼ teaspoon salt. Prepare couscous without added salt or oil. One serving of this recipe consists of 1 cup of the chicken and vegetables over ¾ cup cooked couscous.

Nutritional info (per serving)

Calories	365
From fat	20%
Fat	8 g
Saturated	2 g
Trans	0 g
Carbohydrates	59 g
Protein	27 g
Sodium	309 mg
Cholesterol	48 mg
Calcium	51 mg
Fiber	5 g

Food exchanges
2 starch, 3 vegetable,
2 lean meat

 Test Kitchen Tip

Choose tomatoes that are plump, firm and feel heavy for their size. The skin should be smooth, richly colored and free of blemishes or deep cracks. Store tomatoes at room temperature, they'll keep several days. It's best not to refrigerate tomatoes, or they will become mealy.

Cashew Chicken

This Cashew Chicken is an easy weeknight meal if you marinate the chicken the night before and have all the ingredients prepped and ready. Using just 2 teaspoons of fresh gingerroot provides a kick to this recipe. Serving this dish over brown rice gives it a whole-grain boost.

 5   **50 mins total**

Ingredients

10 ounces boneless, skinless chicken breast cut into small strips

2 tablespoons reduced-sodium soy sauce, divided

2 teaspoons brown sugar

2 teaspoons minced gingerroot

2 teaspoons cider vinegar

½ cup apple juice or apple cider

2 tablespoons cooking sherry

1 tablespoon chili sauce

1 tablespoon cornstarch

1 tablespoon peanut or canola oil, divided

⅛ teaspoon red pepper flakes

2 cloves garlic, peeled, minced

1 cup sliced celery

1 cup onion, cut into ½-inch pieces

1 can (8 ounces) water chestnuts, drained and rinsed

⅓ cup dry roasted, unsalted cashews

½ teaspoon salt

¼ teaspoon fresh ground black pepper

2 ½ cups cooked brown rice, prepared without salt or oil

Directions

Place chicken strips in a small glass bowl. In a measuring cup or small jar, combine 1 tablespoon soy sauce, brown sugar, gingerroot and cider vinegar. Pour marinade over chicken and toss to coat. Marinate chicken strips in the refrigerator at least 2 hours or overnight.

In a separate bowl, combine the remaining soy sauce, apple juice, sherry, chili sauce and cornstarch and set aside.

In a large nonstick skillet, heat 2 teaspoons oil over medium heat. Add chicken and cook until golden brown and cooked through, about 5 to 8 minutes. Transfer chicken and its juices to a dish and keep warm. To the same skillet, add the remaining one teaspoon of oil and heat red pepper flakes for 1 minute. Add garlic and continue to sauté an additional minute. Add celery, onion, water chestnuts and cashews and continue cooking, stirring constantly until the vegetables begin to soften, about 3 to 5 minutes. Add chicken and its juices to the skillet and stir to combine.

Whisk sauce and add it to the skillet. Cook until the sauce thickens, about 1 minute. Season with salt and black pepper and serve over the rice.

Test Kitchen Tip
Fresh gingerroot, used in this recipe, freezes well and keeps for several months. Place it in a plastic bag with the air squeezed out. To use, there's no need to thaw, break off what you need and grate, or mince it. You also can grate from the whole piece and return the unused portion to the freezer.

Nutritional info (per serving)

Calories...................... 325
    From fat 25%
Fat ....9 g
    Saturated................2 g
    Trans ....0 g
Carbohydrates ....39 g
Protein .... 19 g

Sodium .... 498 mg
Cholesterol .... 39 mg
Calcium .... 45 mg
Fiber ....3 g
Food exchanges
    2 starch, 2 lean meat,
    2 vegetable, ½ fat

Chicken Breasts with Dijon Cream Sauce

Cream sauces can add plenty of fat and calories to recipes. In this recipe, the fat and calories are reduced by using fat-free half-and-half in place of heavy cream. Just a small amount of Dijon mustard adds texture and a slightly tangy edge.

 4 30 mins total

Ingredients

- 4 (4 ounces each) boneless, skinless chicken breasts
- ½ teaspoon coarsely ground black pepper
- ½ teaspoon salt
- 2 tablespoons canola oil
- ⅓ cup fat-free, less-sodium chicken broth
- ⅓ cup dry white wine
- ⅓ cup fat-free half-and-half
- 1 ½ tablespoons Dijon mustard
- 1 teaspoon cornstarch
- 3 tablespoons cold water

Directions

Sprinkle both sides of chicken breasts evenly with black pepper and salt.

Add canola oil to a large nonstick skillet, and place it over medium-high heat until it's hot.

Add chicken breasts to the skillet; cook 7 to 10 minutes on each side or until the chicken is tender and no longer pink (165 degrees). Remove chicken from the skillet, and keep it warm.

Reduce heat to medium-low. Add broth and wine to the skillet, stirring to loosen browned bits.

In a small bowl or measuring cup, combine the half-and-half and Dijon mustard; add mixture to the skillet. Reduce heat and simmer 5 minutes or until sauce has thickened slightly.

In a small bowl, combine the cornstarch and water, stirring until the cornstarch is dissolved. Gradually add the cornstarch mixture to the sauce; heat to boiling, stirring constantly. Boil and stir 1 minute.

Serve the chicken with sauce over rice.

Nutritional info (per serving)

Calories	244	Sodium	480 mg
From fat	36%	Cholesterol	64 mg
Fat	9 g	Calcium	32 mg
Saturated	1 g	Fiber	0 g
Trans	0 g	Food exchanges	
Carbohydrates	3 g	3 lean meat, 1 fat	
Protein	26 g		

Test Kitchen Tip

Fat-free half-and-half tends to be thicker than traditional half-and-half. Many contain carrageenan, a natural thickener. Stirring a cornstarch/water mix into the half-and-half helps stabilize it so it does not curdle.

Chicken Burgers with Sliced Avocado

Using ground chicken breast is a welcome change from ground turkey for burgers. It's also a great source of lean protein when you're looking to cut calories and fat. But keep in mind that chicken or turkey burgers can dry out quickly. In this recipe, egg white, milk and soy sauce keep it moist.

Nutritional info (per serving)

Calories	347	Sodium	533 mg
From fat	23%	Cholesterol	54 mg
Fat	9 g	Calcium	91 mg
Saturated	1 g	Fiber	7 g
Trans	0 g		
Carbohydrates	40 g		
Protein	28 g		

Food exchanges
2 starch, 1 vegetable,
3 lean meat

Test Kitchen Tip

When buying ground poultry, pay attention to labels. If the package is labeled simply "ground chicken" — and not "ground chicken breast" — it will have more fat. A 4-ounce raw portion of ground chicken can have 9 grams of fat. To be considered very lean, ground poultry has to be 97% or more fat-free. Some labels will state this.

 4 45 mins total

Ingredients

- 1/3 cup finely diced onion
- 1 teaspoon canola oil
- 1 egg white
- 2 tablespoons skim milk
- 1 tablespoon Worcestershire sauce
- 1 teaspoon reduced-sodium soy sauce
- 1/4 cup plain bread crumbs
- 1/4 teaspoon garlic powder
- 1/4 teaspoon poultry seasoning
- 1/8 teaspoon freshly ground black pepper
- 1/8 teaspoon ground mustard
- 12 ounces ground chicken or turkey breast
- 4 (2 ounces each) whole-wheat hamburger buns
- 4 teaspoons reduced-fat mayonnaise
- 4 slices avocado
- 4 slices tomato
- 4 slices red onion
- 4 lettuce leaves

Directions

Place onion and oil in a small nonstick skillet and sauté over medium heat until softened, about 5 minutes.

In a small bowl whisk together the egg white, skim milk, Worcestershire sauce and soy sauce. In another larger bowl combine the bread crumbs, garlic powder, poultry seasoning, black pepper and ground mustard. Add the egg white mixture to the bread crumb mixture and stir to combine. Stir in the ground chicken until incorporated.

Divide the mixture into 4 equal portions and shape into patties. The mixture will be rather sticky. Shaping patties between wax paper works well. Refrigerate patties for at least 20 minutes before cooking.

To cook, place patties in a nonstick skillet over medium-high heat or grill directly over medium coals. Cook patties about 4 to 6 minutes on each side or until thoroughly cooked through.

Serve each patty on a whole-wheat bun with 1 teaspoon mayonnaise and a slice of avocado, tomato, red onion and a lettuce leaf.

Chicken Cordon Bleu

The only way to distinguish low-fat cheese from high-fat cheese involves reading the food label. A low-fat cheese will have no more than 3 grams of fat and no more than 2 grams of saturated fat in a 1-ounce serving. If you can't find anything that suits your palate in that category, try a reduced-fat cheese with no more than 5 grams of fat and 3 grams of saturated fat per ounce.

 4   1 hour 5 mins total

Ingredients

Vegetable oil cooking spray

4 boneless, skinless chicken breasts (4 ounces each)

4 slices (½ ounce each) lean, reduced-sodium ham

4 slices (½ ounce each) reduced-fat Swiss cheese

⅓ cup bread crumbs

3 tablespoons grated Parmesan cheese

⅛ teaspoon freshly ground black pepper

¼ cup low-fat buttermilk

2 tablespoons melted trans fat-free margarine

1 teaspoon fresh snipped parsley, optional

Directions

Preheat oven to 375 degrees. Coat the bottom of a glass baking dish with the vegetable oil cooking spray; set aside.

Flatten chicken breasts between plastic wrap to about a ½-inch thickness using a meat mallet, a small, heavy frying pan or a closed fist. You also can slice the chicken breast in half horizontally almost all the way through. Open the chicken breast up and press out to flatten. Lay 1 thin slice of ham and a ½-ounce of Swiss cheese on the flattened breast. Roll up carefully, beginning at the narrow end and secure with wooden picks. Repeat the process with the remaining chicken breasts.

In a bowl, combine the bread crumbs, Parmesan cheese and black pepper. Place the buttermilk in a separate bowl. Dip the chicken rolls in the buttermilk and then the bread crumb mixture. Place chicken pieces in the prepared baking dish. Brush each roll with the melted margarine. Bake for 35 to 40 minutes or until golden brown. Garnish with parsley.

Test Kitchen Tip

To avoid pounding thick chicken breasts to flatten them, slice them in half horizontally. This is better than pounding because you end up with nice, neat and even cuts of chicken. Start out with very cold chicken breasts from which the tenders (the long, narrow piece under the breast) have been removed, saving them for another use. Place the breasts on a clean work surface and hold them in place with your hand. Slice the breasts in half horizontally, starting at the thickest end, working away from you.

Nutritional info (per serving)

Calories...................... 284	Sodium .... 342 mg
From fat 35%	Cholesterol .... 90 mg
Fat .... 11 g	Calcium .... 224 mg
Saturated .... 4 g	Fiber .... 0 g
Trans .... 0 g	Food exchanges
Carbohydrates .... 8 g	½ starch, 4 lean meat
Protein .... 37 g	

Chicken with Cherry Balsamic Glaze

This easy-to-prepare chicken dish is ready in 30 minutes and served with a sweet and tangy sauce. The chicken breasts are pounded thin for quick cooking. Balsamic vinegar gives the sauce a tangy flavor. The chicken is topped off with crunchy almonds.

 4   30 mins total

Ingredients

1 tablespoon trans fat-free margarine

1 tablespoon olive oil

¼ cup all-purpose flour

½ teaspoon salt, divided

¼ teaspoon ground black pepper, divided

4 (4 ounces each) boneless, skinless chicken breasts, pounded to ¼-inch thickness

½ cup cherry preserves

2 tablespoons balsamic vinegar

2 tablespoons slivered almonds, toasted

Directions

In a large nonstick skillet, heat margarine and olive oil over medium heat until margarine melts.

In a shallow dish or pie plate, combine flour, ¼ teaspoon salt and ⅛ teaspoon black pepper. Dredge the chicken breasts in flour and sauté until golden brown on each side and cooked through, about 5 minutes on each side.

Remove the chicken to a serving platter and keep warm. In a small saucepan, heat cherry preserves and balsamic vinegar until warm. To serve, season chicken breasts with remaining salt and pepper, top with cherry sauce and sprinkle with toasted almonds.

Nutritional info (per serving)

Calories......................354
    From fat 25%

Fat ....10 g
    Saturated.................1 g
    Trans ....0 g

Carbohydrates ....36 g

Protein ....28 g

Sodium .... 337 mg

Cholesterol ....72 mg

Calcium .... 32 mg

Fiber ....1 g

Food exchanges
    2 starch, 3 lean meat

Test Kitchen Tip

Almonds tend to burn easily when toasted so watch them carefully. Use a toaster oven or toast them in a skillet, shaking the skillet often to prevent them from burning.

Curried Chicken Salad with Pineapple and Grapes

If you're new to curry powder, this Curried Chicken Salad is an easy one to try. It's a nice change to plain chicken salad. Curry powder adds wonderful flavor to soups, stews and vegetables as well as meat, fish and poultry dishes. Curry powder is a pulverized blend of as many as 20 spices and seeds. This dish makes great use of leftover chicken.

8   15 mins total

Ingredients

2 ¾ cups cooked skinless chicken breast, cubed

1 can (8 ounces) pineapple tidbits, drained

1 cup red or green grapes, halved

¾ cup chopped celery

⅓ cup chopped red onion

⅓ cup golden raisins

½ cup reduced-fat mayonnaise

½ cup reduced-fat sour cream

½ teaspoon curry powder

½ teaspoon salt

¼ teaspoon black pepper

8 cups bibb lettuce, chopped

Directions

In a large bowl, toss chicken breast cubes, pineapple, grapes, celery, onion and raisins. In a small bowl or measuring cup, combine mayonnaise, sour cream, curry powder, salt and black pepper. Add dressing mixture to chicken mixture and gently mix until well combined. Serve chilled on a bed of lettuce.

Nutritional info (per serving)

Calories......................... 187
    From fat................. 29%
Fat .... 6 g
    Saturated .... 2 g
    Trans .... 0 g
Carbohydrates .... 18 g
Protein .... 17 g
Sodium .... 307 mg
Cholesterol .... 49 mg
Calcium .... 66 mg
Fiber .... 2 g
Food exchanges
    1 fruit, 1 vegetable,
    2 lean meat

Test Kitchen Tip

Curry powder typically comes in two forms: sweet and mild (Indian) and hot (Madras). The heat level depends on the amount of chili pepper used. Many brands may not indicate its form, so be sure to read the ingredient list and see how many types of pepper are used in the blend and where they fall on the list. If they are first on the list, it's hot.

Chicken Frangelico

This super-easy Chicken Frangelico earned a spot as a Best of the Free Press Test Kitchen recipes in 2009. Replacing regular half-and-half with fat-free half-and-half in the sauce cut 150 calories. The sauce has a terrific nutty flavor boost from Frangelico (a hazelnut-flavored liqueur).

 4 30 mins total

Ingredients

3 tablespoons trans fat-free margarine, divided

¼ cup all-purpose flour

⅛ teaspoon plus ¼ teaspoon salt, divided

⅛ teaspoon ground black pepper

4 (4 ounces each) boneless, skinless chicken breasts, pounded to ½-inch thickness

¼ cup diced onion

1 clove garlic, peeled, minced

¼ cup Frangelico (hazelnut-flavored liqueur)

1 cup fat-free half-and-half

2 teaspoons cornstarch

2 tablespoons slivered almonds, toasted

Directions

In a large skillet, heat 2 tablespoons margarine over medium-high heat until melted. In a shallow dish or pie plate, combine flour, ⅛ teaspoon salt and black pepper. Coat chicken breasts in flour mixture and sauté in margarine, turning until golden brown on each side and cooked through. Transfer chicken to a platter to keep warm.

Add the remaining tablespoon of margarine to the skillet along with onion and garlic. Sauté 3 to 5 minutes, scraping up any browned bits on the bottom of the pan. Add the Frangelico and continue to sauté an additional 3 to 5 minutes.

In a small bowl or measuring cup, combine half-and-half and cornstarch. Reduce heat to medium-low and gradually add the half-and-half mixture to the skillet. Allow the sauce to thicken. Pour sauce over the chicken, top with toasted almonds and serve. Serve with brown rice, couscous or no-yolk egg noodles.

Nutritional info (per serving)

Calories	331	Sodium	361 mg
From fat	24%	Cholesterol	72 mg
Fat	9 g	Calcium	84 mg
Saturated	2 g	Fiber	1 g
Trans	0 g		
Carbohydrates	20 g		
Protein	30 g		

Food exchanges
1 starch, 3 lean meat, ½ milk

Test Kitchen Tip
To cut the chicken breast into even strips, freeze it for about 20 minutes.

Grilled Tandoori Chicken

This chicken recipe is marinated in a mixture of spices and Greek-style yogurt. Thicker and creamier than traditional yogurt, Greek yogurt has a texture similar to custard or sour cream. This rich texture is achieved through a straining process that removes more whey and water from the yogurt. Traditional Greek yogurt is made with whole milk or a combination of whole milk and cream, making some varieties high in fat — more than 20 grams of fat in an 8-ounce serving. Opt for fat-free or low-fat Greek yogurt, which is just as rich and creamy.

 8   40 mins total

Ingredients

2 pounds boneless skinless chicken breasts, cut into eight 4-ounce pieces

1/3 cup chopped onion

1 tablespoon, plus 1 teaspoon canola oil

3 cloves garlic, peeled, minced

1 tablespoon chopped fresh gingerroot

1 1/2 teaspoons garam masala

1 teaspoon paprika

1/2 teaspoon ground cumin

1/2 teaspoon curry powder

1/2 teaspoon dried turmeric

1/2 teaspoon salt

1/4 teaspoon red pepper flakes

1 container (7 ounces) low-fat Greek-style yogurt

1 1/2 tablespoons fresh lemon juice

Nutritional info (per serving)

Calories......................... 191	Sodium .... 193 mg
From fat................28%	Cholesterol .... 74 mg
Fat................................. 6 g	Calcium .... 54 mg
Saturated.................1 g	Fiber ....1 g
Trans ....0 g	Food exchanges
Carbohydrates .... 3 g	3 lean meat
Protein ....29 g	

Directions

With a fork, poke holes in chicken pieces. Using a knife, cut diagonal slices about 1-inch apart and no more than a 1/4-inch deep into the larger pieces. Place chicken in a glass baking dish or plastic bag. In a blender, combine onion, 1 tablespoon canola oil, garlic and gingerroot; process on high speed to form a paste. Add garam masala, paprika, cumin, curry powder, turmeric, salt, red pepper flakes, yogurt and lemon juice. Process until smooth, scraping down the sides. Pour the marinade over the chicken, turning to coat evenly and rubbing the marinade into the holes and slits. Cover with plastic wrap or seal bag and refrigerate for 6 to 24 hours, turning occasionally.

Prepare the outdoor grill and brush the grill grate with the remaining 1 teaspoon of canola oil to prevent sticking. Place chicken on the grill and discard any remaining marinade. Grill chicken for 5 to 8 minutes on each side or until an internal temperature of 165 degrees is reached. Serve with sautéed vegetables or brown rice.

Test Kitchen Tip

Greek yogurt typically cost more than traditional yogurt. Use Greek yogurt the same way you use regular yogurt — over cereal with fruit, in creamy salad dressings, smoothies and chilled soups. It's also a great low-fat substitute for mayonnaise and sour cream. Greek yogurt contains almost twice the amount protein as traditional yogurt and about half the sodium.

Indian Lemon Chicken

This recipe from chef Frank Turner, director of Culinary Wellness at Henry Ford West Bloomfield Hospital, opts for boneless, skinless chicken thighs for a meatier flavor. They add a little more fat, but are a change from boneless, skinless chicken breast.

 4    40 mins total

Ingredients

2 pieces (1 inch) fresh gingerroot, peeled and coarsely chopped

2 garlic cloves, peeled

¼ cup water

Vegetable cooking oil spray

1 tablespoon canola oil

4 (4 ounce) boneless, skinless chicken thighs

½ cup chopped cilantro

1 finely diced jalapeño pepper

1 ½ teaspoons ground cumin

½ teaspoon coriander seed

¼ teaspoon ground turmeric

½ teaspoon salt

½ cup lemon juice

1 teaspoon lemon zest

Directions

Place gingerroot, garlic cloves and water in a food processor or blender. Process to a smooth paste and set aside. Lightly coat a nonstick skillet with vegetable oil cooking spray.

Add the oil and place over medium high heat. Add chicken thighs in a single layer and brown on both sides, about 4 to 5 minute per side. Transfer chicken thighs to a heated plate. To the skillet, add the cilantro, jalapeño, cumin, coriander seed, turmeric and salt. Stir constantly until the herbs and spices become fragrant, about 1 minute. Stir in reserved ginger paste, lemon juice and lemon zest. Return the chicken thighs to the skillet and spoon sauce over the tops. Cover and simmer for 5 minutes. Turn chicken over and simmer, covered for additional 5 minutes, until chicken is cooked through. Transfer chicken thighs to a serving platter, spooning sauce over the top. Serve immediately.

Nutritional info (per serving)

Calories...................... 222
    From fat 53%

Fat .... 13 g
    Saturated............... 3 g
    Trans ....0 g

Carbohydrates .... 4 g

Protein ....23 g

Sodium .... 323 mg

Cholesterol ....81 mg

Calcium .... 23 mg

Fiber ....1 g

Food exchanges
    3 medium-fat meat

Test Kitchen Tip

When chicken thighs are on sale, it's a good idea to stock up and freeze them. If you buy with the bone and skin on, remove both. Flash freeze the thighs by placing them on a tray and placing them in the freezer. Once nearly frozen, remove and transfer to a plastic sealable bag. This way they will not be stuck together, but frozen individually so you can take out the amount you need later.

Spicy Chicken Stir-Fry in a Peanut Sauce

Colorful fruits and vegetables are filled with healthy antioxidants and phytochemicals. One of the easiest ways to get these substances is to enjoy a variety of brightly colored fruits and vegetables every day. This stir-fry incorporates several vegetables from just about every color group.

  6   45 mins total

Ingredients

2 cups cooked whole-wheat angel hair pasta, reserving 2 tablespoons pasta cooking water

2 tablespoons reduced-sodium soy sauce, divided

2 tablespoons dry sherry

12 ounces boneless, skinless chicken breast, cut into strips

3 tablespoons peanut butter

2 tablespoons honey

2 teaspoons grated gingerroot

1 clove garlic, peeled, minced

¼ teaspoon red pepper flakes

1 tablespoon sesame oil or canola oil, divided

1 ½ cups julienned carrots

1 ½ cups sliced red bell pepper

1 ½ cups snow peas, halved

1 ½ cups sliced onion

½ teaspoon salt

1 tablespoon chopped cilantro, optional

6 lime wedges, optional

Nutritional info (per serving)

Calories	274
From fat	26%
Fat	8 g
Saturated	2 g
Trans	0 g
Carbohydrates	32 g
Protein	20 g
Sodium	364 mg
Cholesterol	36 mg
Calcium	51 mg
Fiber	4 g

Food exchanges
1 starch, 3 vegetable, 2 lean meat

Directions

Cook the pasta according to package directions, omitting the salt. Reserve 2 tablespoons of the pasta cooking water and drain the pasta.

In a medium bowl, combine 1 tablespoon soy sauce, sherry and chicken strips; toss well to coat. In a small bowl, combine remaining soy sauce, peanut butter, honey, gingerroot, garlic, red pepper flakes and 2 tablespoons reserved pasta water.

In a large skillet or wok, heat 1 teaspoon oil over medium-high heat. Add the chicken breast strips and sauté 5 to 8 minutes or until chicken is lightly browned. Remove chicken from pan. Add remaining 2 teaspoons of oil to the pan. Add carrots, red bell pepper, snow peas and onion; sauté vegetables 3 to 5 minutes. Add the chicken and cooked pasta to the vegetable mixture; gently toss. Top mixture with the peanut butter sauce and gently stir to combine. Sprinkle with salt; stir to combine. If desired, top each serving with a sprinkle of chopped cilantro and a squeeze of fresh lime.

Test Kitchen Tip

To julienne means to cut a food, such as the carrots in this recipe, into matchstick size pieces.

Watch This!

Scan this QR code with your smartphone to watch the Heart Smart® video.

Szechuan Chicken

Once the prep work of cutting the chicken and vegetables is done, this recipe is a breeze to put together. Serving it over brown rice gives it a fiber boost.

 4   20 mins total

Ingredients

3 tablespoons cornstarch

1 teaspoon ground ginger

1 pound boneless, skinless chicken breast cut into small strips

2 tablespoons canola oil

3 cloves garlic, peeled, minced

$\frac{1}{4}$ teaspoon red pepper flakes

2 $\frac{1}{2}$ cups sliced mushrooms

$\frac{1}{3}$ cup fat-free, less-sodium chicken broth

2 tablespoons reduced-sodium soy sauce

2 tablespoons rice wine vinegar

1 tablespoon chili sauce

1 teaspoon sugar

$\frac{1}{8}$ teaspoon cayenne pepper

4 green onions, sliced diagonally into $\frac{1}{4}$-inch pieces

2 cups cooked brown rice, prepared without salt or oil

Nutritional info (per serving)

Calories	371	Sodium	467 mg
From fat	27%	Cholesterol	72 mg
Fat	11 g	Calcium	42 mg
Saturated	2 g	Fiber	3 g
Trans	0 g		
Carbohydrates	35 g		
Protein	32 g		

Food exchanges
2 starch, 3 lean meat
1 vegetable, $\frac{1}{2}$ fat

Directions

Combine cornstarch and ground ginger and place in sealable bag. Add the chicken strips to the bag, and toss to coat. In a wok or large skillet, heat oil over medium-high heat. Add garlic and red pepper flakes, and sauté 1 to 2 minutes. Add chicken, and continue to sauté, stirring constantly until chicken is lightly browned. Add mushrooms, and continue to cook an additional 2 to 3 minutes.

In a measuring cup, combine the chicken broth, soy sauce, rice wine vinegar, chili sauce, sugar and cayenne pepper. Add the sauce to the wok, and continue to cook until the sauce has thickened and the chicken is cooked through, 3 to 5 minutes. Garnish with the sliced green onions, and serve over brown rice. Each serving consists of 1 cup Szechuan Chicken over $\frac{1}{2}$ cup cooked brown rice.

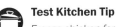 **Test Kitchen Tip**
Freeze chicken for about 20 minutes to make it easier to slice into uniform strips. You can also use chicken breast tenders, cutting them in half.

Turkey and Pepper Moussaka

This hearty Moussaka gets a veggie boost from green and red peppers. The surprise ingredient in this recipe is the small amount of cinnamon mixed in with the ricotta and Parmesan cheese for an added spice flavor.

 8   1 hour 30 mins total

Ingredients

1 tablespoon canola oil

2 large red bell peppers, cored, seeded and cut into strips

2 large green peppers, cored, seeded and cut into strips

1 ¼ pounds ground turkey breast

1 medium onion, peeled, chopped

2 cans (14.5 ounces each) no-added-salt diced tomatoes

1 can (6 ounces) tomato paste

1 teaspoon dried oregano

1 teaspoon dried basil

½ teaspoon salt

¼ teaspoon black pepper

Vegetable oil cooking spray

⅔ cup plain bread crumbs, divided

1 container (15 ounces) low-fat ricotta cheese

½ cup fat-free egg substitute

½ cup shredded Parmesan cheese

½ teaspoon cinnamon

Directions

Preheat oven to 375 degrees. In a large nonstick skillet, heat oil over medium-high heat. Add red and green pepper strips; sauté 8 minutes. Remove to a medium-size bowl.

In the same skillet, cook the ground turkey and onion, stirring to break up clumps, until the turkey is no longer pink, about 8 minutes. Add tomatoes, tomato paste, oregano, basil, salt and pepper to the turkey mixture; cook 3 minutes. Remove from heat.

Spray a 4-quart oval baking dish with vegetable oil cooking spray and sprinkle the bottom with ⅓ cup bread crumbs. Arrange half the pepper strips over the bread crumbs. Layer with the turkey mixture; top with the remaining ⅓ cup bread crumbs and pepper strips.

In a medium bowl, stir together ricotta cheese, egg substitute, Parmesan cheese and cinnamon until well blended. Spread the cheese mixture over the turkey and pepper mixture. Cover and bake until bubbly around the edges, about 45 minutes.

Remove the cover and increase the oven temperature to broil. Broil until the topping is browned, about 3 minutes.

Let stand 10 minutes before serving.

Test Kitchen Tip

Hard cheeses, such as Parmesan, freeze well. You can freeze a block of Parmesan and grate or shred as needed. You can also shred or grate and freeze the cheese.

Nutritional info (per serving)

Calories...................... 263
    From fat................ 21%
Fat................................6 g
    Saturated...............3 g
    Trans ....0 g
Carbohydrates ....23 g
Protein ....28 g

Sodium .... 422 mg
Cholesterol ....61 mg
Calcium .... 196 mg
Fiber ....4 g
Food exchanges
    1 starch, 2 vegetables,
    3 lean meat

Turkey Piccata

A hefty 5 cloves of garlic is used in this Turkey Piccata recipe. The way garlic is cut and cooked influences how strong it tastes. The finer garlic is chopped, the stronger it tastes. Garlic cloves can be used whole, sliced, slivered, chopped, minced, pressed or pounded. Garlic mellows the longer it is cooked.

 6    25 mins total

Ingredients

½ cup all-purpose flour

¾ teaspoon salt, divided

¼ teaspoon ground black pepper

1 package (1 ¼ pounds) turkey breast cutlets

2 tablespoons olive oil, divided

2 tablespoons trans fat-free margarine, divided

5 cloves garlic, peeled, minced

½ cup white wine

¼ cup fresh squeezed lemon juice

½ of a red bell pepper, julienned

1 tablespoon fresh flat-leaf parsley, chopped

Lemon slices for garnish

4 ½ cups hot cooked couscous

Directions

Place flour in a shallow dish. Add ¼ teaspoon salt and ground black pepper to flour and stir to combine. Dredge turkey cutlets in flour mixture. (Most 1 ¼ pound packages of turkey cutlets will contain 6 to 7 cutlets.)

In a large skillet, heat 1 tablespoon oil over medium-high heat. Add 3 or 4 cutlets and cook 2 to 3 minutes on each side or until browned. Remove turkey from pan; keep warm and repeat process with remaining 1 tablespoon oil and floured cutlets. Once browned, remove cutlets from pan and keep warm.

Add 1 tablespoon margarine to the skillet and sauté garlic, about 3 minutes. Add wine, lemon juice, red bell pepper, remaining ½ teaspoon salt and remaining 1 tablespoon margarine to pan; scrape pan to loosen browned bits, stir to combine.

Layer turkey cutlets over sauce, cover and cook an additional 3 to 5 minutes. Sprinkle with parsley and garnish with lemon slices if desired. Serve with ¾ cup cooked couscous, prepared without salt and margarine or oil.

Nutritional info (per serving)

Calories	355
From fat	23%
Fat	9 g
Saturated	1 g
Trans	0 g
Carbohydrates	39 g
Protein	24 g
Sodium	382 mg
Cholesterol	52 mg
Calcium	31 mg
Fiber	2 g

Food exchanges
2 ½ starch, 2 lean meat, 1 fat

Test Kitchen Tip

Choose firm, plump bulbs of garlic with dry skins. Avoid heads with soft or shriveled cloves, and those stored under refrigeration. At home, store fresh garlic in an open container away from other foods, in a cool, dark place. Properly stored, unbroken bulbs should last about eight weeks.

Turkey Sausage

Traditional breakfast meats aren't exactly heart-healthy. Four slices of bacon contain about the same amount of fat as three Twinkies. Three sausage patties have the same amount of fat as a quarter pound burger with cheese. These Turkey Sausage patties have just 4 grams of non-artery-clogging fat and can fit into a Heart Smart® eating plan.

6 (2 patties each) · **35 mins total**

Ingredients

1 pound ground turkey breast

1/3 cup finely diced dried cherries

1 1/2 tablespoons canola oil

1 clove garlic, peeled, finely minced

2 tablespoons brown sugar

1 teaspoon rubbed sage

1/2 teaspoon salt

1/2 teaspoon freshly ground black pepper

1/2 teaspoon fennel seed

1/8 teaspoon crushed red pepper flakes

1/8 teaspoon cayenne pepper

Directions

In a medium-sized bowl, thoroughly combine all the ingredients. Divide the sausage mixture into 12 equal portions and shape into patties, about 2 1/2 inches in diameter. To cook, working in batches if necessary, place patties in a nonstick skillet over medium-high heat. Cook patties about 5 to 6 minutes on each side or until done.

Nutritional info (per serving)

Calories	143
From fat	25%
Fat	4 g
Saturated	0 g
Trans	0 g
Carbohydrates	10 g
Protein	17 g
Sodium	192 mg
Cholesterol	47 mg
Calcium	15 mg
Fiber	0 g

Food exchanges
1/2 fruit, 2 lean meat

Turkey Tetrazzini

This Turkey Tetrazzini is a great way to use leftover turkey. Using whole-wheat pasta provides fiber to the recipe. Try using cremini mushroom for a heartier flavor.

 6   1 hour total

Ingredients

5 ounces dry whole-wheat spaghetti or angel hair pasta

2 tablespoons trans fat-free margarine

¾ cup chopped onion

2 cloves garlic, peeled, minced

1 cup sliced mushrooms

3 tablespoons all-purpose flour

1 ½ cups skim milk

½ teaspoon salt

½ teaspoon poultry seasoning

½ teaspoon mustard powder

¼ teaspoon white pepper

¼ cup white wine

1 ounce reduced-fat cream cheese, softened

¾ cup reduced-fat sour cream

3 cups cooked turkey breast, cubed

Vegetable oil cooking spray

3 tablespoons Parmesan cheese

Nutritional info (per serving)

Calories......................345	Sodium ....359 mg
From fat.................29%	Cholesterol ....85 mg
Fat................................11 g	Calcium ....180 mg
Saturated...............4 g	Fiber ....4 g
Trans ....0 g	Food exchanges
Carbohydrates ....28 g	2 starch, 3 lean meat,
Protein ....33 g	1 fat

Test Kitchen Tip

To cut the turkey breast into even strips, freeze it for about 20 minutes.

Directions

Prepare pasta according to package directions, omitting the salt. In a large skillet, heat margarine over medium heat. Add onion and garlic and sauté until onions become soft, about 5 minutes. Add mushrooms and continue to sauté an additional 3 to 5 minutes. Stir in flour until blended, then gradually stir in milk so that no lumps form. Season with salt, poultry seasoning, mustard powder and white pepper.

Preheat oven to 375 degrees.

Cook sauce mixture over medium heat, stirring constantly until it thickens. Add wine and combine. Add cream cheese and stir until it is melted. Remove the sauce from the heat and add the sour cream and turkey and stir to combine. Toss the sauce with the cooked pasta and place in a 9- or 10-inch round oven-safe quiche dish coated with vegetable oil cooking spray. Sprinkle the top with Parmesan cheese. Bake for 20 to 25 minutes.

The sauce should bubble slightly and the cheese on top should be golden brown. Let stand a few minutes before slicing and serving.

Ultimate Enchilada Casserole

A serving of this Heart Smart® Ultimate Enchilada Casserole provides a good source of fiber and just five grams of fat per serving.

  10   1 hour 15 mins total

Ingredients

Vegetable oil cooking spray

1 pound ground turkey breast

½ cup chopped onion

½ cup chopped green pepper

1 ½ teaspoons dried oregano

2 teaspoons chili powder

½ teaspoon garlic powder

½ teaspoon ground cumin

¼ teaspoon cayenne pepper

1 tablespoon vinegar

6 medium corn tortillas

1 can (15 ounces) pinto beans, rinsed and drained

2 cans (10 ounces each) enchilada sauce, divided

1 cup shredded, reduced-fat cheddar cheese

1 can (10.5 ounces) reduced-fat, low-sodium cream of chicken soup

1 tablespoon chopped, canned green chilis

Directions

Preheat oven to 350 degrees.

Spray a 2-quart baking dish with vegetable oil cooking spray.

In a large nonstick skillet, cook the ground turkey. Add the onion, green pepper, dried oregano, chili powder, garlic powder, ground cumin, cayenne pepper and vinegar; cook until the onion is tender.

Remove the pan from the heat.

Cut the tortillas into 1-inch strips and then into thirds.

Line the baking dish with half of the tortillas. Top them with half of the meat mixture. Layer with the beans, the remaining meat mixture, one can of enchilada sauce, cheese and the remaining tortillas.

In a small mixing bowl combine the soup, the remaining can of enchilada sauce and the chopped green chilies; pour the sauce over the tortillas.

Bake uncovered for 30 minutes or until the casserole is bubbly and heated through.

Nutritional info (per serving)

Calories	188
From fat	24%
Fat	5 g
Saturated	2 g
Trans	0 g
Carbohydrates	19 g
Protein	17 g
Sodium	595 mg
Cholesterol	39 mg
Calcium	117 mg
Fiber	4 g

Food exchanges
1 starch, 1 vegetable, 2 lean meat

White Bean Chicken Chili

This chili is a Heart Smart® favorite and packs a bite thanks to the canned chilies. You can use more or less chilies to your taste. The Great Northern beans provides an excellent source of fiber to this chili with 13 grams per serving.

 8 (1 ¾-cup servings)   1 hour 10 mins total

Ingredients

2 tablespoons olive oil

¾ pound boneless, skinless chicken breasts, cut into 1-inch cubes

2 large sweet onions, peeled, diced

8 cloves garlic, peeled, minced

1 teaspoon oregano

½ teaspoon ground coriander

½ teaspoon cayenne pepper

2 teaspoons ground cumin

1 cup fresh sliced mushrooms

1 jar (48 ounces) Great Northern beans, rinsed and drained

4 cups fat-free less-sodium chicken broth

2 to 4 cans (4 ounces each) chopped green chilies

1 cup fresh chopped cilantro

Nutritional info (per serving)

Calories........................ 266
    From fat 23%
Fat ....7 g
    Saturated................ 2 g
    Trans .... 0 g
Carbohydrates .... 37 g
Protein ....25 g
Sodium .... 764 mg
Cholesterol .... 33 mg
Calcium .... 212 mg
Fiber .... 13 g
Food exchanges
    2 starch, 1 vegetable
    2 lean meat

Directions

In a large stock pot, heat olive oil over medium heat. Add the cubed chicken breast and cook over medium heat, stirring occasionally, until it's cooked through, about 10 to 15 minutes.

Remove the chicken and set it aside.

Place onions, garlic, oregano, coriander, cayenne pepper, cumin and mushrooms in the pot and cook over medium heat, stirring occasionally, for 15 minutes or until the onions appear translucent.

Add beans, chicken broth and green chilies. Simmer for 30 minutes over medium heat, stirring occasionally. Stir in the chicken and cilantro. Simmer for 10 minutes over medium heat.

Test Kitchen Tip
To easily peel cloves of garlic, place on counter and press down firmly on it with the side of a chef's knife. The skin should split so it's easy to remove.

Fish and Shellfish

Fish and Shellfish

Research findings on the health benefits of adding fish to your weekly menu continue to grow. The studies are so promising that the American Heart Association recommends eating at least two servings of fish per week to promote heart health. The 2010 Dietary Guidelines for Americans echo that recommendation, advising the general public to consume eight ounces of seafood per week.

Not only is seafood low in artery-clogging saturated fat, it offers the omega-3 fatty acids, eicosapentaenoic acid (EPA) and docosahexaenoic acid (DHA). While the ways in which these omega-3 fatty acids reduce heart disease are still being studied, research has shown they make blood platelets less sticky, which helps prevent plaque build-up that can lead to heart attack and stroke. They also may help reduce blood triglyceride levels and may lower blood pressure in some people.

It is fine to select seafood that is lower in omega-3 fatty acids, just be sure to include choices with higher amounts, such as salmon, tuna, trout and Atlantic or Pacific mackerel. Try the recipes in this chapter. Sweet and Sour Shrimp, Oven-Fried Catfish, Parmesan-Encrusted Rainbow Trout and Grilled Salmon with Orange Glaze are just few of our favorites. While the American Heart Association

and other health authorities remain in favor of eating fish, the Food and Drug Administration and the Environmental Protection Agency have a few recommendations for pregnant women, women who might become pregnant, nursing mothers and young children.

• Do not eat shark, tilefish, swordfish, or king mackerel, due to high levels of mercury.

• Choose a variety of fish and seafood, and avoid eating the same type more than once a week. It is safe to eat up to 12 ounces a week of a variety of fish and shellfish that are lower in mercury. Five of the most commonly eaten fish that are low in mercury are: shrimp, canned light tuna, salmon, pollock and catfish. Since canned white albacore tuna has more mercury than canned light tuna, no more than six ounces of albacore tuna should be consumed in a week.

• Check local advisories about the safety of fish caught in local rivers, lakes and streams. If no advice is available, eat no more than six ounces per week and don't consume any other fish that week.

Baked Orange Roughy

Seafood is low in saturated fat and offers a special type of fat called omega-3 fatty acids or omega-3s. Research shows that omega-3s help prevent plaque build-up that can lead to heart attack and stroke. They may also reduce blood triglyceride levels. Mackerel, lake trout, herring, sardines, albacore tuna, whitefish and salmon are highest in omega-3s, but eating any fish — such as this Heart Smart® Baked Orange Roughy — is a healthy choice.

4   **30 mins total**

Ingredients

Vegetable oil cooking spray

1 pound orange roughy fillets

2 tablespoons olive oil

2 teaspoons lemon juice

1 teaspoon paprika

1 teaspoon garlic powder

1 teaspoon onion powder

¼ teaspoon ground black pepper

¼ teaspoon salt

¼ teaspoon ground white pepper

¼ teaspoon ground cayenne pepper

3 tablespoons grated Parmesan cheese

1 tablespoon dry bread crumbs

Directions

Preheat oven to 425 degrees. Coat a shallow baking pan with vegetable oil cooking spray; place fish fillets in the pan.

In a small bowl, combine olive oil, lemon juice, paprika, garlic powder, onion powder, black pepper, salt, white pepper and cayenne pepper. Spoon or brush half the mixture over fish.

To the remaining oil mixture, add the Parmesan cheese and bread crumbs; mix well. Spoon onto fish and spread evenly. Bake 10 to 15 minutes (depending on thickness of fish), or until fish flakes easily with a fork.

Nutritional info (per serving)

Calories...................... 181
    From fat................45%

Fat.................................9 g
    Saturated................2 g
    Trans ....0 g

Carbohydrates ....3 g

Protein ....21 g

Sodium .... 252 mg

Cholesterol .... 71 mg

Calcium .... 59 mg

Fiber ....1 g

Food exchanges
    3 lean meat, 1 fat

Test Kitchen Tip

The general rule-of-thumb for cooking fish is to cook it 10 minutes per 1-inch of thickness. This is often referred to as the Canadian rule.

Barramundi Piccata

Barramundi is a mild tasting, white-flesh fish farmed-raised by Australis Aquaculture, based outside Boston. Barramundi is known for its high amounts of omega-3 fatty acids, which are good fats that promote heart and brain health, with 833 milligrams in a 5-ounce serving. By comparison, wild Coho salmon has 900 milligrams. Barramundi can be baked, broiled and sautéed.

 4   30 mins total

Ingredients

2 teaspoons plus 1 tablespoon olive oil, divided

2 tablespoons finely diced shallots

2 cloves garlic, peeled, minced

¼ cup fresh squeezed lemon juice

¼ cup dry white wine

2 tablespoons capers, rinsed

1 tablespoon trans fat-free margarine

4 (4 ounces each) barramundi fillets or favorite firm white fish

4 cups baby spinach leaves

¼ teaspoon salt, divided

¼ teaspoon freshly ground black pepper, divided

1 tablespoon finely chopped parsley, optional

Directions

In a large skillet, heat 2 teaspoons oil over medium heat. Sauté the shallots and garlic until softened, about 3 minutes. Stir in the lemon juice, wine, capers and margarine. Combine ingredients and simmer 3 minutes. Place the fillets in the sauce and simmer for an additional 5 to 8 minutes or until fish flakes.

In a bowl, drizzle the spinach leaves with remaining 1 tablespoon oil and season with an ⅛ teaspoon salt and ⅛ teaspoon black pepper. Place the fillets on top of the spinach, drizzle with the wine caper sauce and season with the remaining ⅛ teaspoon salt and ⅛ teaspoon black pepper.

Garnish with parsley if desired.

Nutritional info (per serving)

Calories......................183
    From fat.................39%

Fat ....8 g
    Saturated.................1 g
    Trans ....0 g

Carbohydrates ....4 g

Protein ....21 g

Sodium ....359 mg

Cholesterol ....47 mg

Calcium ....51 mg

Fiber ....1 g

Food exchanges
    3 lean meat, 1 fat
    1 vegetable

Broiled Salmon with Yogurt Sauce

Research findings on the health benefits of adding fish to your weekly menu continue to mount. The studies are so promising that the American Heart Association recommends eating at least two servings of fish per week to promote heart health. Not only is seafood low in artery-clogging saturated fat, it offers a special type of fat called omega-3 fatty acids. The American Heart Association recommends eating fatty, cold-water varieties such as trout, herring, sardines, whitefish and salmon.

 4   **35 mins total**

Ingredients

Vegetable oil cooking spray

4 small salmon fillets, about ¾-inch thick (about 1 pound)

YOGURT SAUCE

6 ounces fat-free, plain yogurt

3 tablespoons reduced-fat mayonnaise

1 teaspoon dried dill weed

2 tablespoons trans fat-free margarine, melted

¼ teaspoon salt

¼ teaspoon freshly ground black pepper

1 teaspoon lemon zest

1 clove garlic, peeled, minced

½ cup peeled, seeded and coarsely chopped cucumber

Directions

Set oven to broil. Spray a broiler pan with vegetable oil cooking spray. Place the salmon fillets on the broiler pan. Brush the salmon with the melted margarine and sprinkle with salt and pepper. Broil fillets about 4 inches from the heat source for about 8 minutes or until cooked through.

To prepare the yogurt sauce: Mix the yogurt, mayonnaise, dill weed, lemon zest, garlic and cucumber together in a small bowl.

Remove salmon from broiler and top each salmon fillet with ¼ cup of yogurt sauce.

Nutritional info (per serving)

Calories........................242
    From fat 48%

Fat ....13 g
    Saturated................ 2 g
    Trans ....0 g

Carbohydrates .... 6 g

Protein ....24 g

Sodium ....302 mg

Cholesterol .... 64 mg

Calcium .... 105 mg

Fiber ....1 g

Food exchanges
    3 meat, 1 fat

Cod Italiano

Olive varieties number in the dozens: Manzanilla, kalamata, niçoise, lugano and picholine, to name a few. While all fresh olives are bitter, the final flavor of the fruit depends on how ripe it is when picked and the processing it receives. Olives are pickled or preserved using oil, water, brine or dry-curing methods. Sodium watchers, take note: Don't overdo this delectable fruit. Ten large olives provide more than 20% of your day's maximum requirement of sodium. The half cup of olives added to this Cod Italiano recipe provides wonderful flavor without causing sodium sticker shock.

4 | 30 mins total

Ingredients

2 cups cooked linguine

2 tablespoons olive oil

1 cup chopped onion

1 cup zucchini, julienned

2 cloves garlic, peeled, minced

½ cup pitted kalamata olives, halved

1 can (14.5 ounces) no-salt-added diced tomatoes

½ cup dry white wine

1 tablespoon balsamic vinegar

1 teaspoon Italian seasoning

½ teaspoon salt

¼ teaspoon ground black pepper

1 pound cod fillets, cut into 4 equal pieces

8 teaspoons grated Parmesan cheese

Test Kitchen Tip

Domestic and imported olives are available bottled, canned and in bulk year-round. Unopened olives may be stored at room temperature for up to two years. Once opened, they can be refrigerated in their own liquid in a nonmetal container for several weeks.

Directions

Cook linguine according to package directions, omitting the salt. Drain and set aside.

In a large skillet, heat oil over medium heat. Add onions, zucchini and garlic and sauté until softened, about 5 minutes. Stir in olives, tomatoes, wine, balsamic vinegar, Italian seasoning, salt and black pepper. Combine ingredients and simmer for 5 minutes. Place the cod fillets directly in the sauce. Cover and simmer for 5 minutes or until fish flakes.

Serve each cod fillet with ½ cup cooked linguine and ⅔ cup tomato sauce. Sprinkle each serving with 2 teaspoons grated Parmesan cheese.

Nutritional info (per serving)

Calories...................... 356
    From fat................. 28%
Fat .... 11 g
    Saturated .... 2 g
    Trans .... 0 g
Carbohydrates .... 33 g
Protein .... 26 g
Sodium .... 550 mg
Cholesterol .... 50 mg
Calcium .... 94 mg
Fiber .... 3 g
Food exchanges
    1 starch, 3 lean meat,
    3 vegetable, 1 fat

Crab Cakes with Remoulade Sauce

Thought you couldn't enjoy crabmeat on a heart-healthy diet? These Crab Cakes with Remoulade Sauce fit well into a Heart Smart® eating plan. All seafood, including shellfish, is low in saturated fat. People who consume more saturated fat tend to have higher levels of bad LDL cholesterol and that increases heart disease risk. Crabmeat also provides heart-healthy omega-3 fatty acids.

 8 2 hour 5 mins total

Ingredients

REMOULADE SAUCE

¼ cup plain fat-free yogurt

¼ cup low-fat mayonnaise

2 tablespoons minced green onion

1 tablespoon sweet pickle relish

1 tablespoon Creole or Dijon mustard

1 tablespoon minced parsley

2 teaspoons lemon juice

1 teaspoon Worcestershire sauce

⅛ teaspoon paprika

3 to 4 dashes hot sauce

CRAB CAKES

1 ½ cups water

½ cup uncooked wild rice

1 pound lump crabmeat, shell pieces removed

¾ cup dry bread crumbs

¼ cup finely chopped celery

¼ cup chopped green onion

¼ cup reduced-fat mayonnaise

2 tablespoons minced parsley

1 tablespoon lemon juice

1 teaspoon dry mustard

⅛ teaspoon cayenne pepper

⅛ teaspoon ground black pepper

2 large egg whites, lightly beaten

4 teaspoons canola oil, divided

Nutritional info (per serving)

Calories	196	Sodium	453 mg
From fat	28%	Cholesterol	57 mg
Fat	6 g	Calcium	107 mg
Saturated	1 g	Fiber	1 g
Trans	0 g	Food exchanges	
Carbohydrates	19 g	1 starch, 2 meat	
Protein	16 g		

Test Kitchen Tip

Most of the cooking time with this recipe is because of the wild rice – which takes an hour to cook. While the rice is cooking prepare all the other ingredients.

Directions

In a small bowl, mix together all ingredients for the remoulade sauce. Cover and store in the refrigerator until ready to serve. To prepare crab cakes, bring water to a boil in a medium saucepan. Add wild rice, cover, reduce heat and simmer 1 hour or until tender. In a large bowl, combine cooked wild rice, crab meat, bread crumbs, celery, green onion, mayonnaise, parsley, lemon juice, dry mustard, cayenne pepper, ground black pepper and egg whites. Divide mixture into 8 equal portions, shaping each into a 1-inch thick patty. Heat 2 teaspoons oil in a large nonstick skillet over medium heat. Add 4 patties; cook 4 minutes. Carefully turn patties over and cook an additional 4 minutes or until golden brown. Repeat procedure with remaining oil and patties. Serve with remoulade sauce.

Crumb-Coated Flounder

The American Heart Association recommends eating at least two servings of fish, particularly fatty fish, every week. One serving is 3 ½ ounces cooked or about ¾ cup of flaked fish. Fatty fish that provide very healthy doses of omega-3s include trout, herring, sardines, whitefish and salmon. This recipe features flounder, and although it isn't listed as one of the omega-3 powerhouses, it's a great choice and contains half the amount of recommended omega-3s. Flounder is a great source of high-quality protein without the artery-clogging saturated fat found in such protein sources as beef, pork and dark poultry meat. In this recipe, you can also use cod, halibut or sole.

 5   1 hour total

Ingredients

1 tablespoon canola oil

5 flounder fillets, about 5 ounces each

10 reduced-fat buttery round crackers (such as reduced-fat Ritz)

¼ cup grated Parmesan cheese

½ teaspoon all-purpose seasoning (such as Old Bay Seasoning)

¼ teaspoon garlic powder

¼ teaspoon ground black pepper

1 tablespoon trans fat-free margarine, melted

Directions

Preheat oven to 400 degrees.

Place oil in a 13-by-9-inch baking dish, tilting to coat the entire bottom. Place fillets in the baking dish, turning once to coat both sides of the fish.

In a resealable bag, crush crackers to a crumb consistency. Add Paremsan cheese, all-purpose seasoning, garlic powder and black pepper, reseal the bag and combine.

In a measuring cup, melt the margarine. Add crumb mixture and combine to coat the dry ingredients. Place the crumb mixture over the fillets and bake, uncovered for 18 to 20 minutes or until the fish flakes easily with a fork.

Test Kitchen Tip

When purchasing fresh fish, select a reputable store and buy only fresh seafood that is refrigerated or displayed on thick layers of ice. The flesh should appear moist, shiny and firm. Fish should have a clean, fresh, mild odor that reminds you of the ocean. It's best to cook and eat fresh fish the day it's purchased. Store fresh fish no more than two days in the refrigerator.

Watch This!

Scan this QR code with your smartphone to watch the Heart Smart® video.

Nutritional info (per serving)

Calories	200
From fat	31%
Fat	7 g
Saturated	1 g
Trans	0 g
Carbohydrates	5 g
Protein	28 g
Sodium	292 mg
Cholesterol	66 mg
Calcium	68 mg
Fiber	0 g

Food exchanges
4 lean meat, 1 fat

Honey Balsamic Glazed Salmon Fillets

These salmon fillets are brushed with a glaze made with balsamic vinegar and orange juice. Balsamic vinegar, made from Trebbiano grapes, is a dark colored, sweet and sour vinegar aged in wood barrels. It's a good match as a glaze for salmon and other fish. To cut calories, make salad dressings from vinegars such as balsamic, champagne, fruit or rice wine vinegar. These are less pungent so you can use a higher ratio of vinegar to oil.

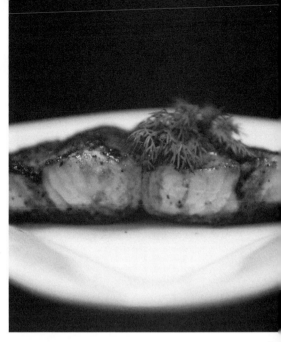

 4    30 mins total

Ingredients

Vegetable oil cooking spray

4 salmon fillets, about ¾-inch-thick and 5 ounce each, skin removed

¼ teaspoon salt

¼ teaspoon ground black pepper

3 tablespoons balsamic vinegar

1 tablespoon honey

1 tablespoon orange juice

2 teaspoons Dijon mustard

4 fresh dill sprigs, optional

Directions

Preheat oven to 400 degrees.

Line a baking sheet with aluminum foil and coat with vegetable oil cooking spray. Arrange the salmon fillets on the baking sheet and season the top of each fillet with salt and black pepper.

In a small saucepan over medium heat, cook balsamic vinegar, honey, orange juice and Dijon mustard. Simmer uncovered for 3 to 5 minutes, or until slightly thickened. Brush fillets with the balsamic glaze and bake for 10 to 14 minutes or until the flesh flakes easily with a fork. Top each salmon fillet with a sprig of fresh dill if desired.

Nutritional info (per serving)

Calories...................... 228
    From fat 36%
Fat ....9 g
    Saturated................1 g
    Trans ....0 g
Carbohydrates ....7 g
Protein .... 27 g
Sodium ....243 mg
Cholesterol ....75 mg
Calcium ....18 mg
Fiber ....0 g
Food exchanges
    4 meat

Test Kitchen Tip

Store vinegar in a cool, dark place. Unopened, most vinegar will last for about two years; opened, it will keep for about six months.

Orange Matcha Salmon

This salmon recipe, from the file of chef Frank Turner, director of Culinary Wellness at Henry Ford West Bloomfield Hospital, is poached in a Matcha tea-infused liquid. It's known for its nutrient and antioxidant qualities because the whole leaf is consumed, not just the liquid brewed from the leaf. Sources say that one glass of matcha tea is equivalent to 10 glasses of regular green tea. If you have salmon leftover from this recipe, it's a terrific addition to any mixed greens salad.

Test Kitchen Tip

When buying salmon, buy a whole salmon fillet, and cut it into individual portions. Wrap it well in freezer-quality plastic wrap and place in a freezer bag. This way you can take out the portions you need, and it's an easier way to cook the thinner, tapered tail section.

 4   25 mins total

Ingredients

ORANGE GLAZE

1 ½ cups fresh squeezed orange juice

1 teaspoon orange zest (from 1 orange)

1 tablespoon reduced-sodium soy sauce

1 tablespoon sugar

POACHING LIQUID

1 cup water

1 tablespoon Matcha green tea leaves

1 bay leaf

½ tablespoon whole black peppercorns

4 salmon fillets, about 4 ounces each (wild caught)

Directions

Preheat broiler. To prepare the glaze, combine the orange juice, orange zest, soy sauce and sugar in a saucepan. Over medium high heat, reduce glaze at least by half or until it thickens slightly; set aside. Combine water, tea leaves, bay leaf and peppercorns in a large shallow pan. On stovetop, bring the poaching liquid to a temperature of 170 degrees. Place salmon fillets in the liquid for 2 minutes. Turn fillets over and poach 1 additional minute. Remove salmon from the liquid, place on a baking sheet and pat dry with paper towel. Cover fillets with glaze and place under the broiler for 2 to 3 minutes until slightly browned. Serve immediately.

Nutritional info (per serving)

Calories.......................215
　　From fat.................29%

Fat ....7 g
　　Saturated.................1 g
　　Trans ....0 g

Carbohydrates .... 14 g

Protein .... 24 g

Sodium .... 178 mg

Cholesterol .... 48 mg

Calcium .... 51 mg

Fiber .... 0 g

Food exchanges
　　3 lean meat, ½ fruit

Oven-Fried Fish Sticks with Mustard Sauce

These easy-to-make fish sticks are a good option for kids. They're oven-fried and served with a tangy mustard sauce that's a good substitute for tartar sauce.

 4   30 mins total

Ingredients

Vegetable oil cooking spray

1 pound cod or other white fish fillet

¼ cup low-fat buttermilk

½ cup yellow cornmeal

¼ cup plain bread crumbs

MUSTARD SAUCE

⅓ cup low-fat mayonnaise

½ teaspoon red wine vinegar

1 teaspoon Dijon mustard

1 teaspoon fresh parsley, chopped

¼ teaspoon salt

¼ teaspoon ground black pepper

¼ teaspoon garlic powder

¼ teaspoon chili powder

1 ½ teaspoons green onions, chopped

½ teaspoon ground mustard

Nutritional info (per serving)

Calories.......................215
    From fat................13%
Fat..................................3 g
    Saturated................1 g
    Trans.......................0 g
Carbohydrates...........23 g
Protein........................22 g

Sodium.................484 mg
Cholesterol.............51 mg
Calcium..................64 mg
Fiber...........................2 g
Food exchanges
    1 ½ starch,
    3 lean meat

 Test Kitchen Tip

Freeze the fish fillets for about 20 minutes for easy slicing.

Directions

Preheat oven to 425 degrees. Coat baking sheet with vegetable oil cooking spray and set it aside.

Cut fish fillets diagonally into 1-inch-wide strips.

In a bowl, combine buttermilk and fish strips, stirring gently.

In a heavy-duty plastic sealable bag, combine the cornmeal, bread crumbs, salt, black pepper, garlic powder and chili powder.

Add fish strips; seal the bag and gently turn the bag to coat the fish. Place the fish strips on the baking sheet.

Gently spray the tops of the fish sticks with cooking spray. Bake for 25 minutes or until the fish is crisp and flakes easily when tested with a fork. Meanwhile, to prepare the mustard sauce, stir together all the sauce ingredients in a bowl and serve the sauce with the fish.

Oven-Fried Catfish

This simple Oven-Fried Catfish is an easy-to-make weeknight option. The catfish is breaded in a cornmeal spiced coating and baked at high temperature so the coating crisps. Round this meal out with a crisp mixed greens salad.

 4   **35 mins total**

Ingredients

½ cup cornmeal

1 ½ teaspoons seafood seasoning blend (such as Old Bay Seasoning)

1 ¼ teaspoons garlic powder

1 ¼ teaspoons onion powder

½ teaspoon ground black pepper

⅛ teaspoon salt

⅓ cup low-fat buttermilk

4 catfish fillets, about 5 ounces each

Vegetable oil cooking spray

Nutritional info (per serving)

Calories........................ 191	Sodium ....381 mg
From fat................. 19%	Cholesterol .... 83 mg
Fat................................. 4 g	Calcium ....37 mg
Saturated ....1 g	Fiber ....1 g
Trans ....0 g	Food exchanges
Carbohydrates .... 14 g	1 starch, 3 lean meat
Protein ....23 g	

Directions

Preheat oven to 425 degrees. In a small bowl or measuring cup, combine cornmeal, seafood seasoning blend, garlic powder, onion powder, black pepper and salt.

Place buttermilk in a shallow dish and cornmeal spice coating in a separate shallow dish. Dip the catfish fillets in buttermilk then dredge in cornmeal mixture. Coat large, rimmed baking sheet with vegetable oil cooking spray. Place the catfish fillets on baking sheet and coat the top of the fillets with vegetable oil cooking spray. Bake about 15 to 20 minutes or until the fish is easily flaked with a fork.

Parmesan-Encrusted Rainbow Trout

This recipe features rainbow trout, which belongs to the same family as heart-healthy salmon. It has a tender but firm flesh and a mild, somewhat nutty flavor. Arctic char, related to both trout and salmon, is a silver fish living in the icy waters of North America and Europe. Arctic char has become more commercially available in recent years. Its pink, tender, somewhat sweet flesh is a cross between trout and salmon. It can be used in this recipe as well.

 4    35 mins total

Ingredients

16 ounces rainbow trout

2 tablespoons paprika

1 tablespoon garlic powder

¼ teaspoon ground black pepper

½ cup grated Parmesan cheese

2 teaspoons dried parsley flakes

1 tablespoon trans fat-free margarine, cut into pieces

3 tablespoons lemon juice

Directions

Preheat oven to 425 degrees.

Place the fish on a large baking sheet lined with foil and sprinkle with paprika, garlic powder and black pepper. In a small bowl, combine the Parmesan cheese and parsley flakes. Sprinkle the mixture on top of the fish and press gently.

Place margarine pieces on top of the fish. Pour lemon juice over the top and sides of the fish.

Loosely cover the fish with a piece of foil and bake for 10 minutes. Remove the foil and bake an additional 5 to 10 minutes to allow the Parmesan cheese to form a crust. For a very crunchy crust, place under the broiler for about 5 minutes.

Remove from the oven, cut into four equal portions and serve.

Nutritional info (per serving)

Calories...................... 233
    From fat 46%
Fat .... 12 g
    Saturated............... 4 g
    Trans .... 0 g
Carbohydrates .... 5 g
Protein ....25 g
Sodium .... 226 mg
Cholesterol ....67 mg
Calcium .... 196 mg
Fiber .... 2 g
Food exchanges
    3 lean meat, 1 fat

Shrimp Enchiladas

These Shrimp Enchiladas are easy enough to make for a weeknight dinner. Using green chili enchilada sauce gives them a slightly spicy kick. When choosing shrimp for this recipe, use a large shrimp and only coarsely chop them. The shrimp pieces should be discernable.

Nutritional info (per serving)

Calories......................158	Sodium ....448 mg
From fat................28%	Cholesterol .... 62 mg
Fat ....5 g	Calcium ....93 mg
Saturated.................1 g	Fiber ....1 g
Trans ....0 g	Food exchanges
Carbohydrates ....18 g	1 starch, 1 lean meat, 1 fat
Protein ....9 g	

Test Kitchen Tip

Having a bag of frozen shrimp on hand is a good go-to ingredient for making easy weeknight meals. When buying shrimp, keep in mind it is sold and labeled by the number of shrimp per pound. For example, large shrimp, used in this recipe, generally has 21 to 30 shrimp per pound and small has 36 to 45 shrimp per pound.

 12   1 hour 15 mins total

Ingredients

Vegetable oil cooking spray

2 tablespoons trans fat-free margarine

1 cup diced onion

1 cup diced red bell pepper

1 minced jalapeño pepper

1 clove garlic, peeled, minced

1 pound peeled, deveined and coarsely chopped large raw shrimp

½ teaspoon ground cumin

½ teaspoon chili powder

2 cans (10 ounces each) green chili enchilada sauce

½ cup (2 ounces) reduced-fat shredded sharp cheddar cheese

2 tablespoons (1 ounce) reduced-fat cream cheese

12 white corn tortillas, 6-inch in diameter

2 tablespoons reduced-fat sour cream

1 can (4 ounces) diced green chilies

¾ cup favorite salsa

Directions

Preheat oven to 350 degrees. Coat a 9-by-13-inch baking dish with vegetable oil cooking spray.

In a large nonstick skillet, heat margarine over medium heat. Add onion, bell pepper, jalapeño pepper and garlic and sauté until vegetables soften, about 3 minutes. Add shrimp, cumin and chili powder and continue to sauté until shrimp are pink and some of the liquid in the pan has evaporated, about 5 to 8 minutes. Stir in ½ cup of the enchilada sauce, cheddar cheese and cream cheese. Spread ¼ cup enchilada sauce in the bottom of the baking dish.

Working with 4 tortillas at a time, place them on a plate and microwave for about 30 seconds to soften. Spoon about ¼ cup of the shrimp mixture on a tortilla and roll up. Place in baking dish. Repeat with remaining tortillas, fitting them snugly in the dish. In a small bowl, combine the remaining enchilada sauce, sour cream and green chilies. Pour the sauce over the enchiladas, cover with foil and place in the oven for 20 to 30 minutes. Remove the foil and continue to bake an additional 10 to 15 minutes. Serve with salsa. One serving consists of one enchilada topped with one table-spoon salsa.

Spicy Cornmeal Cod with Tartar Sauce

If you like tartar sauce with fish, try this Heart Smart® version. Using low-fat yogurt and reduced-fat mayonnaise cuts the calories, while sweet pickle relish and red wine vinegar give it a tangy flavor.

 6   1 hour 15 mins total

Ingredients

SAUCE

¾ cup plain low-fat yogurt

¼ cup reduced-fat mayonnaise

2 tablespoons minced green onion

2 tablespoons minced parsley

1 tablespoon lemon juice

2 tablespoons sweet pickle relish

2 teaspoons red wine vinegar

1 teaspoon Worcestershire sauce

¼ teaspoon freshly ground black pepper

⅛ teaspoon ground red pepper

COD

1 ½ pounds cod fillets

¾ cup yellow cornmeal

¼ cup all-purpose flour

2 tablespoons Parmesan cheese

½ teaspoon salt

¼ teaspoon ground black pepper

¼ teaspoon garlic powder

⅛ teaspoon ground cayenne pepper

¼ cup fat-free egg substitute

¼ cup skim milk

Vegetable oil cooking spray

Directions

In a small bowl, mix together all the sauce ingredients. Cover the sauce with plastic wrap and refrigerate at least 1 hour.

Preheat oven to 425 degrees.

Cut the cod fillets into 4-inch-by-2-inch pieces.

In a heavy-duty zip-top plastic bag, mix the cornmeal, flour, Parmesan cheese, salt, black pepper, garlic powder and cayenne pepper.

In a bowl, combine the egg substitute and milk. Dip the fish pieces into the egg mixture, then place them in the zip-top bag, seal the bag and gently turn the bag to coat the fish.

Place the fish on a baking sheet coated with cooking spray.

Bake for 10 to 15 minutes, turning the fish once, or until the fish is crisp and flakes easily when tested with a fork. Remove the fish from the oven and serve it with the tartar sauce.

Nutritional info (per serving)

Calories...................... 249	Sodium ....451 mg
From fat................. 18%	Cholesterol .... 54 mg
Fat .... 5 g	Calcium ....,. 109 mg
Saturated..................1 g	Fiber .... 2 g
Trans .... 0 g	Food exchanges
Carbohydrates ....23 g	1 ½ starch,
Protein .... 25 g	3 lean meat

Smoked Salmon Salad

Fruits and vegetables contain soluble fiber, the type of fiber shown to have heart health benefits by lowering blood cholesterol levels. The oranges and carrots in this smoked salmon salad are great sources of soluble fiber. This refreshing main-dish salad qualifies as a good source of fiber, with 7 grams per serving.

 2   35 mins total

Ingredients

½ cup orange juice

2 teaspoons olive oil

2 teaspoons rice vinegar

1 teaspoon Dijon mustard

1 teaspoon orange marmalade

¼ teaspoon freshly ground black pepper

4 cups torn fresh spinach

1 can (15 ounces) mandarin orange segments, drained

6 ounces smoked salmon, cut into chunks

6 tablespoons shredded carrots

½ red onion, thinly sliced into rings

Directions

In a small bowl, whisk together orange juice, olive oil, rice vinegar, Dijon, orange marmalade and black pepper. Set the dressing aside. Place 2 cups of torn spinach on two salad plates. Divide the mandarin orange segments between the plates. Top each salad with salmon, shredded carrots and red onion slices. Drizzle with the dressing.

Nutritional info (per serving)

Calories...................... 244
    From fat................. 31%
Fat................................. 9 g
    Saturated.................1 g
    Trans ....0 g
Carbohydrates ....24 g
Protein .... 19 g

Sodium .... 784 mg
Cholesterol .... 20 mg
Calcium .... 90 mg
Fiber ....7 g
Food exchanges
    2 meat, 1 fruit,
    2 vegetable

Sweet and Sour Shrimp

Because of its slightly elevated cholesterol content, shrimp was once considered unhealthy for those pursuing a heart-healthy diet. Although shrimp has about twice as much cholesterol as other meat, it is extremely low in artery-clogging saturated fat and total fat. Research suggests that dietary cholesterol is less of a heart danger than saturated fat. Just keep the portion size moderate — 3 to 4 ounces — and enjoy it baked, grilled, broiled, boiled or stir-fried.

 4   **40 mins total**

Ingredients

2 tablespoons cornstarch, divided

½ teaspoon salt, divided

1 egg white

8 ounces large raw shrimp, peeled and deveined

1 can (8 ounces) pineapple chunks, packed in juice

3 tablespoons sugar

3 tablespoons ketchup

3 tablespoons cider vinegar

2 tablespoons canola oil

1 clove garlic, peeled, chopped

½ cup ¾-inch onion pieces

½ cup ¾-inch green pepper pieces

½ cup red bell pepper strips

½ cup carrot strips

3 cups cooked brown rice (prepared without salt or fat)

Directions

In a medium bowl, whisk together 1 tablespoon cornstarch, ¼ teaspoon salt and egg white. Add shrimp and stir well to coat. Cover and marinate in the refrigerator for 15 minutes. Drain pineapple chunks and reserve the juice. Dissolve the remaining 1 tablespoon of cornstarch in the reserved pineapple juice.

In a small bowl, combine remaining ¼ teaspoon salt, sugar, ketchup, cider vinegar and cornstarch/pineapple juice mixture; set aside.

In a wok or large skillet, heat oil over medium-high heat. Remove shrimp from the marinade and discard the marinade. Add the garlic and shrimp to the wok and stir-fry 1 minute. Add the onion, green pepper, red bell pepper, carrots and pineapple and stir-fry an additional 2 to 4 minutes. Add the ketchup sauce and continue to cook 1 minute or until sauce has thickened and bubbles. One serving contains 1 cup of shrimp sauce over ¾ cup cooked brown rice.

Nutritional info (per serving)

Calories	395
From fat	21%
Fat	9 g
Saturated	1 g
Trans	0 g
Carbohydrates	65 g
Protein	15 g
Sodium	332 mg
Cholesterol	83 mg
Calcium	59 mg
Fiber	5 g

Food exchanges
2 starch, 1 lean meat,
3 vegetable, 1 fruit, 1 fat

Test Kitchen Tip

When purchasing fresh, raw shrimp let your nose be your guide. Raw shrimp should smell of the sea with no hint of ammonia. Most shrimp is frozen immediately after being caught and then thawed. Use raw, unfrozen shrimp the same day it's purchased. Shrimp meat should be firm and the shells should be shiny. Avoid shrimp with black spots, which is a sign of aging.

Meatless and Vegetarian

Meatless and Vegetarian

Vegetarian diets have gained mainstream acceptance and popularity in recent years. Even the latest Dietary Guidelines for Americans, while not discouraging consumption of meat, urge Americans to eat a diet consisting mostly of vegetables, fruits and whole grains.

Plant-based diets offer many health advantages. Vegetarians tend to have lower incidences of obesity, cardiovascular disease, hypertension and certain types of cancer than nonvegetarians. Vegetarian diets are typically lower in calories, total fat, artery-clogging saturated fat and cholesterol. They also tend to include more beneficial nutrients such as folate, vitamins C and E, potassium and fiber.

Vegetarian eating patterns vary widely. The lacto-ovo vegetarian enjoys grains, vegetables, fruits, legumes, nuts, seeds, dairy products and eggs, but exclude meat, fish and poultry. The vegan, or total vegetarian, excludes all animal products, as well as dairy and eggs. And some individuals classify themselves as part-time vegetarians — called flexitarians — and they focus on plant foods but also dabble in meat.

Following a part-time vegetarian diet just means eating more plant-based meals without having to forgo meat entirely. In fact, you might already be a part-time vegetarian and not even know it. If peanut butter and jelly, pasta with marina sauce, or veggie pizza frequently appear on your kitchen table, you are a part-time vegetarian.

The recipes in this section can inspire you to include more meatless meals throughout the week without drastically changing your favorite dishes. Try our Eggplant Rolatini or Farfalle and Mushrooms with Walnut Sauce. And if you want a vegetarian alternative to your favorite lasagna recipe, our Roasted Vegetable Lasagna is a winner and was selected as one of the Best Free Press Test Kitchen recipes for 2010.

Angel Hair Pasta with Marinara

Much of the sodium we consume is hidden in prepared and processed foods like lunch meats, canned soups and frozen dinners. Eating less sodium might be easier than you think. This marinara sauce recipe calls for no-added-salt whole tomatoes as a way to reduce the sodium. Depending on the brand, two 28-ounce cans of whole tomatoes could add more than 3,000 milligrams of sodium to this recipe. Using no-added-salt tomatoes add about 200 milligrams of sodium — a huge sodium savings.

  8 · 55 mins total

Ingredients

- 2 cans (28 ounces each) no-added salt whole peeled tomatoes
- 4 tablespoons olive oil, divided
- 1/8 teaspoon crushed red pepper flakes
- 1 cup chopped onion
- 3 cloves garlic, peeled, minced
- 1/2 cup shredded carrots
- 2 teaspoons dried oregano
- 2 teaspoons dried basil
- 1/2 cup red wine
- 1 bay leaf
- 2 teaspoons sugar
- 3/4 teaspoon salt
- 1/2 teaspoon black pepper
- 8 cups cooked whole-wheat angel hair pasta
- 1/2 cup grated Parmesan cheese

Directions

Pour tomatoes into a strainer over a large bowl, reserving the liquid; set aside.

In a large skillet, heat 2 tablespoons olive oil over medium heat. Add red pepper flakes and sauté 1 minute. Add the onion and continue to sauté until softened, about 6 to 8 minutes. Add the garlic, carrots, oregano and basil and cook, stirring constantly, until garlic is fragrant, about 30 seconds.

Increase heat to medium high and add the drained tomatoes to the skillet, gently crushing and squeezing excess liquid from each one before adding to the skillet. Cook, stirring every minute until the liquid has evaporated and the tomatoes begin to stick to the bottom of the pan and brown bits (called fond) form about 10 to 12 minutes.

Add the red wine and cook until thickened, stirring to loosen browned bits from the bottom of the pan, about 1 minute. Add the reserved tomato liquid and bay leaf and bring to a simmer; reduce heat to medium and cook, stirring occasionally until the sauce is thick, about 8 to 10 minutes. Add the sugar, salt, black pepper and remaining 2 tablespoons olive oil. Serve sauce over pasta; sprinkle with cheese. One serving consists of 1 cup cooked pasta topped with 2/3 cup marinara sauce and 1 tablespoon Parmesan cheese.

Nutritional info (per serving)

Calories 334
    From fat 24%
Fat .... 9 g
    Saturated .... 2 g
    Trans .... 0 g
Carbohydrates .... 50 g
Protein .... 13 g

Sodium .... 299 mg
Cholesterol .... 4 mg
Calcium .... 80 mg
Fiber .... 4 g
Food exchanges
    2 starch, 3 vegetable,
    1 fat

Black Bean and Brown Rice Burritos

In association with Johns Hopkins Bloomberg School of Public Health, the Meatless Monday national public health campaign is designed to help Americans prevent four of the leading causes of premature death — heart disease, stroke, diabetes, and cancer. Meatless Monday encourages Americans to move toward a more balanced approach to healthy eating by limiting their intake of meat and artery-clogging saturated fat, and adding more fruits, vegetables and whole grains to the diet. Going meatless once a week is a simple way to lower saturated fat intake. Try these Black Bean and Brown Rice Burritos as a meatless meal to serve on Monday, or any day of the week.

 6   25 mins total

Ingredients

6 flour tortillas (6-inch each)

1 tablespoon olive oil

¾ cup chopped onion

¾ cup chopped red bell pepper

1 clove garlic, peeled, minced

1 tablespoon finely diced jalapeño pepper

2 teaspoons chili powder

1 teaspoon ground cumin

1 can (15 ounces) black beans, drained and rinsed

3 ounces reduced-fat cream cheese

¾ cup salsa, divided

⅔ cup cooked brown rice

¼ cup reduced-fat sour cream

Directions

Preheat oven to 350 degrees. Wrap tortillas in foil and bake for 10 to 15 minutes or until heated through. In a large skillet, heat olive oil over medium heat.

Place onion, red bell pepper, garlic and jalapeño in skillet and cook for 5 minutes, stirring occasionally. Add chili powder and cumin and continue cooking for 1 to 2 minutes. Add beans to the skillet and cook 3 minutes more. Cut cream cheese into cubes and add to the skillet. Continue to cook until cream cheese is melted. Add ½ cup of salsa and cooked rice to the bean mixture and heat through. Spoon about ⅓ cup of the bean mixture evenly down the center of each warmed tortilla. Top each tortilla with 2 teaspoons salsa and 2 teaspoons sour cream and roll up. Serve immediately.

Nutritional info (per serving)

Calories......................281	Sodium ....525 mg
From fat.................32%	Cholesterol ....15 mg
Fat .... 10 g	Calcium ....124 mg
Saturated ....4 g	Fiber ....5 g
Trans ....0 g	Food exchanges
Carbohydrates ....39 g	2 starch, 1 lean meat,
Protein ....9 g	1 vegetable, 1 fat

Eggplant Rolatini

Eggplant comes in many varieties, ranging in color from rich purple to white, in length from 2 to 12 inches and in shape from oblong to round. This nearly fat- and sodium-free vegetable is a good source of fiber. Keep in mind, however, that sliced eggplant absorbs oil like a sponge. Healthier ways to prepare this vegetable include baking, broiling or grilling. This recipe is a good source of fiber with 7 grams per serving.

 4   45 mins total

Ingredients

2 medium eggplant

1 egg

¼ cup skim milk

1 cup plain bread crumbs

Vegetable oil cooking spray

¼ cup diced onion

1 clove garlic, peeled, minced

4 ounces part-skim mozzarella cheese, shredded

½ cup low-fat ricotta cheese

¼ teaspoon dried oregano

1 can (15 ounces) pizza sauce

¼ cup Parmesan cheese

Directions

Peel eggplant and slice it lengthwise, getting at least 5 slices from each eggplant. In a shallow dish, combine the egg and milk. Place bread crumbs in a separate shallow dish. Dip eggplant slices in the egg mixture, then coat them with bread crumbs. Arrange eggplant slices on a baking sheet coated with vegetable oil cooking spray and coat the top of each slice of eggplant with vegetable oil cooking spray. Broil 5 to 7 minutes on each side of the eggplant slices to soften them; set aside.

Preheat oven to 350 degrees. Coat a nonstick skillet with vegetable oil cooking spray. Add the onion and garlic and sauté until they are soft, about 4 to 5 minutes; set aside. In a small bowl, combine mozzarella cheese, ricotta cheese, oregano and the sautéed onion and garlic mixture. Using a tablespoon measure, spoon a heaping dollop of the cheese mixture onto an eggplant slice and roll it up. Repeat this process with each eggplant slice. Spray a 13-by-9-inch glass baking dish with cooking spray. Spoon ⅓ cup pizza sauce into the baking dish and spread it around. Place the eggplant rolls in the baking dish and top them with the remaining pizza sauce. Sprinkle with Parmesan cheese; cover and bake 30 to 35 minutes. Remove from oven and serve.

Nutritional info (per serving)

Calories	265
From fat	27%
Fat	8 g
Saturated	4 g
Trans	0 g
Carbohydrates	32 g
Protein	17 g
Sodium	415 mg
Cholesterol	42 mg
Calcium	413 mg
Fiber	7 g

Food exchanges
1 starch, 3 vegetable, 2 meat

Test Kitchen Tip

When selecting eggplant choose firm, smooth-skinned eggplants that are heavy for their size. A good eggplant should not be seedy, small- and medium-sized eggplants have fewer seeds than larger, overly mature eggplants. Eggplants become bitter with age and are very perishable. They should be stored in a cool, dry place and used within a day or two of purchase. If longer storage is needed, store eggplant in the refrigerator vegetable drawer.

Farfalle and Mushrooms with Walnut Sauce

Plenty of substances in nuts offer heart-healthy attributes. They contain monounsaturated and polyunsaturated fats, vitamin E, folate, magnesium, copper, potassium and dietary fiber. Eating as little as 1 ounce of nuts per day can provide many health benefits. But that's not a license to overindulge. Nuts are a very concentrated source of calories — about 150 to 200 calories per ounce. One ounce of nuts will easily fit in the palm of your hand. If you decide to add a handful or two of nuts to your diet every day without cutting calories elsewhere, expect to be 30 to 40 pounds heavier at the end of a year. Walnuts bring this pasta dish to life with the addition of them in the sauce.

 5   30 mins total

Ingredients

2 tablespoons plus 1 teaspoon trans fat-free margarine, divided

1 package (12 ounces) mushrooms, coarsely chopped

3 cloves garlic, peeled, minced

1 tablespoon dry white wine

3/4 teaspoon salt, divided

1/4 teaspoon white pepper, divided

1 tablespoon plus 1 teaspoon flour

1 cup skim milk

1 ounce (about 1/4 cup) walnuts, toasted

6 ounces dried farfalle pasta, cooked and drained

3 tablespoons grated Parmesan cheese

Test Kitchen Tip

Here's a few ways to incorporate nuts into your diet. Sprinkle chopped nuts on top of low-fat yogurt and cereal. Use nuts to replace croutons on salads. Add nuts to steamed or sautéed vegetables.

Directions

In a large skillet, heat 1 tablespoon margarine over medium heat. Add mushrooms and garlic and sauté for 3 to 5 minutes. Add wine and continue to sauté an additional 2 to 3 minutes. While mushrooms and garlic are cooking, season with 1/2 teaspoon salt and 1/8 teaspoon white pepper.

To make the walnut sauce: Melt 1 tablespoon plus 1 teaspoon margarine in a heavy saucepan. Whisk in flour; cook, whisking constantly for about 1 minute. Gradually whisk in the skim milk, 1/4 teaspoon salt and 1/8 teaspoon white pepper. Bring sauce to a boil, whisking constantly. Reduce heat to medium-low and continue to cook until sauce is thickened, 1 more minute. Add walnuts to the sauce. While the sauce is cooking, prepare pasta according to package directions, omitting the salt. Toss the sauce with the hot cooked pasta, top with Parmesan cheese and serve.

Nutritional info (per serving)

Calories	268	Sodium	432 mg
From fat	37%	Cholesterol	4 mg
Fat	11 g	Calcium	114 mg
Saturated	2 g	Fiber	2 g
Trans	0 g		
Carbohydrates	33 g		
Protein	11 g		

Food exchanges
1 1/2 starch, 2 vegetable, 1 meat, 1 fat

Grilled Veggie Stack

A stack of grilled vegetables served on its own or between slices of grilled bread is perfect for casual, alfresco dining. Vegetables are best grilled about al dente (just slightly firm to the bite). This recipe features grilled portabella mushrooms, roasted red pepper, sweet onion and eggplant. Another veggie to try is zucchini sliced on the diagonal or cut in half lengthwise if small, say 6 inches or so and only about 1 inch in diameter.

 6 30 mins total

Ingredients

MARINADE

⅓ cup balsamic vinegar

⅓ cup olive oil

1 tablespoon sugar

¼ teaspoon salt

Black pepper to taste

1 tablespoon fresh chopped parsley

VEGETABLES

6 portabella mushroom caps with stems, washed well

1 tablespoon olive oil

2 tablespoons plain bread crumbs

2 tablespoons grated Parmesan cheese

6 slices (¼ inch thick each) eggplant

6 slices (½ inch thick) red or white onion left whole

3 small red peppers, cored and cut in half lengthwise, or substitute a 12-ounce jar of roasted peppers

6 slices favorite reduced-fat sliced cheese, optional

6 slices (¼ inch thick) tomato

6 whole-wheat thin-style buns

Directions

In a small bowl, mix the marinade ingredients and set aside. Remove the stems from the mushrooms and make them finely chopped. In a small skillet, heat the olive oil and sauté the stems until they are softened. Sprinkle in the bread crumbs and Parmesan cheese. Set aside.

Place the mushroom caps, eggplant, onion and red pepper slices on a baking sheet and brush sides with the marinade mixture. Let stand about 10 minutes.

Prepare the grill or preheat the broiler. When the grill is ready, brush the grates with oil and wait 5 minutes before grilling.

Grill or broil the vegetable slices. Put the mushrooms and onions on first because they will take the longest to grill. The eggplant grills rather quickly so put it on last. If using roasted red peppers from a jar, just toss them on the grill for a minute or two to heat through. Turn the vegetables once halfway through cooking.

Remove from the grill and stack the vegetables on the bun. Top each with a tomato slice and, if desired, a cheese slice. Spread the reserved mushroom stem mixture on the top roll.

Nutritional info (per serving)

Calories......................331	Sodium ....257 mg
From fat.................35%	Cholesterol ....15 mg
Fat...............................13 g	Calcium .... 387 mg
Saturated...............4 g	Fiber ....11 g
Trans ....0 g	Food exchanges
Carbohydrates...........42 g	2 starch, 2 vegetable,
Protein ....19 g	1 meat, 1 fat

Test Kitchen Tip

It's best to slice onions at least ½ inch so they hold together while grilling. To make sure onions don't fall apart, secure the slices with 6-inch skewers. You can also cut the grilled vegetables into big chunks and toss them with hot cooked pasta. Use your favorite sauce or a drizzling of olive oil and Parmesan cheese shavings.

Italian Rotolo

Making the dough for this Heart Smart® Italian Rotolo sounds tricky, but is worth the effort. The filling is creamy and a good way to sneak in some folate-rich spinach. One hearty serving of this recipe has only 165 calories and 6 grams of fat.

 6   1 hour 40 mins total

Ingredients

½ cup plus 2 tablespoons all-purpose flour, divided

¼ teaspoon salt

1 egg, white and yolk separated

2 tablespoons water

1 teaspoon olive oil

Vegetable oil cooking spray

1 tablespoon finely chopped onion

1 package (10 ounces) frozen chopped spinach, cooked, drained and squeezed dry

⅓ cup low-fat ricotta cheese

¼ cup grated Parmesan cheese, divided

2 tablespoons finely chopped walnuts

⅛ teaspoon ground nutmeg

2 cups low-fat mushroom spaghetti sauce

Nutritional info (per serving)

Calories..........................165	Sodium ....453 mg
From fat..................33%	Cholesterol ....42 mg
Fat ....6 g	Calcium ....132 mg
Saturated................2 g	Fiber ....3 g
Trans ....0 g	Food exchanges
Carbohydrates ....20 g	1 starch, 2 vegetable,
Protein ....7 g	1 fat

Directions

In a small mixing bowl, stir together ½ cup flour and the salt. Make a well in the center. Combine the egg yolk, water and oil; add to the flour. Mix well. Sprinkle a clean work surface with 2 tablespoons flour. Turn the dough onto the floured surface. Knead until the dough is smooth and elastic, about 8 minutes. Cover; let rest for 10 minutes.

On a lightly floured surface, roll the dough into a 12-by-12-inch square. Let stand, uncovered, for 15 minutes. Bring water to a boil in a 4 ½-quart pot. Carefully immerse the pasta sheet into boiling water. Return to boiling; simmer 1 to 2 minutes or until just tender. Carefully drain into a large colander. Rinse with cold water; drain well.

Spread dough on a damp cloth. Let stand 15 minutes to dry. Preheat oven to 375 degrees. Spray a skillet with vegetable oil cooking spray. Add onion and cook until tender, 3 to 5 minutes. In a medium bowl, beat egg white. Add spinach, cooked onion, ricotta cheese, 3 tablespoons Parmesan cheese, walnuts and nutmeg, and mix well.

Trim dough to 12-by-14-inch rectangle (the dough extends during cooking). Spread the spinach filling over the dough to within ½ inch of the edges. Sprinkle with 1 tablespoon Parmesan cheese. Starting at the short side, roll up the dough jelly roll style, using the towel to aid in rolling. Coat a 13-by-9-by-2-inch baking pan with vegetable oil cooking spray. Place the dough in the prepared pan. Spoon the spaghetti sauce over roll. Bake, covered, for 20 to 25 minutes. Remove from the oven and slice to serve.

Lettuce Wraps

This recipe from chef Frank Turner, director of Culinary Wellness at Henry Ford West Bloomfield Hospital, features oven roasted tofu nestled in soft lettuce leaves. Tofu, or soybean curd, is bland but takes on the flavors of foods with which it is cooked. In this recipe it takes on soy and sesame flavors and is topped with sautéed vegetables.

 2 (3 lettuce wraps per serving)   45 mins total

Ingredients

6 Boston bib or butter crunch lettuce leaves (romaine lettuce can also be used)

2 teaspoons canola oil, divided

1 clove garlic, peeled, minced

2 teaspoons fresh peeled, grated gingerroot

1 tablespoon reduced-sodium soy sauce, divided

4 ounces extra-firm tofu, cut into large matchsticks

½ cup shredded carrots

½ cup sliced shiitake mushrooms, stems removed

½ cup bean sprouts

½ cup sliced green onions

¼ teaspoon sesame oil

2 tablespoons chopped peanuts

2 tablespoons finely chopped cilantro

½ teaspoon crushed red pepper, optional

Directions

Rinse whole lettuce leaves and pat dry with paper towel, being careful not to tear. Set aside. In a small bowl, whisk together 1 teaspoon canola oil, garlic, gingerroot and ½ tablespoon soy sauce. Add tofu and gently toss to coat, being careful not to break the tofu pieces. Place tofu in the refrigerator, allowing it to marinate at least 30 minutes.

Preheat oven to 325 degrees. Place the tofu along with the marinade on a baking sheet and roast for 15 to 20 minutes. Heat the remaining canola oil in a sauté pan. Add carrots, mushrooms and sprouts and sauté for 2 to 3 minutes, or until slightly soft. Add green onions, remaining ½ tablespoon soy sauce and sesame oil; stir to combine. Divide the mixture evenly into the lettuce leaves. Top with the roasted tofu, peanuts, cilantro and, if desired, crushed red pepper. Fold in sides, roll tightly and serve.

Nutritional info (per serving)

Calories....................... 206
   From fat 57%

Fat .... 13 g
   Saturated.................. 1 g
   Trans .... 0 g

Carbohydrates .... 13 g

Protein .... 11 g

Sodium .... 308 mg

Cholesterol .... 0 mg

Calcium .... 108 mg

Fiber .... 4 g

Food exchanges
   2 meat, 3 vegetable,
   1 fat

Test Kitchen Tip

Tofu comes in several varieties. Use extra-firm in this recipe so it holds its shape. When using shiitake mushrooms, always remove the stems before cooking as they tend to be tough and rubbery.

Mediterranean Chopped Salad with Penne, Feta and Sun-Dried Tomatoes

 5 40 mins total

Crisp romaine lettuce, chickpeas, artichoke hearts, sun-dried tomatoes, red onion and cucumbers drizzled with a classic Greek vinaigrette are the highlights of this main dish. This salad gets a huge fiber boost from chickpeas, also known as garbanzo beans. As a main dish, this salad has 7 grams of fiber.

Ingredients

- 1 cup dry penne pasta
- ½ cup sun-dried tomatoes (not packed in oil)
- 5 cups romaine lettuce, torn into bite-size pieces
- 1 can (15 ounces) chickpeas, drained and rinsed
- 1 can (13.75 ounces) water-packed artichoke hearts, drained, rinsed and quartered
- ½ cup cucumbers, peeled and diced
- ¼ cup pitted black olives
- ½ cup (2 ounces) feta cheese, crumbled
- ¼ cup red onion slices
- 2 tablespoons red wine vinegar
- 1 tablespoon water
- 1 tablespoon olive oil
- 1 teaspoon dried oregano
- 1 teaspoon sugar
- ¼ teaspoon black pepper
- 1 clove garlic, peeled, minced

Test Kitchen Tip

Canned beans often are high in sodium. Always drain and rinse canned beans to rid them of excess sodium. Some brands now offer no-salt-added canned beans.

Nutritional info (per serving)

Calories...................... 235
    From fat................35%
Fat ....8 g
    Saturated...............2 g
    Trans ....0 g
Carbohydrates ....34 g
Protein ....9 g
Sodium ....471 mg
Cholesterol ....10 mg
Calcium ....131 mg
Fiber ....7 g
Food exchanges
    2 starch, 1 vegetable,
    1 lean meat, 1 fat

Directions

In a large saucepan of unsalted boiling water, cook pasta one minute short of al dente. Add sun-dried tomatoes and cook one more minute. Drain and rinse under cold water; transfer to a large bowl. Add the lettuce, chickpeas, artichoke hearts, cucumbers, olives, feta cheese and red onion. Combine the red wine vinegar, water, olive oil, oregano, sugar, black pepper and garlic in a small jar; shake well. Pour over vegetable mixture, tossing gently to coat.

Oven-Fried Falafel with Tzatziki Sauce

Falafel is ground chickpeas (garbanzo beans) made into a ball and typically deep fried. In this version, it's oven-fried and served with a cool and creamy tzatziki sauce. These falafel are great for lunch.

Nutritional info (per serving)

Calories	294	Sodium	375 mg
From fat	31%	Cholesterol	56 mg
Fat	10 g	Calcium	118 mg
Saturated	2 g	Fiber	7 g
Trans	0 g		
Carbohydrates	39 g		
Protein	15 g		

Food exchanges
2 starch, 2 lean meat, 1 vegetable

 4   1 hour 15 mins total

Ingredients

- 1 container (7 ounces) low-fat Greek-style yogurt
- 2 tablespoons lemon juice
- 4 cloves garlic, peeled, minced, divided
- 2 teaspoons dill weed
- ¼ teaspoon black pepper
- ⅛ teaspoon salt
- ¼ cup chopped yellow onion
- 1 tablespoon plus 2 teaspoons olive oil, divided
- 1 can (15 ounces) chickpeas (garbanzo beans), drained and rinsed
- ¼ cup parsley leaves
- 1 teaspoon ground cumin
- 1 egg
- 1 tablespoon all-purpose flour
- Vegetable oil cooking spray
- 2 (6 inches each) whole wheat pitas
- 4 leaf lettuce leaves
- ¼ cup thinly sliced red onion

Directions

To make the tzatziki sauce, combine the yogurt, lemon juice, 1 minced garlic clove, dill weed, black pepper and salt in a medium bowl. Cover and refrigerate until ready to assemble the sandwiches. In a small nonstick skillet, sauté the yellow onion and remaining 3 minced garlic cloves in 2 teaspoons olive oil for 3 to 5 minutes. Place the chickpeas, sautéed onions and garlic, parsley and cumin in a food processor. Process until the mixture is coarsely pureed. Place the chickpea mixture in a small bowl and add the egg and flour. Cover and refrigerate until ready to bake.

Preheat oven to 450 degrees. Pour the remaining 1 tablespoon of olive oil into a 9-inch square baking dish and place in the preheated oven; heat oil for 4 to 5 minutes. Remove the baking dish from the oven and quickly shape the falafel mixture into 4 patties and place in the heated pan. Note the falafel mixture will be very moist. Spray each patty lightly with nonstick cooking spray, return to the oven and bake for 25 to 30 minutes, turning once during the cooking process. To assemble each sandwich, slice each pita in half and fill each half with a baked falafel, one lettuce leaf, sliced red onion and drizzle with a quarter of the tzatziki sauce.

Heart Smart® Pesto with Pasta

Pesto is a fresh-tasting, fragrant sauce made from basil, olive oil, garlic, pine nuts and Parmesan or pecorino cheese. Use pesto in soups, as a pizza sauce, spread on crusty bread, tucked in an egg white omelet or in with pasta. Pesto has a powerful flavor and a little goes a long way. This Heart Smart® Pesto has about half the fat of typical recipes because we used less olive oil and fewer nuts.

 5   30 mins total

Ingredients

3 cups tightly packed basil leaves (about 2 ounces)

6 tablespoons grated Parmesan cheese

3 tablespoons chopped almonds

3 tablespoons water

2 cloves garlic, peeled, finely chopped

½ teaspoon salt

¼ teaspoon coarsely ground pepper

⅛ teaspoon ground nutmeg

2 ½ tablespoons olive oil

8 ounces cellentani pasta or other favorite short pasta

¼ cup hot water or reserved pasta water

Directions

In a food processor, place basil, Parmesan cheese, almonds, 3 tablespoons water, garlic, salt, pepper and nutmeg. Purée until a paste forms. With motor running, add oil in a thin stream and process until smooth, about 1 minute.

Cook pasta in a large pot according to package directions, omitting the salt. Reserve ¼ cup hot pasta water; drain pasta and return to pot. Add the pesto and reserved hot pasta water or hot tap water and toss to coat pasta.

Nutritional info (per serving)

Calories	222	Sodium	287 mg
From fat	46%	Cholesterol	5 mg
Fat	11 g	Calcium	102 mg
Saturated	2 g	Fiber	2 g
Trans	0 g		
Carbohydrates	24 g		
Protein	7 g		

Food exchanges
1 ½ starch, 1 meat, 1 fat

Test Kitchen Tip
You can replace high-priced pine nuts, which are typical in pesto, with almonds or walnuts. Toast the nuts about 5 to 8 minutes in a 350 degree oven until fragrant.

Pasta Primavera

Primavera means "spring style" and using fresh vegetables in dishes. Pasta Primavera is one of the more popular dishes which you top cooked pasta with julienned cooked vegetables. This recipe has a cream sauce made with fat-free half-and-half for a lighter fat and calorie load.

 6   50 mins total

Ingredients

2 tablespoons olive oil

¾ finely diced onion

4 garlic cloves, peeled, minced

8 ounces sliced mushrooms

1 cup sliced red bell pepper

1 cup julienned zucchini

1 can (13.75 ounces) artichoke hearts, drained and rinsed

¾ teaspoon salt

¼ teaspoon black pepper

3 ounces reduced-fat cream cheese, softened

¾ cup fat-free half-and-half

1 tablespoon fresh lemon juice

⅛ teaspoon cayenne pepper

½ cup Parmesan cheese

6 ounces dried angel hair pasta

Directions

In a large skillet, heat olive oil over medium heat. Add the onions and garlic and sauté until onions become soft, about 5 minutes. Add mushrooms, red bell pepper, zucchini and artichoke hearts and continue to sauté an additional 5 to 8 minutes.

While vegetables are sautéing, season with salt and black pepper. Clear an area in the center of the skillet. Place cream cheese in the center of the skillet, allowing it to melt. Add half-and-half, lemon juice and cayenne pepper and stir to combine. Reduce heat to medium-low and continue to cook until sauce is heated through, about 5 minutes. While sauce is cooking, prepare pasta according to package directions, omitting the salt. Toss sauce with the cooked pasta and Parmesan cheese and serve.

Nutritional info (per serving)

Calories...................... 269
   From fat 33%

Fat .... 10 g
   Saturated................ 4 g
   Trans .... 0 g

Carbohydrates .... 33 g

Protein .... 11 g

Sodium .... 482 mg

Cholesterol .... 16 mg

Calcium .... 136 mg

Fiber .... 3 g

Food exchanges
   1 ½ starch, 2 vegetable,
   1 meat, 1 fat

 Test Kitchen Tip

To julienne vegetables means to cut them into matchstick size pieces.

Roasted Vegetable Lasagna

Don't be discouraged by the long recipe. Once you prep all the ingredients and roast the vegetables, the lasagna goes together fairly quickly.

 10   1 hour 30 mins total

Ingredients

3 cups sliced zucchini

3 cups sliced mushrooms

3 cups eggplant, peeled and quartered

2 red bell peppers, seeded and sliced

5 tablespoons olive oil, divided

3 teaspoons dried oregano, divided

¾ teaspoon salt, divided

¾ teaspoon ground black pepper, divided

8 cups plum or Roma tomatoes, quartered

3 cloves garlic, peeled, sliced

½ teaspoon fennel seed

⅛ teaspoon red pepper flakes

2 teaspoons sugar

1 container (15 ounces) low-fat ricotta cheese

2 cups shredded mozzarella cheese

½ cup grated Parmesan cheese, divided

2 tablespoons fresh parsley, chopped

Vegetable oil cooking spray

9 no-boil lasagna noodles

Nutritional info (per serving)

Calories........................277	Sodium ....369 mg
From fat.................42%	Cholesterol ....25 mg
Fat...............................13 g	Calcium ....284 mg
Saturated................5 g	Fiber ....4 g
Trans ....0 g	Food exchanges
Carbohydrates ....26 g	1 starch, 2 vegetable,
Protein ....14 g	2 lean meat, 1 fat

Watch This!

Scan this QR code with your smartphone to watch the Heart Smart® video.

Directions

Preheat oven to 400 degrees. Have ready 2 large sided baking sheets, such as a jelly roll pan.

On one baking sheet place the zucchini, mushrooms, eggplant and red bell peppers. Drizzle with 3 tablespoons olive oil, 2 teaspoons oregano, ½ teaspoon salt and ¼ teaspoon black pepper and toss to coat.

On the other baking sheet, toss the tomato wedges with the remaining 2 tablespoons olive oil, garlic, remaining 1 teaspoon oregano, fennel seed, ¼ teaspoon black pepper and red pepper flakes.

Place both in the oven and roast uncovered for 15 minutes. Turn the vegetables over and bake an additional 15 to 20 minutes. Remove roasted vegetables and roasted tomatoes from oven. Carefully place the tomatoes and all pan juices in a bowl and add the sugar and remaining ¼ teaspoon salt. Mash the tomatoes to create a sauce.

In a medium-sized bowl, combine the ricotta cheese, mozzarella cheese, ¼ cup Parmesan cheese, parsley and remaining ¼ teaspoon black pepper; set aside.

Coat a 9-by-13-inch baking pan with vegetable oil cooking spray. To begin layering the lasagna, place about ⅓ cup of tomato sauce in the baking dish, spreading to cover the bottom of the dish. Top with 3 noodles, half the ricotta cheese mixture, half the roasted vegetable mixture and one-quarter of the tomato sauce. Begin again with 3 noodles, remaining cheese mixture, remaining roasted vegetables and remaining 3 noodles. Top noodles with remaining tomato sauce and a ¼ cup Parmesan cheese. Bake lasagna uncovered for 30 to 35 minutes or until edges are bubbly and the cheese topping is golden brown.

Spinach Feta Crustless Quiche

If you're looking for a way to ward off heart disease, eating foods rich in folate might help. Folate-rich foods include citrus fruits and juices, strawberries, leafy green vegetables such as spinach and romaine lettuce, dried beans such as navy beans and chickpeas (garbanzo beans) and wheat germ. This Spinach-Feta Crustless Quiche provides more than 25% of the daily requirement for folate.

 4   1 hour 25 mins total

Ingredients

2 teaspoons olive oil

¼ cup diced onion

1 clove garlic, peeled, minced

1 package (10 ounces) frozen chopped spinach, thawed and squeezed dry

1 container (15 ounces) low-fat ricotta cheese

¼ cup crumbled feta cheese

¾ cup fat-free egg substitute

1 tablespoon freshly squeezed lemon juice

½ teaspoon ground black pepper

½ teaspoon salt

Vegetable oil cooking spray

Directions

Preheat oven to 350 degrees.

In a small nonstick skillet, heat the olive oil. Add onion and garlic and cook about 5 minutes or until the onion is tender; set it aside.

In a large bowl combine the spinach, ricotta cheese, feta cheese, egg substitute, lemon juice, black pepper and salt.

Stir in the sautéed onions and garlic.

Pour the mixture into a 1 ½-quart round baking dish coated with vegetable oil cooking spray. Bake 55 to 60 minutes or until the center is set.

Remove the quiche from the oven and let it stand 10 minutes.

Slice into wedges and serve.

Nutritional info (per serving)

Calories	193	Sodium	664 mg
From fat	37%	Cholesterol	27 mg
Fat	8 g	Calcium	640 mg
Saturated	4 g	Fiber	2 g
Trans	0 g		
Carbohydrates	10 g		
Protein	22 g		

Food exchanges
2 ½ lean meat,
2 vegetable

 Test Kitchen Tip

Most quiche freeze well wrapped in foil and placed in a freezer-quality bag. To reheat, place in a 350-degree oven until thoroughly heated.

Wild Rice Casserole

This Wild Rice Casserole is a nice side dish addition to the holiday table. It's also a way to sneak in some whole grains. The dish has a creamy texture from using the condensed soup and fat-free half-and-half. By not using the seasoning packet included with the rice, the sodium is reduced.

 10   1 hour total

Ingredients

1 box quick-cooking wild rice blend (such as Uncle Ben's, without the seasoning packet)

Vegetable oil cooking spray

1 cup sliced mushrooms

½ cup chopped onion

2 cloves garlic, peeled, minced

1 can (10.75 ounces) reduced-fat, less-sodium condensed cream of mushroom soup, undiluted

¾ cup fat-free half-and-half

¼ teaspoon dried basil

¼ teaspoon dried tarragon

½ teaspoon curry powder

½ teaspoon salt

¼ teaspoon pepper

¼ cup pecans, chopped

Directions

Cook wild rice blend according to package directions, omitting the seasoning packet and optional butter and salt. Coat a large nonstick skillet with vegetable oil cooking spray, sauté mushrooms, onion and garlic about 5 minutes. Reduce heat and add soup, half-and-half, basil, tarragon, curry powder, salt and pepper. Heat mixture slowly for about 10 minutes.

Preheat oven to 350 degrees. Combine the cooked rice and cream sauce mixture. Coat a 2-quart casserole dish with vegetable oil cooking spray and add the rice mixture. Sprinkle the top with chopped pecans. Bake for 20 to 30 minutes or until edges of casserole begin to bubble. Remove from oven and serve.

Nutritional info (per serving)

Calories	188
From fat	14%
Fat	3 g
Saturated	1 g
Trans	0 g
Carbohydrates	34 g
Protein	5 g
Sodium	253 mg
Cholesterol	2 mg
Calcium	113 mg
Fiber	2 g
Food exchanges	2 starch, ½ fat

Test Kitchen Tip

Toast the pecans in a preheated 350-degree oven for 6 to 8 minutes to intensify the flavor. Be sure to watch carefully and remove the pecans from the oven when you can smell the nutty aroma or they will burn.

Sweet Endings

Fitting Desserts into a Healthy Diet

Heart Smart® desserts have to be the ultimate oxymoron. But in the Heart Smart® kitchen, we use many tricks to lighten dessert recipes without compromising taste. A few of our favorites are:

Sugar Sense. Sugar has an important role in baking. It provides sweetness and contributes tenderness, texture and volume. Since flavor often is compromised in reduced-fat baking, sugar is needed to preserve or enhance flavor, making this ingredient difficult to reduce. With baked good recipes, you may only be able to cut the amount of added sugar by a quarter. While that may seem insignificant, doing so cuts almost 200 calories from the recipe. If you are going to cut back on the amount of sugar, add a pinch of cinnamon or nutmeg. These spices can give the perception of sweetness without the added calories.

Another way you can reduce the sugar content of cakes is to forgo the frosting as we did with our Graham Cracker Cake, adding just a dollop of light whipped topping. If frosting is a must, add it only between the cake layers, not to the sides. This trick worked perfect for the Pumpkin Torte and the Carrot Cake.

Fat Cuts. When it comes to reducing fat in a recipe, we tend to rely on three substitution tricks. The first is replacing some or all the fat (oil, margarine, or butter) in baked good recipes with applesauce or other type of pureed fruit. The Black Forest Cake and Vanilla Almond Cake provide two examples. Admittedly, this replacement technique can sometimes leave a cake or brownie with a spongy texture. To lessen that side effect, leave in a tablespoon or two of oil and replace the remaining oil with applesauce. For example, if your cake recipe calls for a 1/2 cup (8 tablespoons) of vegetable oil, add 6 tablespoons of applesauce and 2 tablespoons of oil.

We also replace some or all of the fat in a dessert recipe with low-fat or fat-free yogurt. This works particularly well with brownie recipes, which we used in the Raspberry Cheesecake Bars and Double Chocolate Walnut Brownies.

When it comes to cookies, we found a mixture of a trans fat-free margarine and reduced-fat cream cheese, also known as Neufchâtel, to be the perfect replacement for butter. Tablespoon for tablespoon, reduced-fat cream cheese contains less fat than margarine or butter. You'll find this substitution in our Apple Walnut Cookies and Chocolate Chip Cookies.

Apple Raisin Bread Pudding

Homemade bread pudding is a simple, delicious baked dessert made with cubes of bread soaked in a mixture of milk or cream, eggs, sugar, vanilla and spices. Unfortunately, a serving of this dessert can provide more than 650 calories and 25 grams of fat. In this Heart Smart® version, skim milk replaces whole milk and egg substitute is used instead of whole eggs. Using whole-wheat bread instead of white bread gives this recipe a fiber boost.

 8   1 hour 40 mins total

Ingredients

Vegetable oil cooking spray

2 ½ cups skim milk

½ cup fat-free egg substitute

⅔ cup sugar

2 teaspoons vanilla extract

2 teaspoons cinnamon

¼ teaspoon salt

6 slices whole-wheat bread, cubed

½ cup shredded Granny Smith or Fuji apple

½ cup dark raisins

2 tablespoons trans fat-free margarine, melted

1 tablespoon cinnamon sugar

Directions

Preheat oven to 350 degrees. Spray an 11-by-7-inch baking dish with vegetable oil cooking spray.

In a large bowl, whisk together milk, egg substitute, sugar, vanilla, cinnamon and salt; add the bread cubes. Cover with plastic wrap, and let stand until bread is soaked through, about 30 minutes.

Stir in shredded apple, raisins and margarine. Pour mixture into the prepared baking dish and sprinkle with cinnamon sugar. Bake until the pudding is set and lightly golden on top, 50 minutes to 1 hour. Serve warm or cold.

Nutritional info (per serving)

Calories.........................247
    From fat.................15%

Fat.................................4 g
    Saturated.................1 g
    Trans......................0 g

Carbohydrates...........47 g

Protein..........................7 g

Sodium ....296 mg

Cholesterol ....2 mg

Calcium ....125 mg

Fiber ....4 g

Food exchanges
    2 starch, 1 fruit, ½ fat

Test Kitchen Tip

Bread pudding should wobble like a gelatin mold when removed from the oven because it continues to cook after it is removed.

Apple Raisin Phyllo Strudel

This strudel is made with phyllo dough instead of puff pastry. Phyllo dough is flaky, tissue-thin sheets of raw, unleavened flour dough best known for use in Greek and Mediterranean sweet pastries and savory dishes. They are low in fat and a perfect substitute for puff pastry and pie crusts. When making this recipe, have the phyllo thawed and all the ingredients ready for assembly.

 12 1 hour total

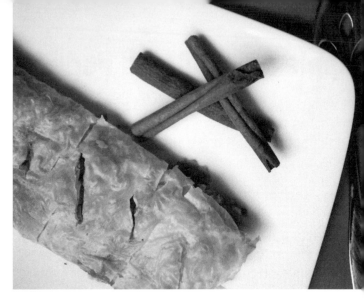

Ingredients

Vegetable oil cooking spray or parchment paper

¼ cup raisins

1 tablespoon brandy (optional)

¼ cup plus 1 tablespoon trans fat-free margarine, divided

4 cups peeled and chopped tart apples (such as Granny Smith)

¼ cup sugar

2 teaspoons fresh lemon juice

1 teaspoon vanilla extract

½ teaspoon ground cinnamon

8 sheets phyllo dough

Nutritional info (per serving)

Calories...........................98	Sodium .... 63 mg
From fat.................28%	Cholesterol ....0 mg
Fat...................................3 g	Calcium ....4 mg
Saturated ....0 g	Fiber ....1 g
Trans ....0 g	Food exchanges
Carbohydrates ....17 g	1 fruit, ½ fat
Protein ....1 g	

Test Kitchen Tip

Thaw unopened frozen phyllo dough in the refrigerator overnight and then at room temperature for about one hour. To prevent phyllo from drying out while layering the sheets, cover it with plastic wrap then place a damp clean cloth or towel on top of the plastic wrap. Lightly brush each sheet of phyllo dough with oil or melted, trans fat-free margarine in streaks when stacking.

Directions

Preheat oven to 350 degrees. Line a jelly roll pan with parchment paper or spray it lightly with vegetable oil cooking spray. In a small bowl, soak raisins in the brandy, if desired; set aside.

In a large nonstick skillet over medium heat, melt 1 tablespoon of margarine and add the apples, sugar, lemon juice, vanilla extract and cinnamon. Stir to combine and sauté until apples are slightly softened, about 5 minutes. Add the soaked raisins to the skillet and heat through.

Meanwhile, melt the remaining ¼ cup of margarine.

Note that this recipe makes 2 strudel rolls. Using 4 sheets of phyllo for each strudel, lightly brush each layer of phyllo with melted margarine, stacking one layer on top of the next. Place half the apple filling mixture on top of one stack of prepared phyllo sheets about 1 inch from the bottom edge. Roll up, folding in the sides. Place strudel seam side down on the prepared pan. Repeat procedure with remaining 4 phyllo sheets, margarine and apple filling. Brush the top of each strudel roll with margarine. Score the top of each strudel into 6 equal sections. Bake for 30 to 40 minutes or until golden brown. Remove and allow the strudel to cool for 15 minutes before slicing. For easier slicing, use a serrated knife.

Apple Walnut Cookies

Walnuts are unique because they contain a significant amount of the omega-3 fatty acid alpha linolenic acid (ALA). The research on the health benefits of walnuts is piling up. The U.S. Food and Drug Administration says that eating 1 ½ ounces of nuts a day may reduce the risk of coronary heart disease. To reap the benefits without consuming too many calories, limit your portion size to 1 or 1 ½ ounces. That portion size will fit in the palm of your hand.

 32   **45 mins total**

Ingredients

Parchment paper or vegetable oil cooking spray

¼ cup trans fat-free margarine

¼ cup (2 ounces) reduced-fat cream cheese

¾ cup packed brown sugar

¾ cup sugar

1 egg

1 teaspoon vanilla extract

2 cups all-purpose flour

1 teaspoon baking soda

⅛ teaspoon salt

1 teaspoon ground cinnamon

1 teaspoon ground nutmeg

¼ teaspoon ground cloves

1 cup peeled, diced apples (Granny Smith work well)

½ cup walnuts, finely chopped

Nutritional info (per serving)

Calories..........................95
    From fat 28%
Fat .... 3 g
    Saturated................1 g
    Trans ....0 g
Carbohydrates ....17 g
Protein ....2 g
Sodium ....68 mg
Cholesterol ....8 mg
Calcium ....9 mg
Fiber ....0 g
Food exchanges
    1 starch, ½ fat

Directions

Preheat oven to 325 degrees.

Line a cookie sheet with parchment paper or coat with vegetable oil cooking spray; set aside. In a large bowl, beat together margarine, cream cheese, brown sugar and sugar. Add egg and vanilla extract and continue to beat until incorporated.

In a separate bowl, combine the flour, baking soda, salt, cinnamon, nutmeg and cloves. Stir the flour mixture into the sugar mixture until smooth. The batter will be very thick. Stir in apples and walnuts. Drop dough by a rounded tablespoon onto prepared baking sheet, making 32 cookies. Bake 15 minutes. Cool slightly and move to wire rack to cool completely.

Test Kitchen Tip

For an intense walnut taste, toast the walnuts in a 350-degree oven for about 6 to 8 minutes. Remove from oven and cool before adding to the batter. Keep shelled walnuts tightly sealed and store in the refrigerator for up to six months or in the freezer for up to one year.

Watch This!

Scan this QR code with your smartphone to watch the Heart Smart® video.

Black Forest Bundt Cake

If made the right way, chocolate cake can be heart-healthy. This Black Forest Bundt Cake uses skim milk and applesauce to replace some of the fat. It's rich tasting and is topped off with reduced-fat whipped topping. This cake is ideal to serve a crowd.

 16   2 hours total

Ingredients

Floured baking spray

1 package (18.25 ounces) trans fat-free chocolate cake mix (such as Duncan Hines Moist Deluxe Dark Chocolate Fudge cake mix)

1 box (4 serving size) chocolate cook-and-serve pudding and pie filling

¾ cup skim milk

½ cup water

½ cup unsweetened applesauce

2 egg whites

1 egg

1 tablespoon almond extract

1 bag (12 ounces) frozen unsweetened dark sweet red cherries, thawed and drained

2 tablespoons sugar

1 tablespoon all-purpose flour

1 cup reduced-fat whipped topping

Nutritional info (per serving)

Calories	193
From fat	14%
Fat	3 g
Saturated	1 g
Trans	0 g
Carbohydrates	38 g
Protein	3 g
Sodium	291 mg
Cholesterol	13 mg
Calcium	50 mg
Fiber	1 g

Food exchanges
2 starch, ½ fat

Directions

Preheat oven to 350 degrees. Coat a 12-cup Bundt pan with the floured baking spray.

In a large bowl, combine the cake mix, dry pudding mix, skim milk, water, applesauce, egg whites, egg and almond extract and beat according to cake mix package directions. Pour batter into the prepared pan.

In a small bowl, combine the cherries, sugar and flour; stir to combine. Gently place the cherries on top of the cake batter. The cherries will sink into the batter as the cake cooks.

Bake for 50 to 55 minutes or until a wooden pick inserted in the cake comes out clean. Let stand 30 to 40 minutes before inverting the pan to release cake. Allow cake to cool completely. Serve each slice with 1 tablespoon whipped topping.

Carrot Cake

Typical carrot cake has a cream cheese frosting and uses whole eggs, oil and nuts in the batter. This version, a two-layer cake with only frosting on the top got a calorie and fat makeover. Vanilla pudding made with skim milk and fat-free whipped topping is used as a filling in between layers and to top the cake with. One slice of this carrot cake has 204 calories and 4 grams of fat.

 16 1 hour 15 mins total

Ingredients

CAKE

Vegetable oil cooking spray

1 cup packed brown sugar

½ cup unsweetened applesauce

½ cup fat-free vanilla yogurt

¼ cup canola oil

1 large egg

2 large egg whites

2 teaspoons vanilla extract

FROSTING

1 cup skim milk

1 box (4 serving size) instant vanilla pudding

1 ½ cups all-purpose flour

1 cup whole-wheat flour

1 ½ teaspoons baking soda

2 ½ teaspoons ground cinnamon

½ teaspoon ground nutmeg

2 cups shredded carrot

1 can (8 ounces) crushed pineapple packed in juice

½ tub or 4 ounces fat-free whipped topping

Directions

Preheat oven to 350 degrees.

Coat two 8-inch round cake pans with vegetable oil cooking spray.

To prepare the cake: In a large bowl, combine the brown sugar, applesauce, vanilla yogurt, canola oil, egg, egg whites and vanilla extract; beat until well blended.

In a separate bowl, combine the all-purpose flour, whole-wheat flour, baking soda, cinnamon and nutmeg; stir well with a fork. Add the flour mixture to the brown sugar mixture and stir until just moist. Fold in shredded carrot and pineapple with juice. Evenly divide the batter between the two prepared cake pans.

Bake for 20 to 25 minutes or until a wooden pick inserted in the center comes out clean. Allow cake to cool in pan a few minutes, then invert on a wire rack to cool completely.

To prepare frosting: Pour skim milk into a large bowl, add instant vanilla pudding mix and beat according to package directions. Fold in whipped topping. Frost the top of each cake layer with frosting, leaving the side of the cake unfrosted. Slice and serve.

Nutritional info (per serving)

Calories....................... 204
    From fat.................17%

Fat................................. 4 g
    Saturated................ 0 g
    Trans .... 0 g

Carbohydrates .... 38 g

Protein .... 4 g

Sodium .... 246 mg

Cholesterol .... 14 mg

Calcium .... 58 mg

Fiber .... 2 g

Food exchanges
    1 ½ starch, 1 fruit, ½ fat

Cherry Rhubarb Cobbler

Though botanically considered a vegetable, rhubarb is typically eaten as a fruit. In this recipe, it's paired with sweet cherries and pineapple for a different twist on a cobbler. One cup of cooked rhubarb is rich in vitamin C as well as dietary fiber.

 10 1 hour total

Ingredients

Vegetable oil cooking spray

2 cups rhubarb, cut into ½-inch pieces

3 tablespoons granulated sugar

4 tablespoons all-purpose flour, divided

¾ cup old-fashioned rolled oats

½ cup packed brown sugar

2 tablespoons trans fat-free margarine

1 can (21 ounces) cherry pie filling

1 can (8 ounces) crushed pineapple, well drained

Directions

Preheat oven to 350 degrees. Spray a 10-inch round oven-safe baking dish with vegetable oil cooking spray.

In a large bowl, combine diced rhubarb, granulated sugar and 1 tablespoon flour. Toss until rhubarb is coated and set aside. In a large bowl, combine oats, brown sugar and remaining flour and toss to combine. Using a pastry cutter or fork, cut in the margarine until the mixture becomes crumbly and set aside. Add the cherry pie filling and drained pineapple to the diced rhubarb and stir until combined. Pour fruit mixture into prepared dish and top with the oatmeal crumb mixture. Bake for 40 to 45 minutes or until the fruit mixture bubbles and crumb topping is lightly golden brown. Serve warm or cold.

Nutritional info (per serving)

Calories........................183
    From fat 15%
Fat ....3 g
    Saturated...............0 g
    Trans ....0 g
Carbohydrates ....38 g
Protein ....2 g
Sodium ....47 mg
Cholesterol ....0 mg
Calcium .... 38 mg
Fiber ....1 g
Food exchanges
    ½ starch, 2 fruit

 Test Kitchen Tip

Be sure to cut the leaves off the rhubarb before storing; stalks will keep for about a week in the refrigerator. Never eat the leaves raw or cooked because they are highly toxic.

Ultimate Heart Smart® Chocolate Chip Cookies

If you're craving a cookie or chocolate, snack on one of these chocolate chip cookies. These chocolate chip cookies have many bits of miniature chocolate chips and one serving (1 cookie) will satisfy your craving.

 24 35 mins total

Ingredients

Parchment paper or vegetable oil cooking spray

¼ cup trans fat-free margarine

¼ cup (2 ounces) reduced-fat cream cheese

¾ cup sugar

¾ cup packed brown sugar

1 egg

1 tablespoon vanilla extract

1 ¾ cups all-purpose flour

1 teaspoon baking soda

⅛ teaspoon salt

¾ cup miniature chocolate chips

½ cup walnuts, chopped

Nutritional info (per serving)

Calories	145
From fat	31%
Fat	5 g
Saturated	2 g
Trans	0 g
Carbohydrates	24 g
Protein	2 g
Sodium	91 mg
Cholesterol	10 mg
Calcium	14 mg
Fiber	1 g

Food exchanges
1 ½ starch, 1 fat

Directions

Preheat oven to 375 degrees. Line a cookie sheet with parchment paper or coat with vegetable oil cooking spray; set aside. In a medium bowl, beat together margarine, cream cheese, sugar, brown sugar, egg and vanilla extract. In a separate bowl, combine flour, baking soda and salt and stir into sugar mixture. Stir in chocolate chips and walnuts. Drop by rounded tablespoons onto prepared baking sheet. Bake 10 to 12 minutes, or until edges begin to brown. Cool on wire rack.

Test Kitchen Tip

 To boost the walnut taste in these cookies, toast them first. Spread them out on a sided baking sheet. Place in a 350-degree oven for 5 to 8 minutes or until they are fragrant. Watch carefully because they can easily burn. Remove and cool before chopping.

Double Chocolate Walnut Brownies

Brownies are a snack favorite. These get a boost from coffee-flavored yogurt as well as a double dose of chocolate from cocoa powder and chocolate chips.

  16   1 hour total

Ingredients

Vegetable oil cooking spray

3 tablespoons cocoa powder

1 tablespoon canola oil

1 cup sugar

3 tablespoons reduced-fat cream cheese

¼ cup low-fat coffee-flavored yogurt

1 egg

1 tablespoon vanilla extract

⅔ cup all-purpose flour

½ teaspoon baking soda

½ cup walnuts, chopped

¼ cup semi-sweet miniature chocolate chips

Directions

Preheat oven to 350 degrees. Spray a 9-by-9-by-2-inch baking pan with vegetable oil cooking spray and set aside.

In a small bowl or measuring cup, combine cocoa powder and canola oil until smooth. In a medium bowl, using an electric mixer, cream together the sugar and cream cheese. Add the cocoa mixture, yogurt, egg and vanilla extract.

Combine flour and baking soda. Using a spoon, combine flour mixture and the cream cheese mixture; do not over mix. Fold in the walnuts and chocolate chips. Pour batter into the prepared pan and bake for 20 to 25 minutes or until a wooden pick comes out almost clean.

Remove from oven and cool before cutting.

Nutritional info (per serving)

Calories	131
From fat	34%
Fat	5 g
Saturated	1 g
Trans	0 g
Carbohydrates	20 g
Protein	2 g
Sodium	58 mg
Cholesterol	15 mg
Calcium	16 mg
Fiber	1 g
Food exchanges	
1 starch, 1 fat	

 Test Kitchen Tip
These brownies freeze well.

Graham Cracker Cake

Cream cheese comes in full-fat, reduced-fat and fat-free versions. Full-fat cream cheese contains a hefty dose of fat — 9 grams in just 2 tablespoons or 1 ounce. Neufchâtel is a reduced-fat cream cheese, which has about 6 grams of fat per ounce. It can replace the butter or oil used in many cake recipes.

Nutritional info (per serving)

Calories	182	Sodium	228 mg
From fat	25%	Cholesterol	21 mg
Fat	5 g	Calcium	55 mg
Saturated	2 g	Fiber	1 g
Trans	0 g	Food exchanges	
Carbohydrates	32 g	2 starch, 1 fat	
Protein	3 g		

 12 1 hour 10 mins total

Ingredients

- Parchment paper or floured baking spray
- 3 tablespoons trans fat-free margarine
- 3 tablespoons reduced-fat cream cheese
- 1 cup packed brown sugar
- 1 egg
- 1 teaspoon vanilla extract
- 1 ½ cups graham cracker crumbs (crushed from 12 full graham cracker sheets)
- ½ cup whole-wheat flour
- 1 teaspoon baking powder
- ½ teaspoon baking soda
- ⅛ teaspoon salt
- 1 cup low-fat buttermilk
- 12 tablespoons reduced-fat whipped topping

Directions

Preheat oven to 350 degrees.

Line a 9-inch springform pan or cake pan with parchment paper and coat it with floured baking spray. Combine margarine, cream cheese and brown sugar in a bowl and beat with an electric mixer until fluffy. Beat in the egg and vanilla until well blended.

In a separate bowl, combine the graham cracker crumbs, flour, baking powder, baking soda and salt. Add crumb mixture to the sugar mixture, alternately with the buttermilk, beating until well blended. Pour batter into the prepared pan and bake 35 to 40 minutes, or until a wooden pick inserted in the center comes out clean. Let the cake cool on a wire rack for 10 minutes. Remove from the pan and cool completely. Top each serving with a tablespoon of whipped topping.

 Test Kitchen Tip

Refrigerate cream cheese, tightly wrapped, and use within 10 days after opening. Discard if any mold develops on the surface.

Heart Smart® Tiramisu

Mascarpone is an Italian curd cheese that resembles a thick whipped cream. It's a main ingredient in tiramisu, a decadent, coffee-flavored dessert. Mascarpone is made from cream and is very high in fat. To reduce the fat content in this Heart Smart® Tiramisu, part-skim ricotta and fat-free cream cheese replaced mascarpone.

  12   30 mins total

Ingredients

1 cup low-fat ricotta cheese

8 ounces fat-free cream cheese

½ cup sugar

14 almond toast cookies (such as Stella D'oro Almond Toast Coffee Treats)

¼ cup Kahlua

¼ cup espresso or very strong coffee

2 teaspoons unsweetened cocoa

12 strawberries for garnish

Nutritional info (per serving)

Calories.........................159	Sodium ....172 mg
From fat..................17%	Cholesterol ....21 mg
Fat .... 3 g	Calcium ....82 mg
Saturated ....1 g	Fiber ....0 g
Trans ....0 g	Food exchanges
Carbohydrates ....25 g	1 ½ starch, 1 fat
Protein .... 6 g	

Directions

In a food processor or blender, combine the ricotta, cream cheese and sugar and process until smooth. Using a serrated knife, carefully cut almond toast cookies in half lengthwise. Arrange 14 halves in a single layer (breaking some up to fill in gaps if necessary) in an 11-by-7-inch baking dish.

In a measuring cup, stir together Kahlua and espresso and drizzle half over the toast cookies. Spread half the cheese mixture evenly over the cookies. Repeat procedure with remaining cookies, Kahlua mixture and cheese mixture. Place in the refrigerator and let set, at least 30 minutes.

Sprinkle with cocoa upon serving. Slice and garnish each serving with a whole strawberry.

Test Kitchen Tip

Keep ricotta tightly covered in the refrigerator in its original container. It should be good for about one week. To help seal out air and keep the cheese fresh, store the tightly sealed container upside down.

Lemon Blueberry Bundt

Blueberries appeared on the health scene when researchers discovered that they contain disease-fighting phytochemicals. Phytochemicals, substances found in plants, may help reduce the risk of chronic diseases such as cancer and heart disease. Blueberries also contain the soluble fiber pectin, which helps lower blood cholesterol levels.

 16 1 hour total

Ingredients

Floured baking spray

1 box (18.25 ounces) trans fat-free lemon or yellow cake mix

1 box (4 serving size) lemon or vanilla cook-and-serve pudding and pie filling

¾ cup skim milk

1 container (6 ounces) low-fat lemon yogurt

2 egg whites

1 egg

2 tablespoons canola oil

1 ½ cups fresh blueberries

2 teaspoons all-purpose flour

Powdered sugar for garnish

Directions

Coat a 12-cup Bundt pan with floured baking spray.

Preheat oven to 350 degrees. In a large bowl, combine cake mix, dry pudding and pie filling mix, milk, yogurt, egg whites, egg and oil; beat according to package directions.

In a small bowl, toss the blueberries with the flour (this helps them not sink to the bottom) and fold into the cake batter.

Pour batter into the Bundt pan. Bake for 35 to 40 minutes or until a wooden pick inserted in the center comes out clean. Let stand 30 to 40 minutes before inverting the pan to release the cake. Cool completely. Dust with powdered sugar before serving.

Nutritional info (per serving)

Calories	200
From fat	23%
Fat	5 g
Saturated	1 g
Trans	0 g
Carbohydrates	35 g
Protein	3 g
Sodium	251 mg
Cholesterol	14 mg
Calcium	33 mg
Fiber	1 g

Food exchanges
2 starch, 1 fat

Test Kitchen Tip

Blueberries keep well in the refrigerator if you use them within a few days. Rinse just before using. Blueberries freeze well. Rinse them with cold water and pat them dry with paper towel. When dry, place them in a freezer bag and freeze up to one year.

Watch This!

Scan this QR code with your smartphone to watch the Heart Smart® video.

Lemon Squares

These lemon squares are a tasty dessert that is easy to make. Be sure to cool the dessert before slicing into squares.

  12 45 mins total

Ingredients

CRUST

Vegetable oil cooking spray

¾ cup low-fat graham cracker crumbs (about 10 squares)

2 tablespoons all-purpose flour

1 tablespoon sugar

2 tablespoons trans fat-free margarine

FILLING

1 ¼ cups sugar

2 tablespoons all-purpose flour

½ teaspoon baking powder

1 egg

2 egg whites

½ cup fresh lemon juice, about 2 lemons

Finely grated zest of 1 lemon

2 to 3 drops yellow food coloring

2 tablespoons powdered sugar

Directions

Preheat oven to 350 degrees.

Spray an 11-by-7-inch baking dish with vegetable oil cooking spray.

In a large bowl, combine graham cracker crumbs, flour, sugar and margarine. Using an electric mixer on low speed, blend the mixture until it's crumbly.

Firmly press crumbs onto the bottom of the baking dish and bake 10 minutes in preheated oven.

For the filling, combine sugar, flour, baking powder, egg, egg whites, fresh lemon juice, lemon zest and yellow food coloring.

Carefully pour this mixture over the hot crust.

Bake 20 to 25 minutes or until the edges are light golden brown and the filling is set.

Cool the dessert completely on a wire rack.

Sprinkle the top with powdered sugar and cut the dessert into squares.

Nutritional info (per serving)

Calories........................ 147	Sodium .... 83 mg
From fat................. 18%	Cholesterol .... 17 mg
Fat .... 3 g	Calcium .... 30 mg
Saturated .... 0 g	Fiber .... 0 g
Trans .... 0 g	Food exchanges
Carbohydrates ....30 g	2 starch, ½ fat
Protein .... 2 g	

Test Kitchen Tip

To get the most juice out a lemon (or lime) roll it around on the counter pressing down on it with the palm of your hand. This breaks down the juice cells. You also can place the lemon in the microwave and microwave on high for 20 seconds.

Lime Snaps

Stopping at your favorite cookie vendor for a double fudge brownie will provide you with more than 420 calories and 25 grams of fat. These Lime Snaps have just 3 grams of fat and less than 130 calories per two-cookie serving and would make a great cookie for a holiday cookie exchange.

 12 1 hour total

Ingredients

Vegetable oil cooking spray or parchment paper

1 ½ cups all-purpose flour

1 teaspoon baking powder

¼ teaspoon baking soda

½ cup plus 2 tablespoons sugar

2 teaspoons lime zest

2 tablespoons trans fat-free margarine

2 tablespoons (1 ounce) reduced-fat cream cheese, softened

1 egg

2 teaspoons vanilla extract

Directions

Preheat oven to 375 degrees.

Coat baking sheets with vegetable oil cooking spray or line with parchment paper; set aside.

In a medium bowl, combine flour, baking powder and baking soda.

Place sugar and lime zest in a food processor or blender. Process 1 minute or until the sugar mixture is lime-colored, scraping the sides of the processor bowl or blender if needed.

Spoon sugar mixture into a large bowl, reserving 2 tablespoons, and set aside. Add margarine and cream cheese to the large bowl that contains the sugar lime mixture and beat on medium speed with an electric mixer until light and fluffy. Add egg and vanilla; beat well. Stir flour mixture into the sugar mixture; dough will be somewhat moist.

Coat hands lightly with cooking spray and shape dough into 24 (1-inch) balls. Roll balls in the reserved sugar mixture and place 2 inches apart on baking sheets. Flatten balls with the bottom of a glass. Bake for 7 minutes or until the edges begin to turn lightly brown. Remove and cool on wire racks.

Nutritional info (per serving)

Calories.......................129	Sodium .... 88 mg
From fat.................21%	Cholesterol ....19 mg
Fat ....3 g	Calcium ....14 mg
Saturated ....1 g	Fiber ....0 g
Trans ....0 g	Food exchanges
Carbohydrates ....23 g	1 ½ starch
Protein ....2 g	

Test Kitchen Tip

When recipes call for the zest of the lime (or other citrus) this refers to only the outer or colored part of the skin. The white pith underneath is bitter. Use a citrus zester or vegetable peeler to remove the skin. Rasp-style graters are popular for removing the zest easily in fine feathery pieces.

Mandarin Orange and Kiwi Cornmeal Cake

Kiwi houses a wide assortment of nutrients. Two kiwifruit contain more vitamin C than an orange, more potassium than a banana and more fiber than two slices of whole-wheat bread. Other nutritional attributes of this fruit include folate, vitamin E and magnesium. Beneath the kiwi's fuzzy brown exterior is a rich, brilliant green flesh speckled with a ring of tiny, edible black seeds. The flavor is often described as a blend of pineapple, strawberry and grape.

 10   1 hour total

Ingredients

Floured baking spray

3 kiwifruit, peeled, divided

1 can (15 ounces) mandarin oranges packed in juice, drained and divided

1 ¼ cups all-purpose flour

½ cup yellow cornmeal

2 teaspoons baking powder

¼ teaspoon salt

1 egg

2 egg whites

½ cup sugar

½ cup skim milk

3 tablespoons melted trans fat-free margarine

Zest of 1 orange

⅓ cup powdered sugar

1 tablespoon orange juice

Nutritional info (per serving)

Calories.........................195
  From fat..................14%
Fat.....................................3 g
  Saturated..................1 g
  Trans.........................0 g
Carbohydrates...........38 g
Protein...........................4 g
Sodium.................145 mg
Cholesterol.............21 mg
Calcium..................50 mg
Fiber.............................2 g
Food exchanges
  2 starch, ½ fruit

Directions

Preheat oven to 350 degrees. Coat an 8-inch round cake pan with floured baking spray.

Line the bottom of the pan with parchment paper and spray the top of the parchment paper with baking spray. Thinly slice 2 of the kiwi and place in the bottom of the pan. Place mandarin oranges, reserving ¼ cup of the oranges to place on top of the cooked cake before serving, in the bottom of the pan. Set aside. In a bowl stir together flour, cornmeal, baking powder and salt. Set aside. In another bowl, whisk together egg, egg whites, sugar, milk and melted margarine.

Add the egg mixture all at once to flour mixture. Stir until combined and pour over fruit in the prepared pan. Bake 30 to 40 minutes or until golden brown and firm to the touch. Cool cake in the pan for 5 minutes. If necessary, run a knife around the edge of the pan to loosen sides. Invert the cake onto a cooling rack, and remove the parchment paper. To prepare glaze, combine the orange zest, powdered sugar and orange juice until smooth.

Drizzle glaze on the top of cake. When ready to serve, dice the remaining kiwi, place on top of the cake with the remaining ¼ cup of oranges.

Test Kitchen Tip

Choose kiwi fruit that is firm, plump and yields to gentle pressure. Avoid those with bruises, soft spots or wrinkles. Kiwi fruit become sweeter after being picked. Unripe kiwi will have a hard core and a tart, bitter taste. To ripen kiwi, place them in a paper bag with an apple or banana and let stand a day or two at room temperature. Ripe kiwis can be stored in the refrigerator up to three weeks.

Oatmeal Raisin Cookies

These Oatmeal Raisin Cookies are so low in fat and calories that most people can eat two without ruining their diet. Two cookies contain 154 calories and just 18% are from fat.

 12 (2 cookies per serving)  **30 mins total**

Ingredients

Vegetable oil cooking spray or parchment paper

½ cup packed brown sugar

¼ cup granulated sugar

⅓ cup unsweetened applesauce

3 tablespoons trans fat-free margarine

2 egg whites

1 teaspoon vanilla extract

¾ cup all-purpose flour

1 teaspoon cinnamon

½ teaspoon baking soda

¼ teaspoon baking powder

¼ teaspoon salt

1 ½ cups quick-cooking oats

½ cup raisins

Directions

Preheat oven to 375 degrees.

Coat baking sheets with vegetable oil cooking spray or line with parchment paper; set aside.

In a medium bowl, beat together brown sugar, granulated sugar, applesauce, margarine, egg whites and vanilla.

In a separate bowl, combine flour, cinnamon, baking soda, baking powder and salt; stir into sugar mixture. Add oats and raisins; stir to combine.

Drop by rounded tablespoons onto prepared baking sheets. Bake 8 to 9 minutes, or until edges begin to brown. Cool on wire racks.

Nutritional info (per serving)

Calories........................154
    From fat 18%

Fat .... 3 g
    Saturated.............0.5 g
    Trans ....0 g

Carbohydrates ....28 g

Protein .... 3 g

Sodium .... 160 mg

Cholesterol ....0 mg

Calcium .... 23 mg

Fiber .... 2 g

Food exchanges
    1 starch, 1 fruit

Pear Crisp

The pear runs neck and neck with the apple as an American favorite. Unlike most fruit, pears improve in texture and flavor after they're picked. Pears are rarely tree-ripened. They're picked when mature but still green and firm. If left to ripen on the tree, the flesh becomes mealy.

Test Kitchen Tip

Choose pears that are fragrant and free of blemishes and soft spots. Store them at room temperature until just ripe. Once ripe, refrigerate and eat within a few days. Any pear variety can be used in this recipe.

8 | 1 hour total

Ingredients

Vegetable oil cooking spray

6 cups cored and cubed pears

3 tablespoons all-purpose flour, divided

2 tablespoons honey

1 tablespoon lemon juice

⅓ cup old-fashioned rolled oats

¼ cup packed brown sugar

½ teaspoon ground cinnamon

¼ teaspoon ground ginger

1 tablespoon trans fat-free margarine

½ cup reduced-fat whipped topping

Directions

Preheat oven to 350 degrees. Spray a 10-inch round baking dish with vegetable oil cooking spray. In a large bowl, combine pears and 1 tablespoon flour, and gently toss to coat pears. In a small bowl or measuring cup, combine honey and lemon juice; pour over pears and gently stir until pears are coated. Place pears in the prepared baking dish. In a large bowl, combine oats, brown sugar, remaining 2 tablespoons flour, cinnamon and ginger; toss to combine.

Using a pastry cutter or fork, cut in the margarine until the mixture becomes crumbly. Top pears with the crumb mixture. Bake for 40 to 45 minutes or until the pear mixture bubbles and crumb topping is golden brown. Serve warm or cold with 1 tablespoon of whipped topping.

Nutritional info (per serving)

Calories........................ 173
    From fat................. 16%
Fat ....3 g
    Saturated ....1 g
    Trans .... 0 g
Carbohydrates ....38 g
Protein ....2 g
Sodium .... 23 mg
Cholesterol ....0 mg
Calcium .... 22 mg
Fiber ....5 g
Food exchanges
    ½ starch, 2 fruit, ½ fat

Pumpkin Chocolate Chip Squares

These Pumpkin Chocolate Chips Squares are a tasty lunch-box or after-school snack. Pumpkin's claim to nutrient fame is the carotenoids it contains, such as beta-carotene and lutein. Carotenoids might protect against chronic diseases like heart disease and cancer and help ward off age-related vision loss such as macular degeneration. Pumpkin provides a healthy dose of fiber, potassium, vitamin C, vitamin E and iron, too.

 24   1 hour total

Ingredients

2 cups all-purpose flour

1 tablespoon pumpkin pie spice

1 teaspoon baking soda

½ teaspoon salt

⅓ cup low-fat buttermilk

⅓ cup applesauce

3 tablespoons canola oil

1 ¼ cups sugar

1 egg

2 teaspoons vanilla extract

1 cup canned pumpkin

4 ounces (about ⅔ cup) minature semi-sweet chocolate chips

Directions

Preheat oven to 350 degrees.

Line the bottom and sides of a 9-by-13-inch baking pan with foil, leaving an overhang on all sides.

In a medium bowl, whisk together flour, pumpkin pie spice, baking soda and salt; set the mixture aside. With an electric mixer, mix buttermilk, applesauce, canola oil and sugar on medium-high speed until the combination is smooth. Beat in egg and vanilla extract until they are combined. Beat in pumpkin.

Reduce the mixer speed to low and mix flour mixture into the liquid ingredients until they are just combined.

Fold in the chocolate chips.

Spread batter evenly in the prepared pan. Bake until the edges begin to pull away from the sides of the pan and a wooden pick inserted in the center comes out with just a few moist crumbs attached, about 35 to 40 minutes. Remove cake from the oven and cool it completely in the pan.

Lift the cake from the pan by gently pulling on the foil overhang. Peel off the foil and cut the cake into 24 squares.

Nutritional info (per serving)

Calories........................127	Sodium .... 109 mg
From fat.................28%	Cholesterol ....9 mg
Fat....................................4 g	Calcium ....12 mg
Saturated.................1 g	Fiber ....1 g
Trans ....0 g	Food exchanges
Carbohydrates ....23 g	1 starch, ½ fruit, ½ fat
Protein ....2 g	

Test Kitchen Tip

If you have leftover canned pumpkin, freeze it for another use. Place it in a freezer-safe container leaving ½-inch headspace or place in freezer bags. It will keep at least six months.

Pumpkin Torte

Try this Pumpkin Torte as an option to the holiday pumpkin pie. The cake layers are mildly pumpkin and vanilla flavored with a creamy pumpkin filling in between.

 16 1 hour total

Ingredients

Floured baking spray

1 box (18.25 ounces) yellow cake mix (trans fat-free)

1 box (4 serving size) vanilla cook-and-serve pudding, divided

1 can (15 ounces) pumpkin, divided

8 ounces diet lemon-lime soda (such as diet 7Up)

2 egg whites

1 ½ teaspoons pumpkin pie spice, divided

3 ounces reduced-fat cream cheese, softened

1 tub (8 ounces) fat-free whipped topping

Directions

Preheat oven to 350 degrees.

Spray two 8-inch round cake pans with the floured baking spray.

In a large bowl, combine dry cake mix, ¼ cup of the vanilla pudding mix, 1 cup pumpkin, the diet soda, egg whites and 1 teaspoon pumpkin pie spice. Beat according to the directions on the cake mix box.

Pour batter evenly into the prepared pans. Bake for 20 to 25 minutes or until a wooden pick inserted in the center comes out clean. Allow cakes to cool completely on a wire rack.

In a medium-sized bowl, beat cream cheese with an electric mixer until it's creamy. Add the remaining pudding mix, the remaining pumpkin and the remaining ½ teaspoon pumpkin pie spice; mix well. Gently stir in the whipped topping.

Remove cake layers from the pans. Carefully cut each layer horizontally in half with a serrated knife, making 4 cake rounds. Place the first layer on a serving plate. Spread one quarter of the cream cheese mixture between the layers and on top of the cake. Do not frost the sides of the cake. Cover and store in the refrigerator until ready to serve.

Nutritional info (per serving)

Calories	203
From fat	18%
Fat	4 g
Saturated	2 g
Trans	0 g
Carbohydrates	38 g
Protein	3 g
Sodium	277 mg
Cholesterol	4 mg
Calcium	11 mg
Fiber	1 g

Food exchanges
2 starch, 1 vegetable, ½ starch

Raspberry Cheesecake Bars

Make these Raspberry Cheesecake Bars, a Best of the Free Press Test Kitchen recipe, when you're looking for a taste of summer. You can use fresh or frozen raspberries in this recipe. They are easy-to-make and ideal for a dessert table.

 20 1 hour 15 mins total

Ingredients

Vegetable oil cooking spray

1 box (19.9 ounces) trans fat-free dark chocolate fudge brownie mix

CHEESECAKE TOPPING

1 package (8 ounces) fat-free cream cheese, softened

1 package (8 ounces) reduced-fat cream cheese, softened

½ cup low-fat vanilla yogurt

2 egg whites

1 egg

½ cup sugar

1 teaspoon vanilla extract

¾ cup fresh or frozen raspberries

Directions

Preheat oven to 350 degrees. Spray a 13-by-9-inch pan with vegetable oil cooking spray.

In a medium bowl, stir brownie mix, yogurt and egg whites until well blended, then pour them into the prepared pan. Bake for 28 to 30 minutes or until a wooden pick inserted 2 inches from side of pan comes out almost clean.

While the brownie is baking, cream together the fat-free cream cheese and reduced-fat cream cheese with an electric mixer. Add egg, sugar and vanilla extract and blend until smooth. Gently fold in the raspberries.

Carefully pour cheesecake mixture over the brownie and spread the mixture so that it completely covers the brownie. Bake an additional 20 to 25 minutes.

Remove from oven and let cool completely on cooling rack. Cover with plastic wrap and refrigerate until ready to serve.

Nutritional info (per serving)

Calories	187
From fat	24%
Fat	5 g
Saturated	2 g
Trans	0 g
Carbohydrates	31 g
Protein	6 g
Sodium	224 mg
Cholesterol	20 mg
Calcium	42 mg
Fiber	1 g

Food exchanges
2 starch, 1 fat

 Test Kitchen Tip

Separate egg whites from egg yolks when the eggs are cold. They will separate easier. Always make sure there is not a speck of yolk in the whites or they will not whip up properly. Make sure the bowl is grease-free. Wipe it out with a bit of vinegar before whipping the whites. When recipes call for whipping egg whites to soft or stiff peaks, make sure they and the bowl you are whipping them in are at room temperature. The egg whites will whip up better and in more volume.

Raspberry Sour Cream Coffee Cake

Raspberries reign superior when it comes to their nutrient profile. One cup of these red jewels supplies more than a third of the daily need for vitamin C along with a hefty dose of fiber. Raspberries also contain ellagic acid, a natural substance that may help prevent certain types of cancer. They are a tasty addition in this coffee cake.

  16   1 hour 20 mins total

Ingredients

Floured baking spray

2 cups all-purpose flour

1 teaspoon baking powder

½ teaspoon baking soda

¼ teaspoon salt

1 cup sugar

2 tablespoons canola oil

2 ounces reduced-fat cream cheese

1 tablespoon vanilla extract

1 egg

2 egg whites

¾ cup reduced-fat sour cream

1 teaspoon lemon zest

2 cups fresh raspberries tossed with 2 tablespoons all-purpose flour

3 tablespoons finely diced pecans

2 tablespoons brown sugar

Nutritional info (per serving)

Calories.........................177
  From fat.................25%
Fat ....5 g
  Saturated.................2 g
  Trans ....0 g
Carbohydrates ....29 g
Protein ....4 g

Sodium ....119 mg
Cholesterol ....21 mg
Calcium ....37 mg
Fiber ....2 g
Food exchanges
  2 starch, 1 fat

Watch This!

Scan this QR code with your smartphone to watch the Heart Smart® video.

Directions

Preheat oven to 350 degrees. Coat an 8- or 9-inch spring-form pan with floured baking spray.

In a large bowl, combine flour, baking powder, baking soda and salt; set aside. In a separate bowl, cream together the sugar, oil, cream cheese, vanilla extract, egg and egg whites.

Alternately beat the flour mixture and sour cream into the sugar mixture on low speed until blended, beginning and ending with the flour.

Fold in the lemon zest and raspberries. Pour the batter into the prepared pan, and sprinkle the top evenly with pecans and brown sugar.

Bake 45 to 55 minutes or until a wooden pick inserted near the center comes out clean. Remove from the oven and cool on a wire rack for about 20 minutes, then release and remove the outer edge of the springform pan. Continue to cool cake until ready to serve.

Test Kitchen Tip

Tossing the raspberries with a little flour helps keep them from sinking to the bottom of the batter. When buying raspberries choose plump raspberries without the hull and avoid soft, shriveled or moldy raspberries. If the containers are stained, the raspberries will likely be crushed or bruised. Raspberries are highly perishable. Store immediately in the refrigerator and eat within 2 to 3 days. To clean berries, rinse them gently in cold water.

Strawberry Pretzel Delight

Strawberries vary in size, shape and color. Strawberry connoisseurs often favor smaller berries for their sweetness; large berries can be watery and less sweet. Nutrition-wise, strawberries are excellent. Eight berries provide more vitamin C than an orange and as much fiber as two slices of whole-wheat bread.

They also contain an abundance of phytochemicals, naturally occurring compounds found in plant foods that may decrease the risk of cancer and heart disease.

 18 | 1 hour total

Ingredients

1 cup finely crushed pretzels

¼ cup plus 2 tablespoons sugar, divided

3 tablespoons trans fat-free margarine, melted

1 ½ packages (12 ounces total) reduced-fat cream cheese

2 tablespoons skim milk

2 cups fat-free whipped topping

2 cups boiling water

1 package (8-serving size or 0.6 ounces) sugar-free strawberry gelatin

1 ½ cups cold water

4 cups (about 1 quart) sliced strawberries

Directions

Preheat oven to 350 degrees. In a small bowl, mix crushed pretzels, 2 tablespoons sugar and margarine. Press mixture onto the bottom of a 13-by-9-inch pan. Bake 10 minutes. Remove and cool completely.

In a medium bowl, beat cream cheese with the remaining ¼ cup sugar and milk until blended. Stir in whipped topping and spread over cooled crust; refrigerate.

In a large bowl, add boiling water to gelatin and stir until completely dissolved. Stir in the 1½ cups of cold water. Refrigerate 45 minutes to one hour or until gelatin begins to thicken. Stir in strawberries and spoon over cream cheese layer. Refrigerate 3 hours or until firm.

Nutritional info (per serving)

Calories.........................117	Sodium .... 184 mg
From fat.................38%	Cholesterol ....13 mg
Fat................................5 g	Calcium ....21 mg
Saturated ....2 g	Fiber ....1 g
Trans ....0 g	Food exchanges
Carbohydrates .... 14 g	1 fruit, 1 fat
Protein ....3 g	

 Test Kitchen Tip

Do not wash strawberries until ready to use. Store berries in a moisture-proof container in the refrigerator for 2 to 3 days. Strawberries freeze beautifully. Rinse them and pat them dry with paper towel. Place them on a tray and freeze until they are nearly frozen. Transfer the berries to freezer bags and freeze up to one year.

Triple Berry Brownie Pizza

This brownie pizza is a terrific snack for kids. And kids can also lend a hand in making it by spreading the brownie batter on the pizza pan and arrange the berries on the topping. This recipe gets a fine berry burst from blueberries, raspberries and strawberries.

 16   1 hour 10 mins total

Ingredients

1 package (19.9 ounces) trans fat-free brownie mix (such as Betty Crocker dark chocolate fudge brownie mix)

½ cup unsweetened applesauce

1 egg

¼ cup water

Floured baking spray

TOPPING

1 package (8 ounces) fat-free cream cheese, softened

1 tablespoon sugar

1 teaspoon vanilla extract

2 cups reduced-fat whipped topping, thawed

1 cup fresh strawberries, divided

½ cup fresh raspberries

½ cup fresh blueberries

Directions

Preheat oven to 350 degrees.

In a large bowl, combine the brownie mix, applesauce, egg and water; mix according to package directions. Spread the batter into a 15-inch round pizza pan coated with floured baking spray. If you do not have a round pizza pan, use a 9-by-13-inch pan.

Bake 18 to 20 minutes or until set. Do not over bake. Remove from oven and cool completely.

To prepare topping: Combine cream cheese, sugar and vanilla extract in a medium-size bowl and mix until well blended. Fold in the whipped topping along with ½ cup diced strawberries. Spread cream cheese mixture evenly over the brownie pizza. Slice the remaining strawberries and arrange on top of the cream cheese mixture along with the raspberries and blueberries.

Nutritional info (per serving)

Calories......................196
   From fat 23%

Fat ....5 g
   Saturated...............0 g
   Trans ....0 g

Carbohydrates ....35 g

Protein ....4 g

Sodium .... 180 mg

Cholesterol ....14 mg

Calcium ....31 mg

Fiber ....1 g

Food exchanges
   2 starch, 1 fat

Vanilla Almond Cake

This cake takes little time to prepare and the rest is all in the baking and cooling time. It's a tasty and terrific cake to serve at a luncheon or to bring to a potluck. This Vanilla Almond Cake contains 180 calories per slice, so be sure to keep that portion to just one slice.

 16　1 hour 30 mins total

Ingredients

Floured baking spray

1 box (18.25 ounces) trans fat-free yellow cake mix

1 box (4 serving size) vanilla cook-and-serve pudding and pie filling

¾ cup skim milk

½ cup water

½ cup applesauce

2 egg whites

1 egg

2 teaspoons almond extract

3 tablespoons semi-sweet chocolate chips, melted

Directions

Preheat the oven to 350 degrees.

Coat a 12-cup Bundt pan with floured baking spray.

In a large bowl, combine cake mix, pudding and pie filling mix, milk, water, applesauce, egg whites, egg and almond extract and beat according to package directions.

Bake for 35 to 40 minutes or until a wooden pick inserted in the center comes out clean.

Let it stand 30 to 40 minutes before inverting pan to release cake from pan. Allow cake to cool completely.

Drizzle melted chocolate over the top of the cake.

Nutritional info (per serving)

Calories......................180	Sodium ....253 mg
From fat.................20%	Cholesterol ....13 mg
Fat................................4 g	Calcium ....17 mg
Saturated ....2 g	Fiber ....1 g
Trans ....0 g	Food exchanges
Carbohydrates ....33 g	2 starch, ½ fat
Protein ....3 g	

Test Kitchen Tip

When melting chocolate chips in a microwave do so in 30 seconds increment stirring each time. Watch them carefully because the chips hold their shape even if melted and can easily burn.

Glossary

Here are some nutrition buzzwords and ingredients found in this cookbook and their definitions.

Antioxidants: These help protect the cells in our body from destructive molecules called free radicals. An overproduction of free radicals can cause cell damage that may lead to the onset of health problems such as cancer, heart disease, cataracts and arthritis. Antioxidants such as beta carotene, and vitamins C and E neutralize free radicals.

Beta carotene: One of 600 plus carotenoids found in food. An antioxidant, it is the orange pigment that gives color to carrots, sweet potatoes, winter squash, dark leafy green vegetables and apricots.

Carotenoids: Colorful pigments found plant foods. The body can turn some of these pigments into vitamin A. This antioxidant may prevent some forms of cancer and heart disease.

Cruciferous vegetables: Members of the cruciferous family include arugula, broccoli, cauliflower, cabbage, Brussels sprouts, collard greens, kohlrabi, mustard greens, kale, radishes, turnip greens, watercress and bok choy. Although research is ongoing, studies suggest that cruciferous vegetables may help ward off certain forms of cancers, especially cancer of the mouth, throat and stomach.

DASH diet: The Dietary Approaches to Stop Hypertension (DASH) resulted from studies that found eating a lower-sodium diet rich in fruits, vegetables, fat-free or low-fat milk and milk products, whole-grain foods, fish, poultry, beans, nuts and seeds also reduced systolic and diastolic blood pressure compared to people consuming a diet high in fat and cholesterol with few fruits and vegetables.

Edamame: Pronounced eh-dah-MAH-meh, these are fresh green soybeans. Soy products provide a healthy substitute for protein sources that are higher in artery clogging saturated fat and cholesterol. Edamame are sold frozen in the pod or shelled. Remove shell before cooking and eating.

Greek yogurt: Thicker and creamier than traditional yogurt, Greek yogurt has a texture similar to custard or sour cream. It contains almost twice the amount of protein as traditional yogurt and about half the amount of sodium. Select low-fat or non-fat varieties.

HDL cholesterol: One component of your total blood cholesterol level. The cholesterol in our blood travels around in different packages called lipoproteins. Low-density lipoprotein, or LDL, is known as the bad cholesterol and high-density lipoprotein, or HDL, is known as the good cholesterol. LDL carries cholesterol through the bloodstream to your cells that can lead to plaque build-up in your arteries, increasing the risk of heart disease. HDL removes excess cholesterol from the blood, which slows the build up in the arteries and ultimately lowers heart disease risk.

Isoflavones: Found in soybeans, these are a class of phytochemicals. The term phytochemicals refers to a wide variety of compounds produced by plants that are being studied for their role in the prevention and treatment of many health conditions including cancer, heart disease and high blood pressure.

Jicama: Pronounced HEE-kah-mah, is often referred to as the Mexican potato. It's a large bulbous root vegetable that has a crisp texture and a nutty, sweet flavor. It can be eaten raw or cooked and provides some potassium and vitamin C.

Jasmine rice: Jasmine rice is long-grain rice grown primarily in Thailand. It is often substituted for the more expensive basmati rice. Jasmine rice is moist and tender with a soft texture and subtle nutty flavor and rich aroma. It is available in white and brown forms. Brown jasmine rice is considered a whole grain and would fulfill the latest Dietary Guidelines for Americans recommendation to make half your grain choices whole grains.

Kale: A member of the cabbage family which resembles collard greens except the leaves are curly at the edges. Kale has a mild, cabbagey flavor and comes in a variety of colors from the traditional deep green to yellow-green, red, or purple. This cruciferous vegetable provides ample amounts of vitamins A and C, along with folate, calcium and iron.

Lactose intolerance: The inability of the body to digest the natural sugar (lactose) in milk due to a lack of lactase (the enzyme that breaks down lactose) in the small intestine. Symptoms commonly experienced by those who are lactose intolerant include gas, bloating, abdominal pain, and diarrhea. Yogurt, certain cheeses and lactose-reduced

Glossary

milk are often tolerated well by those with lactose intolerance. Some people with lactose intolerance can even handle small amounts (one-half cup at a time) of milk.

Legumes: Plants that have edible seeds within a pod. These include beans, peas and lentils. Most legumes are an excellent source of fiber. Four to eight grams of fiber are packed into every half-cup serving. Legumes contain soluble fiber, the same type of fiber found in oat bran that can help lower cholesterol. Most nutrition experts recommend that healthy people consume 25 to 30 grams of dietary fiber every day.

Lycopene: A disease-fighting antioxidant found in tomato products. Its pigment gives tomatoes, pink grapefruit, watermelon, guavas, and papayas their red color. Lycopene from processed tomatoes such as canned tomatoes and tomato sauce is more readily absorbed by the body than lycopene from raw tomatoes.

Monounsaturated fat: An unsaturated fat that tends to lower blood cholesterol levels. Oils high in monounsaturated fats are canola oil, olive oil and peanut oil. Foods that are high in monounsaturated fat include avocados, olives and peanuts.

Nutrient dense foods: Provide generous amounts of vitamins, minerals and other nutrients, and relatively few calories. Low nutrient-dense foods supply calories but relatively small amounts of nutrients, sometimes none at all. Spinach would be a very nutrient-dense food, potato chips would not.

Omega-3 fatty acids: This is a type of polyunsaturated fat found in fish such as salmon, trout, and tuna, as well as in flaxseed, canola oil and soybeans. Research suggests that omega-3 fatty acids, especially those from seafood, have beneficial effects in preventing and treating heart disease. The American Heart Association recommends eating at least two servings of fish per week to get a healthy dose of omega-3 fatty acids.

Pre-diabetes: Also known as impaired glucose tolerance. This condition places you at a higher risk for developing type 2 diabetes. In pre-diabetes, blood glucose levels are higher than normal but are not high enough for a diagnosis of diabetes. A fasting plasma glucose level of 100 to 125 milligrams per deciliter indicates pre-diabetes. Results from the Diabetes Prevention Program (DPP) study showed that people with pre-diabetes can prevent the development of type 2 diabetes by changing their diet and increasing their level of physical activity. Being physically active nearly every day is one of the best ways to postpone or prevent type 2 diabetes. Walking just 30 minutes a day, five days a week had a positive impact on study participants.

Quinoa: Pronounced keen-wah, this whole-grain has a delicate, almost bland flavor similar to couscous. It is considered a complete protein because it contains all the essential amino acids. Often referred to as a supergrain, quinoa provides an impressive array of nutrients including iron, potassium, folate, zinc as well as dietary fiber.

Sea salt: Results from the evaporation of sea water rather than being mined from underground salt deposits like table salt. Depending on the source of the sea water, trace minerals may remain in the salt. Sea salt has the same amount of sodium as table salt by weight, so don't look to it as a low sodium alternative to table salt.

Trans fatty acids: Also referred to as trans fats. These are created when an oil is partially hydrogenated. Most of the trans fats we eat come from commercially fried and baked foods, stick margarines and snack foods containing partially hydrogenated oils. Trans fats act like saturated fats and raise bad LDL cholesterol levels, increasing the risk for heart disease.

Zeaxanthin: Along with lutein, are two carotenoids that may reduce the risk of age-related macular degeneration, the leading cause of blindness in older adults. Foods providing these two compounds include dark green vegetables such as kale, spinach, and, broccoli as well as corn, oranges, and egg yolks.

Recipe Index

Recipe Index

Recipe Index

Recipe Index

Measuring Tips

- Use dry metal or plastic measuring cups and measuring spoons (teaspoons and tablespoons) to measure: baking powder, baking soda, brown sugar, cocoa powder, confectioners' (powdered) sugar, flour, nuts, spices and sugar.

- When measuring flours, use the spoon-and-sweep method. Spoon the flour into a measuring cup until filled and mounded. Use a straight edge to level off the excess.

- Use measuring spoons for small amounts of liquids and extracts.

- For yogurt, sour cream, ricotta cheese, use dry measuring cups.

- Use a glass or plastic liquid measuring cup to measure: all liquids, such as water, milk, buttermilk, broths and wine.

Common measurements

Pinch or a dash is less than ⅛ teaspoon

1 teaspoon = ⅙ fluid ounce

3 teaspoons = 1 tablespoon or ½ fluid ounce

2 tablespoons = ⅛ cup

4 tablespoons = ¼ cup

5 tablespoons plus 1 teaspoon = ⅓ cup

8 tablespoons = ½ cup

10 tablespoons plus 2 teaspoons = ⅔ cup

12 tablespoons = ¾ cup

16 tablespoons = 1 cup

1 cup = 8 fluid ounces or ½ pint

2 cups = 1 pint or 16 ounces

4 cups = 1 quart or 32 fluid ounces

8 cups = 64 fluid ounces or ½ gallon

4 quarts = 1 gallon or 128 fluid ounces

16 ounces = 1 pound

Heart Smart®

Learn more about the Heart Smart® Program by scanning this QR code with your smartphone. To download a free QR code scanner, visit your smartphone's application store.

Heart Smart® Kitchen Secrets

At Heart Smart® we believe that healthy eating doesn't mean sacrificing taste. For more than two decades, we've experimented with cooking techniques, ingredient substitutions, new products and flavor combinations to create delicious and healthy recipes.

A few simple ingredient tweaks can reduce the amount of fat, saturated fat, trans fat, cholesterol, sodium and calories that wind up in your recipes. Our favorite makeover secrets are revealed below.

When you recipe calls for	Use
Whole or 2% milk	Skim, ½% or 1% milk, or low-fat buttermilk
Cream or evaporated milk	Evaporated fat-free milk or fat-free half-and-half
Sweetened condensed milk	Low-fat or fat-free sweetened condensed milk
Sour cream	Reduced-fat or fat-free sour cream or low-fat or no-fat plain Greek yogurt
Cottage cheese or ricotta cheese	Low-fat or fat-free cottage or ricotta cheese
Cream cheese	Reduced-fat (Neufchâtel) cream cheese, fat-free cream cheese, whipped part-skim ricotta cheese or yogurt cheese
Full-fat cheese	Fat-free, low-fat (3 grams of fat or less per ounce) or reduced-fat cheese (4 to 7 grams of fat per ounce)
Butter, shortening or stick margarine for sautéing	Liquid oil in a reduced amount, no trans fat margarine, vegetable oil cooking spray, reduced-sodium broth, fruit juice, wine or water
Mayonnaise	Low-fat or fat-free mayonnaise
Whole egg	Two egg whites, or ¼ cup egg substitute, equal one whole egg. For a more tender product, when substituting egg whites for whole eggs in baked goods, beat the egg whites until soft peaks form before incorporating them into the recipe.
Nuts	Reduce the amount by half and toast them to intensify the flavor.
Chocolate chips	Reduce the amount by half and use mini chocolate chips.
Cake frosting	Top cakes with fresh fruit, fruit sauce, low-fat or fat-free whipped topping, or sprinkle lightly with powdered sugar.
Pastry crust	Reduced-fat graham cracker crust or phyllo dough
White flour	Replace half the amount of white flour with whole-wheat flour.

(Continued on next page)

Pasta or white rice	Whole-wheat pasta or brown rice
Bacon	Canadian bacon or lean ham (keep in mind, these alternatives are still high in sodium)
Ground beef	Ground turkey or chicken breast, ground sirloin or extra-lean ground beef

Shaking the Salt

Lowering the sodium content of recipes is a bigger challenge than reducing the fat. If your recipe calls for one teaspoon of salt, you will add 2,300 milligrams of sodium to that recipe.

There are a number of things you can do to reduce the amount of sodium in recipes.

- Use less salt or no salt at the table and in cooking. If a recipe calls for salt, start by cutting the amount you add in half.
- Use herbs, spices and sodium-free seasoning blends in place of salt.
- Drain the liquid from canned vegetables and legumes and rinse well.
- Check food labels and compare the sodium content of similar food items and purchase the item with the least amount of sodium.
- Cook pasta, rice and hot cereals without adding salt.
- When cooking rice and pasta mixes, use only half of the seasoning packet provided.
- Use fresh poultry, fish and lean meat rather than canned, smoked or processed varieties.

Table Salt vs. Kosher Salt vs. Sea Salt

Whether it's table salt, kosher salt or sea salt, all are made up of the same two minerals – sodium and chloride. The major difference is due to their origin and the way they are processed.

Table salt, mined from underground salt deposits, is made up of small, uniformly shaped crystals. Table salt is processed to eliminate trace minerals and usually contains an additive to prevent clumping.

Kosher salt is an additive-free coarse salt. Some describe kosher salt as having a clean, mild flavor. Chefs prefer kosher salt because the coarse texture is easier to pinch.

Sea salt is the result of the evaporation of sea water. Depending on the source of the sea water, trace minerals may remain in the salt. These trace minerals can add flavor as well as color, making sea salt gray, pink, red, or even black.

The reason these salts differ in sodium content is due to the size of the granules. Because of the larger granules, sea salt and kosher salt contain less sodium than the same volume of table salt. Comparing them by weight however, demonstrates the sodium content is essentially the same.

	1 teaspoon	**¹⁄₈ ounce**
Table salt	2,300 milligrams sodium	1,403 milligrams sodium
Kosher salt	1,920 milligrams sodium	1,428 milligrams sodium
Sea salt	1,560 milligrams sodium	1,392 milligrams sodium

Salt Substitutes

Some salt substitutes contain potassium in place of the sodium. For people with kidney disease, or those taking certain medications, potassium-containing substitutes can be harmful. Check with your doctor before using salt substitutes containing potassium.

Keeping Your Kitchen Safe

Healthy cooking also involves keeping food safe to eat. Despite the fact that America's food supply is among the safest in the world, the unappetizing truth is that food-related illness remains a serious public health concern. Foodborne illness affects more than 76 million individuals in the U.S. each year and leads to more than 300,000 hospitalizations.

These suggestions can help you keep foods fresh and safe.

- Wash your hands with hot, soapy water for a full 20 seconds before and after handling food.

- Always use clean utensils and serving plates for cooked foods. Never place cooked food on a plate that previously held raw meat, poultry or seafood unless the plate has been washed.

- Keep hot food hot and cold food cold. Hot food should be kept at least 140 degrees. Cold food should be kept at least 40 degrees or lower.

- Never leave perishable food at room temperature for more than two hours; one hour if the temperature is 90 degrees or higher. Bacteria that cause food poisoning grow quickly at warm temperatures.

Notes

Notes

Notes

Notes

Notes

Notes